border oasis

ENVIRONMENTAL HISTORY OF THE BORDERLANDS

Thomas E. Sheridan, series editor

Border Oasis

WATER AND THE

POLITICAL ECOLOGY

OF THE

COLORADO RIVER DELTA,

1940-1975

Evan R. Ward

The University of Arizona Press Tucson

The University of Arizona Press
© 2003 The Arizona Board of Regents
First printing
All rights reserved
♾ This book is printed on acid-free, archival-quality paper.
Manufactured in the United States of America
08 07 06 05 04 03   6 5 4 3 2 1

Library of Congress Cataloging-in-Publication Data
Ward, Evan R. (Evan Ray), 1971–
Border oasis : water and the political ecology of the Colorado
River Delta, 1940–1975 / Evan R. Ward.
p. cm. — (Environmental history of the borderlands)
Includes bibliographical references (p.) and index.
ISBN 0-8165-2223-5 (cloth : alk. paper)
1. Water-supply—Government policy—Colorado River (Colo.
-Mexico) 2. Water resources development—Colorado River
(Colo.-Mexico) 3. Colorado River Delta (Mexico)—Environmen-
tal conditions. I. Title. II. Series.
TD225.C665W35 2003
333.91′009791′3—dc21
2002010960

British Library Cataloguing-in-Publication Data
A catalogue record for this book is available from the British Library.

Imagine . . . that you are immediately south of the city of Yuma, seated comfortably and contemplatively on the serrated sandy edge of the Yuma Mesa . . . The date is immaterial, except that it is in the far distant past—a thousand, two thousand, possibly twenty thousand years ago . . . You are looking out to the west, over the site of the Yuma Valley . . . [but] you are seated on a beach, and what you see is a vast and nameless body of salt water. In the [sixteenth] century it became known as the Sea of Cortez. . . .

At the time of which we speak this long arm of the Pacific Ocean covered the site of [the entire delta] . . . and for its eastern shore followed the beach line of the Yuma and Sonora Mesas. Northwestward for a hundred and twenty-five miles it washed the selfsame mountains, high mesas and sand-hills which today form the border of the Basin, its floor still far below the level of the sea, in which lie the fertile and verdant Valleys of Coachella and Imperial.

Out of the north, through a gash in the earth a hundred and fifty feet deep, pours a mighty river. This will serve as your introduction to the Colorado. I have said the month is June. An incredible flood is discharging into the sea at your feet, but what strikes you most . . . is the color and consistency of the flood. It has more the appearance of a torrent of mud than of water. I leave you to ponder the phenomenon.[1]

—Mulford Winsor Jr.
"The Menace of the Colorado"

contents

Maps

Figures

Acknowledgments

This project would not have been possible without the assistance of many people in Mexico and the United States. First, Dr. Lester D. Langley helped me to conceive the project as a graduate student at the University of Georgia (UGA) and bring it to fruition. Dr. William Stueck (UGA) challenged me to apply a comparative approach to environmental diplomacy. Dr. Thomas Whigham (UGA) wrote grant recommendations and reviewed the manuscript. Dr. Catherine Pringle, from the Institute of Ecology (UGA), challenged me to add an ecological perspective to these writings. Finally, Dr. James Cobb's study of the Mississippi Delta, *The Most Southern Place on Earth*, provided a conceptual standard for regional studies that I strove to emulate.

The Center for Latin American and Caribbean Studies, the Center for Humanities and Arts, and the Department of History, all at UGA, provided crucial financial assistance for the project.

Numerous archivists in Mexico City, Mexicali, Imperial County, Yuma County, Phoenix, and Washington, D.C., provided the materials that brought the delta and those involved in making decisions for the region's development to life. They are too numerous to list individually, but I will always gratefully remember their assistance. Some, however, went beyond the call of duty, including Linda L. Sanchez and Lynda Trimm (Imperial Irrigation District), Robert Spindler (Arizona State University's Hayden Library), Jane Gubash (U.S. Bureau of Reclamation [USBR] Photo Lab, Boulder City, Nevada), and Bill Garrity (USBR Library, Boulder City). In Yuma, Tamara R. Stover (Yuma County Water Users Association) granted open access to her organization's historical files. Finally, in Washington, D.C., Kelli Hoover and George Franchois (U.S. Department of the Interior Library) prepared materials for me prior to my visit. The International Boundary and Water Commission, through the efforts of Carlos Duarte, granted permission to use data on salinity in the delta. At the University of North Alabama, Lisha Guscke provided invaluable secretarial assistance.

In Mexico City, the staff at the Archivo Histórico del Agua led me to important documents in their archives. In Mexicali, Claudia E. Schroeder Verdugo, then coordinator at the Museum of the Universidad Autónoma de Baja California, graciously provided access to the Rafael Martínez Retes papers as well as facilitated access to photographs for use in the book. Gina Walther, director of the museum, granted permission to use the images, and Virginia Aldana prepared the photos for use in the book. Salvador Vizcarra Schumm, chief of the Historical Archives of the State of Baja California, opened the archive's doors to me on a state holiday.

At the University of Arizona Press, I am indebted to a fine acquisitions editor, Patti Hartmann, who took an early interest in the project, and the editor of the Environmental History of the Borderlands series, Dr. Thomas Sheridan, whose editorial suggestions have made this a better book. Copyeditor Mary M. Hill ably polished the manuscript for publication.

Finally, for the support and peace of mind to finish this project, I thank my family and God. This work is dedicated to my wife, Jennie, and my parents, Roger and Virginia Ward. Jennie actively supported my research, which took me across North America. She also prepared the images for publication. My parents also provided financial and moral support.

Some of the chapters that follow have been adapted from previous articles I have written on the delta region. An earlier version of chapter 1 was published in *Pacific Historical Review* 70 under the title "The Twentieth-Century Ghosts of William Walker: Conquest of Land and Water as Central Themes in the History of the Colorado River Delta." The Gale Group has granted permission to use portions of "The Mexican Water Treaty," from the edited collection *History in Dispute,* volume 7, *Water and the Environment since 1945: Global Perspectives* (St. James Press, 2001), in chapter 2. An earlier version of chapter 3 was previously published in the *Journal of Arizona History* (fall 1999) under the title "Saline Solutions: Arizona Water Politics, Mexican-American Relations, and the Wellton-Mohawk Valley." An earlier version of chapter 6 was published by the *Journal of Political Ecology* 6 (1999) under the title " 'The Politics of Place': Diplomatic and Domestic Priorities of the Colorado River Salinity Control Act (1974)." Portions of the deltascapes have been adapted from an article in *Environment and History* 7, no. 2 (2001) under the title "Geo-

Environmental Disconnection and the Colorado River Delta: Technology, Culture, and the Political Ecology of Paradise." Finally, portions of "Two Rivers, Two Nations, One History: The Transformation of the Colorado River Delta since 1940," an article that originally appeared in *Frontera Norte* 22, have been used in the text. Chapter 4 has been adapted from an article in *Frontera Norte* 26 entitled "Salt of the River, Salt of the Earth: Politics, Science, and Ecological Diplomacy in the Mexicali Valley, 1961–1965." All these fine journals have granted permission to use my material in this book.

Introduction

An International Wedding

[In] no part of the wide world is there a place where Nature has provided so perfectly for a stupendous achievement by means of irrigation as in that place where the Colorado River flows uselessly past the international desert which Nature intended for its bride. Sometime the wedding of the waters will be celebrated, and the child of that union will be a new civilization.
—William Ellsworth Smythe[1]

A round us, on every side, stretched the primeval desert, wrapped in sunshine and in silence," wrote William Ellsworth Smythe, the preeminent evangelist of irrigation, from the veranda of a home on the east bank of the Colorado River near Yuma, Arizona. Smythe had traveled to the delta to promote settlement in the region at the turn of the twentieth century. "But just where we sat," he continued, contrasting a new vista with that of the arid landscape he had just described, "the desert had been vanquished for a space of one hundred and thirty acres. Here were the deep green of alfalfa fields and the long lines of vineyard and orchard. The air was fragrant with odors of growing oranges, lemons and limes." Smythe's description of the irrigated landscape also captured something of the changing social landscape of the delta at the turn of the century: "On the bottom lands below we could see the Mexican laborers harvesting the crops."[2] Farther beyond, the Colorado River wound its way toward the Sea of Cortés.

Smythe's writings offered some of the earliest descriptions of the delta as a landscape fit for capital-intensive agricultural development. He took two reconnaissance trips during his visit, one southwesterly into the Mexican delta and a second to the Imperial Valley. His commentaries concerning the trip also revealed a great deal about attitudes toward the

Figure 1 Prior to irrigation, the valleys of the Colorado River Delta resembled the arid lands pictured here at the Imperial Irrigation District Experimental Farm, Number 2, in 1956. (Used by permission of the Imperial Irrigation District)

desert and Colorado River at the opening of the twentieth century. For Smythe, the Colorado Desert represented a vast sea of opportunity, awaiting only the waters of the Colorado River to reclaim it. Chiding those who believed that land was no good unless leafy trees naturally grew there, Smythe countered, "If the ancient civilizations bloomed in the arid deserts—as Egypt, Asia Minor and Syria . . . why not the new?"[3]

Smythe proclaimed the chalky brown floor of the Colorado River Delta fit for transformation into an agricultural oasis. During his trip to the Mexican delta, Smythe crossed the Colorado River, commenting that its "dark, deep water [flowed] uselessly to the ocean past an empire that has waited for centuries to feel the thrill of its living touch." Translating this metaphor into economic terms, he noted, "It is like a stream of golden dollars which spendthrift Nature pours into the sea."[4] Heading south

Figure 2 The Alamo Canal, pictured here, was the artery that made the border oasis possible. Since it flowed downhill toward the low-lying Imperial Valley, it offered the cheapest option for moving water from the Colorado River to the Mexicali Valley and the Imperial Valley without building expensive aqueducts across the sandy dunes between Yuma and the Imperial Valley. (Used by permission of the Imperial Irrigation District)

toward the Mexican border, he encountered some of the desert flora that lent personality to the delta: "Almost immediately we entered dense growths of mesquite trees and rank weeds of several varieties. The soil was a rich dark brown loam, formed by deposits of water." The fertile soil soon gave way to gravel as the travelers inched closer to the border. At a ranch near the border, Smythe's group stopped to admire an oasis of date palms, "from thirty to fifty feet high, bearing luxurious, ripening fruit." Mr. Hanlon, owner of the ranch, also exhibited other products of this desert Eden. Smythe reported, "We found that his prunes, figs, pome-granates, grapes, melons and garden vegetables were growing luxuri-antly." Hanlon also assured Smythe that he had produced green corn in forty days.[5]

Foreshadowing the work that the California Development Company and the Colorado River Land Company would undertake in creating a cotton empire in the Mexicali and Imperial Valleys, Smythe commented on the international aspects of reclamation of the delta. In reference to the Alamo Canal, an ancient canal through which water could be diverted to both valleys, he recorded: "Nature has also decreed that the diverted stream make its highway through these Mexican lands . . . which have [also] been procured as a part of the foundation of this superb enterprise."[6] Smythe foresaw few problems between the two nations in relation to the Colorado River, believing that the United States would control the terms of diversion as well as provide most of the capital to redeem the desert landscapes in the Mexicali Valley.

Smythe continued to extol the quality of the soil and desert flora growing in the delta. Mesquite trees reached forty feet into the sky, and their branches spanned outward as much as eighty-five feet in width. Gangly arrow weeds grew as high as fifteen feet, and grass for pasturing livestock and horses intermittently broke the flat landscape. Cocopah natives grew corn, melons, and beans in scattered settlements, and waterfowl hunted for food in the numerous lagunas and streams adjacent to the Colorado River. Moving closer to the Cocopah Mountains and the Laguna Salada, an inland lake south of Mexicali, Smythe rejoiced in the "soft, sweet atmosphere, the rich, level soil, the graceful mesquite trees, the abundance of pure spring water, the warm river in which we took a plunge, [and] the sky, alive with ducks, geese, storks and pelicans."[7] In contrast, volcanic mudflats near the Hardy River emitted a sulfurous smell and discouraged plant growth. Altogether, Smythe found the Mexican delta enchanting. Even the volcanic activity manifested a more benign side in the form of "warm mineral water, which might offer bathing facilities for thousands."[8]

Smythe's descriptions of Mexicans and Cocopah natives in the delta were limited but revealed prevalent attitudes toward non-Anglos during the early twentieth century, a period when Manifest Destiny and American imperialism intersected. Although the Cocopah had lived in the region for hundreds of years, Smythe questioned their ability to subdue the delta. In reference to the daily routine of his guide, Charley Cocopah, he noted, "Charley's family [gets] up. They go to bed." Smythe subsequently predicted the role of the Cocopah in the irrigated delta: "They are peaceful work-loving folk, who have earned their living by rude farming for

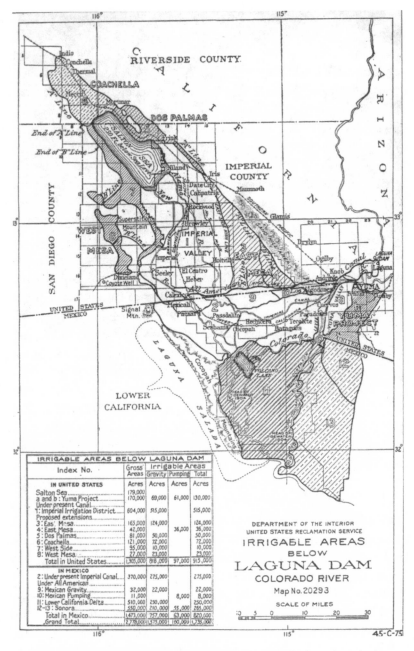

IRRIGABLE AREAS BELOW LAGUNA DAM				
Index No.	Gross Areas	Irrigable Areas		
		Gravity	Pumping	Total
IN UNITED STATES	Acres	Acres	Acres	Acres
Salton Sea	179,000			
a and b : Yuma Project	170,000	69,000	61,000	130,000
Under present Canal				
1: Imperial Irrigation District	604,000	515,000		515,000
Proposed extensions				
3: East Mesa	165,000	124,000		124,000
4: East Mesa	42,000		36,000	36,000
5: Dos Palmas	81,000	50,000		50,000
6: Coachella	121,000	72,000		72,000
7: West Side	95,000	10,000		10,000
8: West Mesa	27,000	23,000		23,000
Total in United States	1,305,000	818,000	97,000	915,000
IN MEXICO				
2: Under present Imperial Canal	370,000	275,000		275,000
Under All American				
9: Mexican Gravity	32,000	22,000		22,000
10: Mexican Pumping	11,000		8,000	8,000
11: Lower California Delta	510,000	250,000		250,000
12-13 : Sonora	550,000	210,000	55,000	265,000
Total in Mexico	1,473,000	757,000	63,000	820,000
Grand Total	2,778,000	1,575,000	160,000	1,735,000

DEPARTMENT OF THE INTERIOR
UNITED STATES RECLAMATION SERVICE

IRRIGABLE AREAS
BELOW
LAGUNA DAM
COLORADO RIVER
Map No. 20293

SCALE OF MILES

45-C-75

Map 1 The lower Colorado River Delta. The Imperial Canal, shown here, is also known as the Alamo Canal. (U.S. Bureau of Reclamation map)

generations. There are about two thousand of them in this locality, and they will make a useful class of laborers when the country is developed."[9]

Smythe also recognized that the creation of an irrigated border oasis would drastically transform the region's ecosystem in a relatively short period of time. He contrasted the desert's imminent fate with the millions of years it had taken the Colorado River to collect silt and rock from the rest of the river basin and deposit them near its mouth in the various valleys that comprised the delta. The flat valley floor of the Mexicali, Imperial, and Yuma Valleys gave way to expansive tidal plains as the river approached the sea. The Santa Rosa, Vallecito, and Juárez Mountains bounded the delta on the west, and Arizona's Dome Rock and Castle Dome Mountains contained the grand valley on the east.

Creative forces of destruction had given rise to the landscapes of the delta. Between 200,000 and 15 million years ago, volcanic activity and subduction of the Pacific Ocean plate by the North American plate parted the California peninsula from the North American mainland. The San Andreas Fault slowly pushed the Baja California peninsula and upper California north. Seismic and volcanic activity formed the mountains that ring the delta today. The resulting gulf between the Baja peninsula and Sonora filled with water from the Pacific Ocean. A great inland sea temporarily blanketed the floor of the present-day delta basin. This union of sea and land would contribute to the alkali character of the delta's soil.

The Colorado River initially flowed into the Colorado Desert and deposited rich silt, soil, and gravel from the entire Colorado River Basin, including the remains of the majestic Grand Canyon. Silt deposits along the river's sides eventually created the high banks of the Colorado River as well as covering the alkali floor of the delta valley. The river eventually found an outlet to the Gulf of California (also known as the Sea of Cortés), and the salts that remained on the delta floor would later test human efforts to sustain intensive agriculture in the Imperial, Mexicali, and Yuma Valleys.

As periodic flooding of the delta basin declined, some five hundred years before Spanish contact with the region, desert flora and fauna created oases of their own on the valley floor. Mesquite trees and cacti dotted the delta's valleys. Coyotes and bobcats hunted desert rabbits, pack rats, and squirrels. In turn, these creatures of the desert floor preyed on the succulent fruit of the saguaro and cardon cacti. Elf owls made their homes in the abandoned holes carved in the cacti by woodpeckers. At night, bats came to life in the cool desert air and immersed their heads in the flowers of the saguaro, feeding on their rich nectar. The bats then spread the saguaro pollen across the desert. Lifeblood of the desert, the various cacti offered water and sustenance to their animal neighbors.[10]

Despite the fact that large-scale irrigation and its attendant technologies would transform the landscape and social order of the Sonoran desert, Smythe believed that the benefits of marrying the desert's soil and water from the Colorado River with the latest technological advances would far outweigh any problems the experiment might create. Indeed, Smythe and his generation believed they were not harming the landscape by transforming it but instead were improving and reclaiming it.

There were potential economic and social advantages to the border oasis. Not only could just about anything be grown in the delta, but its citrus would be ready for market several weeks before citrus grown in central California. Smythe believed that the fecundity of the soil would require families to farm only five acres of land in order to prosper. The abundance of land would allow families to buy it for as little as ten to fifteen dollars an acre. As a result of such a high concentration of people per square mile, he believed, a new urban center would emerge in the delta on a par with the great cities of the Middle East. Basing his model for irrigated communities in the western United States on the commonwealth experience of Mormon communities in Utah during the nineteenth century, Smythe envisioned a new civilization where city and countryside would be linked by the border oasis. In such a region, "people will be independent, for individually and collectively they can produce everything they consume." He continued: "They will not go on making the old mistakes, these twentieth-century farmers. . . . No, we shall have another Holland here, full of genius and enterprise, and sufficient within itself. Nature has made it possible. The aspiration of men will demand it. This will be a commonwealth, and it will be true to its best possibilities, for we have the broad foundation for a life that should be truly great."[11]

Morally, Smythe believed, a civilization based on small farms with

Figure 3 In the early 1970s, the Environmental Protection Agency commissioned prominent photographers to travel throughout the United States and document in photographs significant examples of environmental change. Charles O'Rear traveled to the delta. This striking fish-eye shot of the Imperial Valley and the Salton Sea captures the gridlike landscape of the irrigated border oasis in 1972. (Courtesy of the National Archives and Records Administration)

limited acreage would encourage the region's residents to "[know] each other and [share] each other's burdens."[12] Smythe capped his vision with a description of the great city that would arise in the delta, "the twentieth century Damascus, fairer than that in the Syrian desert . . . and blessed with American liberty."[13]

By the end of the twentieth century, the delta had undergone an extraordinary transformation, just as William Ellsworth Smythe had predicted. However, the conditions Smythe had envisioned were much different from those that existed at the turn of the century. Socially and ecologically, the delta never developed into a cohesive region. What would Smythe find if we revived him and took him to the delta today? In 1997 journalist Frank Clifford lamented that the once-vibrant delta had become "a barren wedge of desert and salt flats where, some days, the only people to be seen for miles are military patrols on the lookout for drug smugglers." Cut off from the river's replenishing waters by the grasp of large western cities, power companies, and agricultural interests, the delta's biologically rich wetlands quickly deteriorated. Major dams upriver endangered numerous plant and animal species and also threatened the livelihood of the Cocopah Indians, who rely on the river for sustenance. Journalist Stan Grossfield succinctly noted that the river's water was "diverted to leaky irrigation channels, pipelines, swimming pools in Los Angeles, golf courses in Palm Springs; to cities like Denver, Salt Lake City, Albuquerque, San Diego, Tucson, Phoenix, and Las Vegas." Similarly, one Mexican writer lamented to Grossfield, "In exchange for all these swimming pools, dams, and lakes, the [Cocopah] people are dying."[14]

Ninety miles northwest of the confluence of the Colorado River and the Sea of Cortés, the New River dumps "a swirling, olive green soup of chemicals and bacteria . . . dead animals, industrial waste, and human excrement" into the Salton Sea.[15] The New River and the Salton Sea were rejuvenated in 1905 when engineers for the California Development Company attempted to open a new intake from the Colorado River to transport water to the Imperial Valley. Enticed by gravity, the entire course of the Colorado River raged through northern Baja California and then returned to the United States at Calexico, California, eventually filling the ancient Cahuilla Basin, now known as the Salton Sea. Intensive farming, *maquila* factories, and local sewage systems continue to pollute the river with wastewater.[16]

Why did these transformations take place? What factors were the most critical in transforming the delta? These are the questions that will be answered in the pages that follow. Academically, the history of the Colorado River Delta as an integrated binational region has been neglected.[17] Yet once the historical lens is focused on the connections between the two nations that geographically comprise the delta as well as

Map 2 The lower Colorado River Basin. (U.S. Bureau of Reclamation map)

the people who live there, we will have a clearer picture of how foreign relations and development have shaped the region. This is best accomplished by bringing diplomatic, borderlands, and environmental history together to examine the effects of development on a region that is geographically peripheral to both Mexico and the United States. In one sense, diplomatic history and environmental history are fundamentally at odds with each other. While diplomatic history defines its areas of interest by political boundaries, environmental history examines space on a landscape scale regardless of the political borders that might intersect that landscape. Yet development along the U.S.–Mexican border during the past century has encouraged historians to make connections between the two seemingly disparate fields. Social, economic, and political spheres of influence do not stop at the border. As a result, borderlands historians have attempted to measure the impact of human communities on the land and people of both nations. Within the context of borderlands history, then, environmental history and diplomatic history are ideal tools to help us understand the ways in which the actions of citizens in both nations overlap and conflict in the delta region.[18]

This book argues that Mexican and U.S. efforts on national, state, and local levels to develop agricultural oases in the delta were the key factors that transformed the region's landscape in less than a century. The political contests for water between the United States and Mexico also played a critical role in shaping the marriage of land and water envisioned by Smythe. Politicians and private individuals in each nation attempted to create their own border oases without considering how such actions affected people living on the other side of the border. U.S. development of the region began around the turn of the century as private interests and governmental agencies linked the Imperial Valley in California and the Yuma Valley in Arizona to global markets. American capitalists also controlled the rise of large-scale agribusiness in the Mexicali Valley. In 1937 Mexican president Lázaro Cárdenas challenged American economic supremacy in the region by expropriating farmlands of the American-owned Colorado River Land Company. Agribusiness interests on both sides of the border encouraged emigration from the interior of Mexico, further exhausting water resources. Ultimately, overemphasis on development in both nations led to an ecological breaking point beginning in the 1960s as salinity, pollution, and water shortages strained agricultural and industrial growth. With existing natural resources inadequate to sustain high levels of development, both nations appealed to nationalistic rhetoric in an effort to maintain the status quo. In 1974 both nations agreed to Minute 242 of the Mexican Water Treaty (signed in 1944), which obligated the United States to construct a desalinization plant near Yuma, Arizona, in order to purify saline drainage from the Wellton-Mohawk Irrigation and Drainage District.

Although William Ellsworth Smythe correctly predicted a transformation of the delta by the union of water from the Colorado River with the fertile delta soil, he misjudged the most volatile union that affected these new landscapes. In less than a century, Mexico and the United States had encouraged exploitation of the Colorado River to the point of causing damage, mainly in the form of salinity damage, to the fields, flora, and fauna on both sides of the border. National, state, and local interests on both sides of the border had failed to recognize the ways in which the border oasis was linked: by geography, irrigation systems, international treaties, and competition for scarce water resources.

Indeed, U.S.–Mexican relations played a transcendent role in the marriage of water and soil in the arid delta.

Deltascape The Spanish Delta

Spaniard José Joaquín Arrillaga served as assistant governor of the Californias in the 1780s and early 1790s, rising to the office of interim governor in 1792. He is best remembered for the four expeditions to Baja California he undertook in 1796 in order to locate suitable sites for Spanish missions between New Spain and Alta California. His fourth voyage, taken in October and November 1796, led him into the heart of the Cocopah communities in the Colorado River Delta.

On October 19, 1796, Arrillaga left Agua Caliente, near the southeastern base of the Juárez Mountains, at 3:30 in the morning. Traveling to the east, he watched the sun cast its first rays on poplar trees lining the banks of the Colorado River. By 9:30 he had arrived at the river, en route to the confluence of the river and the Gulf of California. Near the river's mouth, his horses refused to drink the water, as tidal bores mixed salt water with the fresh, muddied river water. By 11:00 in the morning Arrillaga could not approach the river's mouth due to the rising tide of the Sea of Cortés. He noted the strength of the river: "The waters leave the course of the river, as there is much dry debris as far away as the distance [of three leagues], and only water could take it there." As for the vegetation of the delta plain, "There are only reed thickets and brush. Poplar and willow trees are seen in the distance."[19]

During his expedition, Arrillaga interacted with the Cocopah and commented on their social organization, economic endeavors, and use of the land. Following the trails the Cocopah used to travel from their *rancherías* to the gulf, Arrillaga moved inland past large willow trees, watering holes, and pastures. As for the land, he noted, "All I covered is flat land with lots of briny soil, except the last two miles, which is evidently good land."[20] The following day, Arrillaga attempted to contact other Cocopah communities, offer-

Figure 4 A portion of the lower Colorado River. Note the four landscape features that characterize the region: the river, riparian vegetation, a thin strand of desert, and the mountain range. (U.S. Bureau of Reclamation photograph)

ing gifts and expressions of friendship to the natives. In exchange for Arrillaga's offering of cigarettes, the Cocopah presented the Europeans with an assortment of melons grown in the delta. These peace offerings led to spirited exchanges between the delta's first cultivators of truck crops and the Spaniards. "I allowed my people to buy from them melons and watermelons for their companions, in exchange for meat, biscuit, and cigarettes. They loaded themselves up with all they could."[21]

Arrillaga then headed north along the Hardy River toward present-day Mexicali. Along the way, melon fields and Cocopah huts impressed him. Shallow lagunas filled with saline water broke the monotony of the desert plain. Chimeras and mirages intermingled with actual lagunas. Clusters of mesquite trees and thickets of reeds shielded the cautious Spanish official as he traveled north. In spite of violent encounters with natives near the Hardy River, Arrillaga was highly impressed by the agricultural skills of the Cocopah: "In the ranchería where I was in the morning there was a plot of ripe melons, watermelons, pumpkins, and beans, the type they call yurimuri. I also saw many squashes and melons sliced up; they preserve them dried. The corn harvest had already been stored away. From this ranchería there are others which follow the riverbank. All the ground is moist."[22] He also noted the land-tenure patterns: "The land was populated with little houses or huts in such a way that each house had its plot, and some of them fairly large ones. Here everything that the eye can reach is populated, and far from the river. I was informed that next to the river it was even more densely [populated]." The Cocopah had also sunk wells into the desert floor to obtain potable water, but Arrillaga noted that when they dried up, the soil became salty, much like the alkali soil that pervaded the delta's floor.[23]

Ultimately, Arrillaga believed, the fertility of the land boded well for the future of agriculture there. Despite the fact that the cultivation of beans, melons, and watermelons limited the amount of arable land available to pasture European animals, Arrillaga averred, "I persuade myself by what I saw, that in those years when it rains regularly in the summer, sizable crops materialize." He concluded his overview by speculating, "Cotton would grow very well if it were sown." As for the condition of the natives, he remembered, "The Indian population I saw is immense, [and they are] very robust. It is evident that they have sufficient food."[24]

Arrillaga's observations provide a benchmark regarding the conditions of the lower delta in the late eighteenth century as well as the centrality of the river in the lives of Cocopah natives living there. Obviously, the absence of massive dams and canals upstream enhanced the agricultural endeavors of the Cocopah. During the nineteenth century, however, the Cocopah found their world rebordered when the United States signed the Treaty of Guadalupe Hidalgo (1848) and completed the Gadsden Purchase (1853). These two treaties effectively split the Cocopah into Mexican and U.S. communities.

border oasis

The Twentieth-Century Ghost
of William Walker

*Prevent Baja California's riches from being carried away to foreign
countries so that Mexico can take advantage of their development.*
—Mexican Federal Territories Development
Commission in Charge, 1936[1]

On October 28, 1853, after a long voyage from San Francisco, Tennessee native William Walker and a crew of adventurers disembarked from their ship, the *Caroline,* at Cabo San Lucas and quickly moved to establish the Republic of Baja California as an "American" colony where southerners could ranch, mine, and farm with their slaves. What the diminutive Walker lacked in physical stature he ably compensated for in ambition, if not wisdom. He recognized the economic potential of the arid landscape: "The mineral and ranching richness of Baja California is very great," he noted. Walker also felt justified in annexing the region, since the Mexican government had not developed its natural resources or protected it from Indian depredations. "Therefore," he trumpeted, "upon abandoning the peninsula, as an orphan in the sea, Mexico cannot complain if others take it and make good use of it."[2] Ironically, a fledgling Mexican militia near the border and the swift currents of the Colorado River, which claimed his supplies, ended Walker's filibustering dreams. In May 1854 he returned to San Diego defeated but not disheartened. Soon thereafter he embarked upon his more grandiose conquest of Nicaragua.

Antonio Meléndez, leader of the Mexican militia, feared that the infamous Walker was not the last American who would challenge Mexican sovereignty along the northwest frontier. "As the notices that they [the Americans] will return multiply," he frantically observed, "I am desperately waiting for the help of the Supreme Government, because the country is in a frightful misery, and we have neither the weapons nor the people to resist a strong coup."[3]

In fact, Walker's actions in Baja California, particularly in the wake of the U.S. war with Mexico (1846–48), foreshadowed the dynamics of conquest and intrigue that would characterize U.S.-Mexican contests over land and water resources in the Colorado River Delta for the next century and a half. Like Walker, a handful of U.S. citizens and politicians concocted schemes to wrest resources from Baja California and Sonora and build agricultural empires in Imperial, California, and Yuma, Arizona, Counties. While methods of conquest changed from physical force to legal and engineering maneuvers, the temptation to take or hold back natural resources from Mexican interests persisted into the twentieth century.

Motivated by economic ambition, American farmers, financiers, developers, and politicians insisted that the United States should be allowed to develop as much water from the Colorado River as possible. Many Mexicans, however, could not forget the realignment of their nation's borders in 1848 or the threat of filibusters during the second half of the nineteenth century.[4] Twentieth-century Mexican leaders thus viewed *Mexican* colonization and development of the region as the appropriate response to American economic ambitions in Baja California. Although Walker's scheme for colonization met an early end, his "ghost" reappeared in the form of new plans on both sides of the border to initiate different models of regional development. Walker's legacy reveals a theme that unifies the history of the Colorado River Delta: the conquest and control of land and water.

Like Walker's filibuster, most of these schemes met with resistance on the part of Mexican citizens and leaders. Attempts at conquest were often countered with measures to stimulate development in Baja California and to reinforce Mexican national identity. The most important example of Mexican resistance to American domination of natural resources in the region occurred during the presidency of Lázaro Cárdenas (1934–40). Building on the efforts of his predecessor, Abelardo L. Rodríguez (1932–34), who had also been governor of the northern district of Baja California territory from 1923 to 1929, Cárdenas made colonization and development of Baja California a priority of the Mexican state. His policies set the stage for federal initiatives in the region over the next forty years. The most dramatic of his reforms was the 1937 expropriation of land around Mexicali owned by the American consortium, the Colorado River Land Company (CRLC).[5]

Water Diplomacy and the Porfiriato

Political transitions in Mexico following Walker's Mexican filibuster facilitated the concentration of the delta's natural resources into the hands of American interests. Ironically, Mexican president Porfirio Díaz (1876–80, 1884–1911) supported the rise of an American agricultural empire in the Mexicali Valley during the first third of the twentieth century. Díaz, an adherent of liberal economic theory, believed that construction of Mexico's "path to modernity" required massive foreign investment.[6] The Porfirian regime allowed foreigners to purchase land, water, and mineral rights in Baja California and throughout Mexico.[7] Prior to Díaz's rise to power, Guillermo Andrade, an ambitious Mexican developer who had worked in San Francisco as a banker and an official for the Mexican government, obtained massive land grants in Baja California and Sonora from President Sebastián Lerdo de Tejada (1872–76). Andrade subsequently initiated colonization of the Mexican delta. In 1888, during the Porfirian regime, Andrade received the titles to the earlier concession,[8] giving him ownership of almost all irrigable land in the Mexican delta. In the three years before his death in 1905, Andrade sold approximately 800,000 acres of that land to the newly incorporated CRLC, headed by Harrison Otis and his son-in-law Harry Chandler, the owners of the *Los Angeles Times*.[9]

With ample capital, Chandler and Otis succeeded where others had failed. In the arid Sonoran desert, the availability of water largely determines the fecundity of the land. For hundreds of years, Cocopah and Quechan natives had waited for the annual spring floods of the Colorado River to irrigate their crops. By the end of the nineteenth century, a small group of U.S. capitalists, known collectively as the Colorado Development Company (CDC), believed that water could be transported through a natural conduit, the Alamo Canal, across the sand dunes from the Colorado River near the international boundary to the Imperial Valley. In 1893 the CDC began preparing the canal for modern use. Unfortunately, the gravity-powered canal crossed the international boundary into Mexico, passing through Mexicali and then returning to the United States at present-day Calexico, California. In exchange for a concession to use the canal, which the corporation bought from Andrade, the Mexican government stipulated that 50 percent of the water be used on Mexican soil. In 1904 the CRLC acquired the majority of Mexico's water rights in the Mexicali Valley from Andrade, the Mexican intermediary for the CDC.

Chandler and Otis took capital integration to a new level in the Mexicali Valley. Through their vast array of interests, the Los Angeles magnates dominated the region's agribusiness. As their constitution stated, the CRLC's owners wanted not only to acquire as much land as possible in the region but also "to have control and superintendence of roads, land and sea communication, bridges, warehouses, waterways, aqueducts, loading docks, furnaces, mills, hydraulic works, factories, storehouses . . . [and also to control] all mercantile, mining, agricultural, and industrial exploitation in all its branches . . . whatever may be its object, duration, and denomination without restrictions as principals, agents, associates, representatives, or of any other way and have rights, faculties, and intervention in the expressed businesses."[10] In order to accomplish this ambitious goal of regional domination, Chandler and Otis subleased land to Mexican brokers, who in turn rented land to tenant farmers over a period of ten years. Chandler and Otis preferred Chinese immigrants to receive contracts, since they were easier to transport (by ship) to the region than Mexicans (from the nation's interior) and less likely to demand outright ownership of land. Contracts stipulated that tenants give 50 percent of each crop to the CRLC as well as agree to process cotton at CRLC-controlled subsidiaries. While this process greatly enriched Chandler and his associates, it raised questions among Mexico's leaders regarding the degree of U.S. influence in Mexicali.[11]

The U.S. government developed a strong interest in the delta region in the wake of a tragic flood, instigated by CDC engineers, that inundated the Imperial and Mexicali Valleys between 1905 and 1907. On January 12, 1907, President Theodore Roosevelt expressed keen federal interest in development of the region, even if it meant paying the CRLC to construct levees on Mexican territory to protect the Imperial Valley from future floods. In a message to Congress, Roosevelt chided the CDC for financial

Figure 5 In 1905, the California Development Company opened an additional intake from the Colorado River to the Alamo Canal, setting in motion a catastrophic flood that wreaked havoc in the Mexicali Valley as well as in the Imperial Valley. (Used by permission of the Imperial Irrigation District)

and engineering mismanagement, yet he also noted that the "entire irrigable area which will be submerged or deprived of water in the Imperial Valley and along the Colorado River is capable of adding to the permanent population of Arizona and California at least 350,000 people, and probably 500,000." The land would soon "be worth from $500 to $1,500 per acre to individual owners, or a total of from $350,000,000 to $700,000,000." Furthermore, once Laguna Dam (near Yuma) was finished, Imperial Valley farmers would have a more reliable intake point from the Colorado River. Accordingly, Roosevelt pledged federal support to protect development in the region.[12]

In the fall of 1910 the U.S. Department of the Interior initiated construction of a twenty-five-mile levee below the shoddy intake that had caused floods beginning in 1905.[13] The Mexican government denied a U.S. request to take control of CRLC-owned land below the border where the levees would be constructed, but the Department of the Interior subsequently subsidized construction of levees that became the property of the CRLC.[14] Fortuitously for Chandler and Otis, these levees not only protected the Imperial Valley but also provided greater security for their investments south of the border.[15]

Díaz's willingness to open land to foreigners and encourage linkages with the U.S. economy seemed more benign than imperialistic military assaults from the north, but it portended much stronger connections to the U.S. economy. At the turn of the century, the Mexicali Valley epitomized liberal patterns of Porfirian development as well as any other region along the border. By 1910 a railroad extension linked Mexicali to the Southern Pacific line that ran from Los Angeles via El Paso to New Orleans. The Alamo Canal linked the region's water supply to that of the Imperial Valley, and the CDC administered the sale of water in the Mexicali Valley. U.S. banks supplied capital for Baja California farmers. And while Mexicali gins sent their cotton to Los Angeles and New Orleans for sale, American corporations supplied Mexican consumers, farmers, and industries with finished goods. Finally, during Prohibition, U.S. capital poured into Mexicali, stimulating a notorious tradition of casinos and bars just across the border from Calexico.[16] As one historian aptly noted, "Mexicali had become so Americanized as to be the equivalent of [the] United States South."[17]

Water, Land, and the Mexican Revolution

For the most part, the delta escaped the massive destruction wreaked in Mexico's interior during the Mexican Revolution. Early on, however, Ricardo Flores Magón, radical visionary and founder of the Partido Liberal Mexicano (PLM), insisted that Mexico needed to embrace a utopian plan whereby each citizen would be given "Land and Liberty." During the first decade of the twentieth century, Flores Magón's contact with radical labor movements in the United States and his memory of the repressive hand of foreign capital in Mexico shaped his plan for revolution. He decided to launch his radical revolution against the Porfirian regime and foreign capitalists from Baja California. The peninsula was sparsely populated. Given the disjointed nature of his organization throughout Mexico, Baja California offered Flores Magón a place in which he could build momentum before reaching the more heavily populated Mexican interior. Baja California was also ideal because U.S. citizens owned most of its productive land and resources. In fact, an attack on Mexicali would pit Mexico's most outspoken anarchist, Flores Magón, against one of the most efficient capitalist organizations in Mexico, the CRLC. As one scholar observed, "To go to Baja California [with Flores Magón] was not merely to participate in a military campaign, but [to participate] fundamentally in a work of social reconstruction." In harmony with his demand for "Land and Liberty," Flores Magón encouraged natives and workers to "take the lands and work them in your own behalf without recognizing the rights of the rich."[18]

In the wake of PLM attacks on Mexicali and Tijuana in January and February 1911, the U.S. State Department warned Mexico that unless protection of the levees could be guaranteed, "the Government of the United States would be prepared to cooperate with the Government of Mexico by using its own military forces for the common purpose." The same report noted that as of February 12, 1911, the PLM rebels had retaken Mexicali and that they intended to "entice the Mexican workmen to join them, to drive off the work animals, and to destroy the property."[19] The Mexican embassy declined U.S. military support but offered instead the services of Col. Celso Vega, President Díaz's military governor on the peninsula, plus two hundred men to protect the levee works. When Vega and his troops were defeated during a skirmish en route to Mexicali, the Mexican government ordered the Eighth Division, under the direction of Colonel Mayol, to travel from Manzanillo to Mexicali to protect the works. In the interim, the Department of the Interior received authorization from the Mexican government for the CRLC to employ "as many [nonuniformed] guards as may be necessary to afford adequate protection of the works." In the end, PLM revolutionaries inflicted only minor damage. Nevertheless, the attacks heightened American interest in developing the delta.[20]

prosperity and conquest in the colorado River Delta

In the wake of the revolution and World War I, the return of relative political calm in Mexico logically should have led to greater cooperation between the two nations over the utilization of natural resources in the delta. However, a strong sense of nationalism emerged in Mexico after the revolution. President Álvaro Obregón (1920–24) emphasized the importance of linking the economy of Baja California to the rest of Mexico. Simultaneously, in the United States, wartime prosperity for farmers and western cities encouraged politicians and businessmen throughout the Colorado River Basin to seek a division of the river's water among themselves in anticipation of future development.

Beginning in 1920, representatives from Colorado, Utah, Wyoming, New Mexico, Arizona, California, and Nevada met to apportion water among the seven Colorado River Basin states. Mexico was not invited to participate in the discussions on the grounds (at least in part) of a 1906 legal ruling involving the division of water from the upper Rio Grande between the United States and Mexico. At that time, Attorney General Judson Harmon had ruled that the country of origin, in cases involving international rivers, retained the right to use as much water as it desired from the stream in question. Accordingly, the State Department informed Mexico: "This Commission presumably will meet at some date in the future to consider the distribution of the mutual interests of each of such States in the waters of the Colorado River, but . . . it is believed the result of any such consideration will not affect Mexico in any way."[21] Nevertheless, at least one newspaper, *El Universal,* a leading Mexico City daily, noted that "cotton-growers of Arizona and California are seeking by means of dams and impoundings altogether to deprive Mexicans of the waters of the Colorado River to which they are justly entitled pursuant to the Guadalupe Treaty signed in 1848."[22]

Some of the strongest proponents of the Colorado River Compact and the Boulder Canyon Dam Project were residents in Imperial and Yuma Counties. Farmers in Imperial County wanted to construct an expensive canal, the All-American Canal, that would transport water from the Colorado River to the Imperial Valley without leaving the United States. Throughout the entire basin, anti-Mexican sentiment also encouraged western politicians to appropriate as much water as possible for their own states. Ironically, much of this xenophobia was directed at the U.S.-owned CRLC, which received its water at a lower cost than other U.S. water users and benefited from U.S. flood-control devices without having to contribute to their maintenance. These exclusionary tactics were not lost on the Mexican media or Mexico's diplomats.[23]

Figure 6 This Charles O'Rear photograph illustrates how the All-American Canal literally divides the United States and Mexico (to the left of the canal) as it carries water to the Imperial Valley. (National Archives and Records Administration photograph)

Arizona senator Henry Ashurst brought the delta and its capacity to generate controversy to the fore in both Mexico and the United States. In January 1931, Ashurst placed a proposal before the U.S. Senate to purchase the Baja California peninsula and ten thousand square miles of Sonora along the Colorado River Delta from Mexico "peaceably and honorably." Ashurst had made a similar proposal in 1919, ostensibly as a measure of protection against the wartime enemies of the United States, but the political context of resource allocation in the delta had changed during the intervening twelve years. Most importantly, the institutionalization of the Mexican Revolution in national politics had placed sovereignty over natural resources at the top of Mexico's agenda. Graciously, Mexican president Pascual Ortiz Rubio (1930–32) treated Ashurst's proposal as a joke. Indeed, a number of Mexican deputies suggested that the peninsula be sold only after Mexico opened "negotiations to buy Arizona, California, New Mexico, Texas, and New Orleans."[24]

Ashurst failed to grasp the gravity of his request and the nationalist fervor that it evoked south of the border. From his perspective, "there is no thought of aggression or of a purpose of taking away by force. It is simply a plan to purchase land similar to transactions effected by the United States in the past." Nevertheless, for many Mexicans even an offer to purchase the peninsula smacked of Walkeresque aggression. Ashurst, like Walker, argued that "lower California is practically useless to Mexico, but would be of value to the United States from a commercial and strategical point of view." The *Literary Digest* linked the proposal to a plan to avoid negotiating a water treaty, similar to the Colorado River Compact, with Mexico. "No great stretch of the imagination is needed," the article observed, "to see a link between the purchase and the Boulder Dam development which involves Mexico's rights in the distribution of the Colorado River waters."[25]

A New York–based magazine, the *Outlook and Independent*, noted that the purchase of land in both Baja California and Sonora would give the United States "complete control of the river and [obviate] all difficulties over the distribution of water." While some Mexican officials had treated the proposal with levity, the same article noted that "if it is pressed, there will be little laughing in nationalistic Mexico." Such was the case with Mexico's highly nationalistic secretary of public works,

Juan Almazán, who linked the recurring threat of American annexation of Baja California to "the lack of communication between that region and the rest of Mexico." Adequate infrastructure was a national necessity, he reasoned, because "to oppose such works, arguing that these are hard times, and that it is a poor commercial investment because trade does not justify it, shows in my opinion, an utter disregard of the very real and immediate danger of a new mutilation of the Fatherland."[26] Almazán played an important role in preparing for increased Mexican control of land and water resources in Baja California that accelerated during the Cárdenas presidency.

More than likely, Senator Ashurst made his proposal out of historical ignorance, not as an attempt to insult Mexicans. However, his plan illustrates that the ghost of William Walker still roamed the region, though in different forms. Control of natural resources had become more legalistic, assuming the form of treaties instead of military attacks. Nevertheless, no matter how much the forms of conquest changed, proximity to the United States kept the memory of nineteenth-century incursions alive in the minds of many Mexicans.

Lázaro Cárdenas and the Mexicanización of the Delta

In 1934 Lázaro Cárdenas assumed the presidency of Mexico. Just as Franklin Delano Roosevelt served as a paragon of optimism for a depressed United States, Cárdenas rekindled the flames of the Mexican Revolution and brought hope to a highly stratified society still largely dominated by foreign capital. Prior to his first year in office, Cárdenas traveled throughout Mexico to assess the needs of the nation. His itinerary included a stop in Mexicali. It was the first visit to the peninsula by a Mexican president or presidential candidate since that of Abelardo Rodríguez, who had also governed in Baja California. After his trip, Cárdenas outlined an ambitious program of social reform and economic nationalization to be carried out during his presidency. One of his goals was to "distribute among Mexicans the enormous latifundio of the Colorado River Land Company that occupies the Mexicali Valley."[27] At the same time, he hoped to colonize the expropriated land with migrant Mexican workers currently laboring in the United States. At the end of his reflections on his visit to

Mexicali, Cárdenas expressed high hopes for the city's future. By building on its agricultural foundations, he observed, "Mexicali should make itself into an industrial city."[28]

Cárdenas's close associates also apprised him of Mexicali's potential for development. On November 3, 1935, Gen. Ernesto Aguirre Colorado expressed the need for immediate action to counteract U.S. influences there. Baja California, he announced, was in a "grandiose dilemma." He enjoined Cárdenas, "Either attend to that piece of your country's land immediately, or it will be gone within ten years." He contrasted U.S. roads to Baja California with Mexico's access. Aguirre also noted that for Mexicans who immigrated to the territory, "the sacrifices are so enormous on these trips, many Mexican lives have been lost while crossing the desert, and many vehicles have never arrived at their destination."[29]

Aguirre focused on the potential for agricultural development in the region. He informed Cárdenas that now was the time to act. U.S. interests were quickly exhausting the water resources of the Colorado River. The U.S. Bureau of Reclamation was diverting water to Los Angeles "to irrigate lands that today are unproductive, converting them later on into fecund lands." If Cárdenas did not act quickly, Aguirre calculated, "a problem will present itself for the very fertile cotton fields of the Mexicali region." He recommended construction of a railway to Sonora from Baja California, building highways to link the region to Mexico's interior, federal promotion of state development, purchase of CRLC lands, and increased irrigation from the Colorado River.[30]

In 1936 Cárdenas unveiled a sweeping plan for increased integration of Baja California and Quintana Roo (in the Yucatan peninsula), two peripheral federal territories, into the economic and political structures of Mexico. He emphasized the importance of racial, ethnic, and cultural unity in those two regions as well as the need to develop the resources of Baja California.[31] Cárdenas wanted to increase the population in Baja California and to construct highways and railways between the peninsula and central Mexico to stimulate domestic trade and migration. He hoped the promise of land in Baja California would attract many Mexicans who were working in the United States. A memo circulating through the executive office stated his objectives even more succinctly: "Three factors are necessary to achieve repopulation and integral resurgence of these zones: cheap land, cheap water, and cheap labor."[32]

In order to stimulate migration to and investment in the region, a federal commission was appointed with the express purpose of promoting the development of Baja California. The commission drew up a list of "Cincuenta Pensamientos" (Fifty thoughts), many of which reflect a conscious effort by the Cárdenas administration to protect the northern frontier from foreign influences. One statement linked regional integration to national duty: "To Mexicanize the territories is to strengthen the Fatherland." Another appealed to the changing role of the peninsula in Mexican memory: "Our grandparents had the luxury of forgetting Baja California and Quintana Roo; today, the imperatives of life require that we remember them always." The lure of irrigated farms and the potential for economic prosperity were also employed by the commission to "Mexicanize" the delta. The official propaganda downplayed the harshness of the region's sweltering climate by emphasizing the opportunities for economic advancement: "The malignity of the climate of Baja California is a fable. In reality, there are not endemic or regional sicknesses. The inconveniences of the climate are recompensed by the fruits of labor in this rich region." Other slogans reemphasized the theme of prosperity on the frontier: "If you like, you can not only make yourself independent but also turn a fortune as you go to a place [Baja California] where you can do it. The Mexican territories offer everything that you need." The commission reiterated the prospect of irrigated fields for those willing to migrate northward: "The territories need irrigation so that crops can break the earth, but irrigation requires colonists." Finally, in an effort to recruit colonists and laborers, the committee appealed to Mexican nationalism to counter continued foreign domination of the region. Perhaps in response to repeated U.S. requests originating at the local and state levels to purchase Baja California, the committee urged, "Decrease foreign covetousness of the territories of Baja California . . . by cooperating to achieve [its] true national integration."[33]

Implementation of Cárdenas's plan occurred through federal and local initiatives. In 1936 the Mexican government signed an agreement with the CRLC, requiring it to liquidate its lands gradually to Mexican nationals.[34] On January 27, 1937, a groundswell of local dissatisfaction with the CRLC's unwillingness to execute that accord inspired numerous factions of land-hungry *campesinos* to take control of leased plots from the company. Shortly thereafter, Cárdenas authorized the accelerated occupation and purchase of lands from the CRLC in the Mexicali Valley. Initially, fields were broken up into farm plots known as *ejidos. Ejida-tarios,* or peasants who received these lands, were granted usufructuary rights to the land by the Mexican government but not awarded outright ownership of the plots. Better quality lands were slowly broken up and sold as private property in areas known as *colonias* whose owners were known as *colonos*. By 1956, 157,781 hectares of land formerly owned by the CRLC had been sold to colonos, while 116,546 hectares had been distributed among ejidatarios.[35] The rapid growth that occurred between 1937 and 1956 stretched local water resources to the limit and often caused tension between colonos and ejidatarios.

The exploitation of water from the Colorado River played a central role in Cárdenas's plan to develop the Mexicali Valley. Cárdenas directed the secretary of agriculture and development to find out which lands could be settled and to assure that those lands could "be sufficiently irrigated."[36] He also asked the secretary of foreign relations to obtain from U.S. officials a definite statement on Mexico's water rights to the Colorado River.[37] Because of the ambivalence of U.S. officials toward Cárdenas's request, the Mexican president encouraged intensive development of the Mexicali Valley. Cárdenas believed that if a treaty ever were drawn up, the United States would have to provide Mexico with enough water to irrigate lands currently in use. While the legal principles related to the apportionment of international rivers remained unclear, most Mexican legal experts believed that Mexico would be granted at least enough water for land under development if the issue went to arbitration. In a letter to Baja California governor Rafael Navarro Cortina, Cárdenas emphasized this belief when he asserted: "It is important to consider that the more land we place under cultivation, the better our prospects for a greater volume of water from U.S. reserves from the Colorado River."[38]

Local leaders in Mexicali and San Luís also influenced Mexican claims to water resources in the delta. On December 24, 1935, Bernardo Batiz of the Department of Public Health in Baja California and Antonio Basich, secretary of agriculture and development of Baja California, expressed their frustrations with U.S. unwillingness to spell out Mexico's water rights to the river. Batiz and Basich also emphasized the importance of that resource in regional development, noting that Colorado River waters were "the only and irreplaceable source of wealth and even of subsistence" in the region. One year later, the same pair of officials suggested to federal officials that a rapid increase in water appropriation would provide Mexico with leverage against the United States in case a treaty were drawn up. They concluded that Mexico was in a better position than the United States to maximize the use of water from the Colorado River for agricultural purposes.[39]

In terms of its effects on the ecosystem, the *mexicanización* of the delta intensified a dramatic process of natural resource exploitation that had been initiated by U.S. farmers, bankers, and speculators during the late nineteenth century.[40] The addition of Mexican pressures on water resources brought about an unprecedented binational competition in the region, abetted by mutual mistrust, that has endured to the present. Demographic, agricultural, and industrial growth placed even greater demands on water and labor resources on both sides of the border after the 1930s. Government officials and residents from both nations shared responsibility for this precipitous increase in water use. Cárdenas may have encouraged residents to bring as many hectares under cultivation as possible to establish additional water rights, yet the unwillingness of U.S. officials to provide a reasonable guarantee of water from the Colorado River for Mexico only intensified his efforts to secure prior-use rights. Conversely, Mexican expropriation of previously American-owned lands in the Mexicali Valley prompted local leaders in the United States to increase their own appropriations from the Colorado River.

On December 1, 1940, Cárdenas passed the tricolor presidential sash to his more conservative successor, Manuel Ávila Camacho (1940–46). After Ávila Camacho delivered his acceptance speech before the Mexican Senate, he accompanied Cárdenas to the president's office in the National Palace, where Cárdenas gave Ávila Camacho several notes. In his journal Cárdenas described three of the messages he had passed on. Each reflected his concern that the United States respect Mexican sovereignty. In the first, which he had written to his successor on January 1, 1940,

Cárdenas recommended that the nation's president "continue working until obtaining the absolute respect of the sovereignty of the [Mexican] nation." Cárdenas believed that this principle of national sovereignty, which he had defended throughout his presidency, was an invaluable legacy of the revolutionary tradition. "[If] the citizen who follows me is in agreement with this principle," the outgoing president observed, "it will serve him well to transmit it to his immediate successor [as well]."[41]

At the same time, Cárdenas left Ávila Camacho with more specific ideas as to how he should defend Mexico's sovereignty in Baja California. "The marked interest that exists on the part of our neighbors to the north concerning the territories of Baja California," Cárdenas noted, "has been demonstrated on various occasions, trying to acquire them with distinct pretexts." He noted that the duty-free zones established around the border regions facilitated not only trade but also "the growth of the [Mexican] population." Cárdenas advocated further development in the Mexican delta and programs to encourage immigration to the territory. Economic growth and immigration, he held, would eventually lead to a population of over one million Mexicans on the peninsula. "Human growth runs like the rivers. It runs toward the low or uninhabited lands."[42]

Despite the ideological shifts of Cárdenas's successors, his encouragement of development in and immigration to the Colorado River Delta remained a firm part of the Mexican presidential agenda during the next thirty-five years. Ultimately, Cárdenas's efforts to promote the mexicanización of Baja California answered Antonio Meléndez's 1854 plea for federal help following William Walker's attempted annexation of the Mexican delta.

The Historical Legacies of Conquest

In spite of Walker's ultimate failure as a filibusterer, he endures for many Mexicans as a symbol of the aggressive tendencies of their neighbors to the north. Furthermore, Walker's incursion into northwestern Mexico offers an appropriate starting point for understanding what, in a different context, Patricia Limerick has called an "unbroken legacy" that connects the history of the West in the nineteenth and twentieth centuries.[43] This

is especially true in the case of the U.S.–Mexican borderlands generally and the Colorado River Delta specifically.

The conquest of land and water links events in the region to larger themes in the history of Mexico and U.S.–Mexican relations. The enduring legacy of agribusiness in Mexicali, for example, reflects the lingering effects of the Porfiriato in the region as well as the community's proximity to the United States. That legacy was further enhanced by the period of peace the area enjoyed, notwithstanding the turmoil during the Mexican Revolution. As María Eugenia Anguiano Tellez reminds us: "This region finds itself [overlooked] by studies and discussions that address capitalism in Mexico, even though it is an example of the diversity of situations created and reproduced by . . . capitalist development."[44]

Contests over land and water in the delta region during the extended revolutionary period (1910–40) also reflect broader national debates concerning the type of development that the Mexican state should pursue. While some historians have concluded that the Flores Magón assault on Baja California was merely a peripheral event during the early revolution, his attempt to take control of the CRLC's operations in the Mexicali Valley pitted the most radical revolutionary voices against one of the most efficient U.S. interests in northern Mexico. This foreshadowed a central theme of twentieth-century Mexican society: the debate over the ways in which wealth and power should be distributed among the nation's people. Cárdenas's expropriation of land and broad federal initiatives in Baja California represented a less radical, although more successful, approach to preserving the state's resources from American interests than Flores Magón's insurrection.

The efforts of the federal government to "Mexicanize" the region also provide a new perspective on the Cárdenas regime. For both U.S. and Mexican citizens living in the delta during the late 1930s, Cárdenas's expropriation of land, distribution of plots among campesinos, and comprehensive plan for economic integration to the Mexican state were revolutionary. Yet Cárdenas's plan for regional nationalization was more of a "halfway revolution," for, due to a lack of federal and private funds, he was unable to achieve the type of development occurring north of the border. In fact, U.S. interests continued to dominate financing, cotton processing, and water distribution through the 1960s, when Mexican cooperatives and the national government finally amassed the capital necessary to take them over from their U.S. counterparts.[45] In the wake of Cárdenas's redistribution of land, U.S. banks financed most of the farms in the Mexicali Valley. U.S. corporations also controlled ginning and fertilizing services in the valley.[46] Finally, the realities of U.S.–Mexican relations demanded that Cárdenas maintain cordial relations with the United States even as he warred against transnational corporate influences within Mexican society.[47]

In terms of binational relations, perhaps no region better exemplifies some of the tensions and complexities of diplomacy between Mexico and the United States. Through the lens of water politics and diplomacy, we witness the greatest paradox of U.S.–Mexican relations up close: a bilateral pursuit for economic independence within the context of asymmetrical interdependence. Despite the tensions generated by filibusters and sometimes abetted by mutual ignorance, neither nation achieved the type of development it desired without some help from the neighboring country. For farmers in Baja California, the quest for politico-economic "independence" could not overcome reliance on private and public organizations in the United States for capital, technology, and protection from floods by dams upstream. For farmers in the United States, capital-intensive agriculture in the region would have been impossible without a cheap migrant labor force from across the border. And although U.S. interests and agencies had an economic advantage over their Mexican counterparts, Mexico aggressively developed the region to the extent that its resources allowed. This approach not only responded to the murmur of U.S. annexationists circulated throughout the region in the early 1930s but also reflected the government's encouragement of agribusiness following the violent phase of the Mexican Revolution.[48] Unfortunately, geography and lack of capital placed farmers in the Mexicali Valley at a disadvantage to exploit natural resources from the Colorado River. Yet the two nations were more apt to cooperate than to resort to armed conflict when resolving differences following the Mexican Revolution.[49]

While the mission of William Walker and that of U.S. and Mexican citizens in the twentieth-century delta were not identical, their intent to maximize control over the region's resources provides a window through which to visualize the delta's economic development and environmental challenges during the past century and a half. By the early twentieth century, Walker and Manifest Destiny were dead, but the scarcity of water in the Colorado River Delta continued to stimulate heated, if at times mundane, legalistic and technical discussions between citizens of the two nations over resource allocation.

Deltascape The Cocopah Delta

The following letter from Henry Frauenfelder, president of the Yuma County Water Users Association, to Sen. Carl Hayden explores some of the challenges the Cocopah faced in the late 1930s as a result of increased competition between the United States and Mexico for water resources and stricter control of the international boundary.

In re: Cocopah Indians of Yuma Valley, Arizona
Dear Senator Hayden:
These people are experiencing more or less difficulty with the United States Immigration Service. Their troubles amount to extreme hardship and suffering when members of this tribe are deported into Mexico. The welfare of these neglected people is important to us who farm here because they furnish the only supply of dependable labor during the hottest part of our summers. Also they are the best cotton pickers available anywhere.

On the whole they are peaceful and law abiding, of necessity always willing to work whenever employment can be found. Never recipients of government help or relief they must depend upon manual labor for a livelihood. This seems hardly fair in view of what is being done for other American Indians, as the Cocopahs have always lived in the river bottom lands along the Colorado even though they did roam at times below the border of our country. They are, at least, as much American as they are Mexican, Indians. Living on the crops raised on overflow lands, they moved from one favored spot to another up and down the river. This habit followed for many generations influenced these Indians even until recent times.

Radical changes in our United States Immigration Laws made about the time of our entry and participation in the World War made the entry of such Indians thereafter illegal. However no one took the trouble to inform these . . . people of the new laws and how it affected them. Neither were they then immediately deported. It was only comparatively recently, about two years ago, that the immigration authorities then stationed at San Luís, made a complete survey of all the Cocopah Indians living in the Yuma Valley. Many were thereupon deported into Mexico. These unfortunates, due to a controlled flow of the Colorado, couldn't raise crops on overflow lands as in former years, and consequently were forced to live in a condition of semi-starvation thereafter.

Aside from the rather selfish motive of wanting these Indians to remain here as our most reliable source of labor supply, I am sincerely interested from a humanitarian standpoint in their welfare. . . . Steps should be taken . . . to aid the whole Cocopah tribe, now residing in the United States. A continual harassing and threatening of these . . . unfortunate people is not at all consistent with our President's sincere desire to help the underprivileged classes. I respectfully ask you to check up on this matter and use your influence toward securing a better deal for these people.

Yours very sincerely,
Henry Frauenfelder, YCWUA President[50]

1940s H₂O shortages → Mx water independence ↑ (Morelos Dam, Water Treaty of 1944). Greater interdependence [join effort to exploit region/workers econmly. Impending ecol crisis.

"Our 'Good Neighbors' "

By 1940 dynamic agricultural and ecological revolutions were under way in the Mexicali, Imperial, and Yuma Valleys.[1] While Mexicans and Americans shared the same creditors, links to the global market, and crop-production patterns, the enduring question of water allocation drove the deepest wedge between them between 1935 and 1974. Mexican leaders were most concerned about the lack of a treaty specifying the amount of water Mexicali and San Luís Río Colorado would receive from the river. Although the United States ignored Mexico's requests to participate in the negotiation of the Colorado River Compact (1928), which apportioned the river's water between the seven U.S. states in the basin, Mexican leaders still believed that at some point the United States would have to recognize Mexico's rights to a portion of the river's water. As a result, President Cárdenas encouraged massive development of the Mexican delta, culminating in the signing of the Mexican Water Treaty (1944), the construction of Morelos Dam (1950), and the purchase of the waterworks infrastructure for Mexicali Valley from the Imperial Irrigation District (1960).

Post-Cárdenas Development of the Mexicali Valley

Cárdenas's ambitious colonization plan in the delta did not go unnoticed by local American officials. During January and February 1938, Arizona state legislator Hugo Farmer made four trips to Mexicali to assess agricultural development there. He reported that over 400,000 acres were either developed or being prepared for cultivation. He also observed that the Mexican government had initiated construction of a railroad between Baja California and Sonora as well as a harbor on the gulf "to ship the produce of Mexicali into Mexico for use by the Mexican people." Farmer's observations later fueled efforts in Arizona to win approval for two irrigation

Figure 7 Imperial Dam, north of Yuma, Arizona. The river narrows after it flows through the dam because much of the water flows into the All-American Canal (to the right of the river below the dam), where it is carried to the Imperial Valley. (U.S. Bureau of Reclamation photograph)

projects, including one in Yuma County's Wellton-Mohawk Valley. The recognition of possible water shortages in the future further stimulated efforts to increase arable lands on both sides of the border in the delta.[2]

New development throughout the Colorado River Basin in the United States also influenced Mexican efforts to develop the Mexicali Valley. The construction and operation of the All-American Canal and Boulder, Parker, and Imperial Dams during the 1930s and 1940s greatly disrupted the river's flow regimes downstream. Instead of being controlled primarily by precipitation and natural runoff, the river was regulated by U.S. Bureau of Reclamation (USBR) engineers, who controlled releases from dams upstream depending on the needs of the states included in the Colorado River Basin.

This method of control profoundly affected Mexican residents in the delta. When residents in Mexicali and San Luís Río Colorado anticipated high flow regimes, local organizations built defensive structures to protect riverside fields from the threat of floods. Conversely, when the river was too shallow to enter the Mexicali Valley's intake at Alamo Canal, local leaders turned to national officials, hoping they could convince the United States to increase water flows south of the border. Over time, this stop-and-go process increased tensions between residents of the two nations and compelled Mexican officials to secure an adequate water supply without having to turn to the United States for help so frequently. E. Aguirre Camacho, a relative of Mexican president Manuel Ávila Camacho, best expressed this guarded mistrust toward *norteamericanos* when he wrote: "The cotton will be lost if our 'good neighbors' don't loosen water from the Colorado River. These gentlemen are our 'good neighbors' since 1847 and they either make war on us or drag us into it according to their desires. Be concerned for us, Manuel, and save the region."[3]

The erratic flow patterns set in motion by U.S. dams adversely impacted recent developments in the Mexican delta. In 1941 the Colorado River flooded 1,500 hectares of land adjacent to the river and destroyed an estimated 400,000 pesos worth of cotton. The flood also immobilized the new bridge that linked Mexicali to Puerto Peñasco. Baja California governor Rodolfo Sánchez Taboada reported that the floods resulted from releases from Boulder Canyon Dam of 850,000 cubic meters per second. Local residents frantically attempted to build levees to guard against the rising river.[4]

Floods returned in February 1942, followed by water shortages during the summer. U.S. officials expressed skepticism toward Mexico's request for greater releases from Parker Dam. The U.S. State Department blamed the water shortage on a "breakdown in the control structure of the Alamo Canal," defective installation of inefficient pumps, and the rapid growth that had taken place in the Mexicali Valley. To be sure, these criticisms had merit. Mexican minister of foreign relations Ezequiel Padilla noted that between 1938 and 1941, irrigated land in the valley had increased from 69,702 hectares to 122,105 hectares. Furthermore, valley pumps and the aging Alamo Canal were chronically inefficient.[5]

Periodic U.S. projections for decreased river flows in Mexico also affected binational water negotiations. At the end of 1942, U.S. officials warned Mexicans in the delta not to expect additional releases in 1943

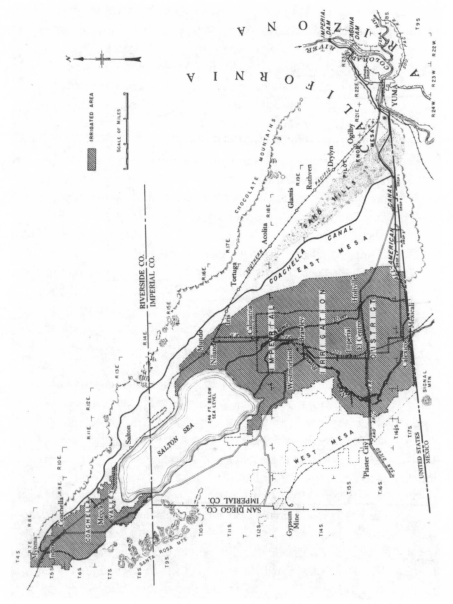

Map 3 The Imperial Valley. (U.S. Bureau of Reclamation map)

because they would be storing as much water as possible behind the dams upriver. The State Department also continued to discourage rapid development of the Mexicali Valley, ostensibly to help the Mexicans conserve enough water to irrigate arable lands. U.S. officials were especially wary of releasing water "when these farmers increase the cultivated acreage with speculative purposes without any security that there will be water available for them and even with the knowledge that under the foreseeable conditions there will not be water."[6]

Despite U.S. warnings that water releases from the dams upstream would be limited, telegrams from Mexicali farmers and politicians requesting diplomatic intervention in order to secure additional water flooded President Ávila Camacho's office in the spring of 1943. "This problem [is the] agricultural life or death of Mexicali," Armando Lizárraga of the Mixed Council of the Regional Economy announced to the president. Territorial Governor Sánchez Taboada requested that a federal official who "knows [the] problem [of a] lack of water" be sent to the valley. Three days later the governor informed the president that the problem was only getting worse, because planting season was approaching and farmers needed water to irrigate their crops. Distributors of farm implements complained that the lack of water "would seriously curtail regional economic interests and especially the situation [of] thousands [of] men from the countryside." In order to resolve the problem, Distribuidora del Pacífico, one of the local farm implement companies, encouraged President Ávila Camacho to "place your valuable influence before authorities in Washington, who now [are] treating the subject [of] providing water [for this] valley." By late April, local and national leaders had petitioned Imperial Irrigation District (IID) leaders to transfer water from the All-American Canal to the Alamo Canal in time for the planting season.[7]

IID leaders were reluctant to sell additional water to Mexicali Valley farmers. They rejected the requests of Mexicali representatives to build a temporary dam that would divert water into the Alamo Canal, since the structure might unleash a flood on the Imperial Valley. However, American diplomats reported that the lack of water in the Colorado River "had aggravated the water situation [in Mexicali] and that the people living on these 36,000 hectares and their lands were in immediate danger of catastrophe." While Imperial Valley farmers did not want to set a precedent by loaning water to Mexico, Ávila Camacho successfully presented the pleas of Mexicali farmers to President Roosevelt and G. S. Messersmith, the ambassador to Mexico, on May 14, 1943. At the request of the State Department, the IID increased the amount of water delivered to Mexico through the Alamo Canal.[8]

Three days later, Undersecretary of State Sumner Welles reported that more water than Mexico could use was passing into the canals. Irritated, Welles warned Messersmith that if such a situation developed again, the ambassador should "recommend to the Mexican authorities that first of all they check with their own people along the border to ascertain the true facts." "Had they done so," Welles continued, "they would have found that there was no shortage of water." Despite Welles's suspicions, Mexicali farmers continued to send telegrams attesting to the lack of water to President Ávila Camacho through June 1943. To add insult to injury, by November floods from the Colorado had smashed through levee works in the Mexicali Valley and threatened cotton fields that were ready for harvest.[9]

Welles's assessment was important for the impression it gave U.S. politicians involved with U.S.–Mexican relations. As a general rule, state and local leaders in the United States were more apt to question Mexico's motives for water requests than were federal officials. Additionally, local leaders generally avoided any agreements that would threaten the water allotments for their own projects. On the other hand, Mexicans developed a strong distaste for working through the bureaucratic mazes of U.S. institutions. Leaders in Mexicali displayed an increased desire to secure waterworks that would free them as much as possible from continual dependence on waterworks in the United States. This was important, as Governor Sánchez Taboada astutely observed, because "the norteameri-canos feel that [because of Mexican requests] they are in some sort of danger, and [our own connection to Alamo Canal from the river] would resolve this problem."[10]

Labor and Demographic Growth in the Delta

Farm labor issues in the binational delta also impacted regional water use, particularly with the implementation of the *bracero* program (1942–

64). During the Great Depression large numbers of Mexican migrants were bussed back to the border. With the onset of World War II, agricultural interests in the United States lobbied Congress for a labor program to bring Mexicans to the United States as temporary workers. For the Mexican government, the bracero program provided many landless campesinos with employment during and after the war and represented a significant contribution to the Allied cause. As a result of large-scale labor and industrial cooperation during World War II, the Mexican and U.S. economies were increasingly integrated after 1945.[11]

Ultimately, the bracero program further encouraged migration to the Mexicali area. During the 1940s, the U.S. Border Patrol deemed Mexicali to be the location where the greatest number of undocumented workers crossed into the delta.[12] By 1944, however, the Mexican deportation center at Mexicali closed it doors to undocumented Mexicans apprehended in the United States, unless they had lived in Baja California for at least six months before crossing the border. The Mexican government requested that undocumented Mexicans who did not fulfill these requirements be delivered to Nogales, Arizona, or El Paso, Texas, where trains could return them to the Mexican interior. This reflected the territory's inability to care for the deluge of workers. Ugo Carusi, commissioner of the Immigration and Naturalization Service, further noted, "Detention facilities are not available for the prolonged detention of such a large number of aliens, and to return them through other points along the Mexican border would only create problems in those communities similar to the ones being faced in Mexicali."[13]

American communities in the delta also felt the impact of increased Mexican migration. A 1945 State Department report noted that 100 to 150 undocumented Mexican nationals were apprehended each day in the Imperial Valley. The same report suggested that "approximately 6,000 more illegal residents [remained] in the vicinity."[14] Local officials were hard-pressed to house and detain the flood of farmworkers.[15] One year later, the situation had intensified. S. E. O'Donoghue, first secretary of the Mexican Embassy, informed the Mexican undersecretary of foreign relations that "more than 10,000 [undocumented] Mexicans [were] now estimated to be in the Imperial Valley in California where they were creating quite a civic problem."[16]

The economic incentives in the region often overpowered the official pronouncements of both nations concerning immigration restrictions. After the Baja California and Mexican governments closed off the port of entry at Mexicali, State Department and Immigration Service officials requested that Mexico allow the undocumented workers to work during the current season in the United States. Mexican officials declined the offer, noting that such a move would "immediately result in a wide-spread movement of workers to the border in the hopes of being recruited and that this movement would cause many additional problems."[17] This official statement was offset by the chronic inability or unwillingness of Mexico to patrol its own borders.[18]

In the American delta, a similar ambivalence, fueled by the economic interests of the region's farmers and politicians, also contributed to increased Mexican immigration after 1940. Farmers in Yuma Valley, especially during World War II, complained about the Immigration Service's rigid standards for procuring Mexican laborers. Yuma's powerful farming and retail magnate, E. F. Sanguenetti, lamented the fact that willing and able Mexicans in San Luís Río Colorado could not cross the border to harvest truck crops.[19] Due to the unstable nature of the labor supply and the bureaucratic red tape that local farmers encountered in obtaining workers from Mexico, farmers employed Papago, Cocopah, and Quechan Indians as well as German and Italian prisoners of war during World War II.[20] With the decline of the bracero program in the 1960s, Arizona farmers scrambled to supplement their labor supply with high school and college students.

U.S. officials recognized that the delta's farming frontier encouraged massive immigration to the region.[21] The inability of government agencies to enforce legal immigration stemmed from several factors. Understandably, the rising number of undocumented immigrants in the delta region forced the U.S. Border Patrol to "discontinue its action looking to the arrest and return to Mexico of Mexican nationals" from time to time.[22] Yet labor shortages often caused the Border Patrol to wink at undocumented immigration. For example, farmers in the Yuma Valley faced a labor shortage during the fall harvest of 1944. Gen. Philip Bruton, director of labor for the U.S. Army, assured U.S. senator Carl Hayden that his people were doing "everything possible to facilitate the handling of this problem on a practical basis." "Handling" problems often meant taking a hands-off approach, reflected in the telegram of Albert Del Guercio, district director of the Immigration and Naturalization Service, to Bruton regarding the resolution of the American delta's labor woes in 1944. He reported, "Personnel Adequate[,] prevent all illegal entries or to apprehend those residing illegally [in] border areas. Ranches [in] Yuma and Imperial Counties not being checked while perishable crops being harvested." Such a policy, while helpful to local farmers, revealed the ambivalent approach U.S. officials took to undocumented entry to the delta region. This only encouraged Mexican immigration to the delta and placed greater demands on existing water supplies.[23]

L exactly how?

The Mexican Water Treaty

Despite official agreement on labor issues, the lack of water in the Mexican delta continued to strain U.S.–Mexican relations in 1944 and 1945. Mexico continued to press for a guaranteed treaty for water from the Colorado and Tijuana Rivers as well as the Rio Grande. Demand for an international treaty had begun as early as discussions for the Colorado River Compact (CRC) during the 1920s. During World War II, prospects for a treaty improved. President Franklin D. Roosevelt and top officials at the U.S. State Department supported a binational water treaty because they wanted to create a hemispheric alliance during World War II.[24] Furthermore, guaranteeing Mexico water from the Colorado River would lend credibility to the Good Neighbor policy. Senators from the upper basin and outside the Colorado River region also supported the treaty based on the need for strong relations with Mexico and to maintain America's positive image during World War II. California's senators, on the other hand, opposed the treaty because it would limit the amount of surplus water they could divert from the Colorado River.

In contrast to California's position, Arizona's governor and congressional contingent championed the Mexican Water Treaty as part of a concerted plan to encourage further development in central Arizona. They also recognized the plight of farmers in the Wellton-Mohawk area by supporting reauthorization of the Gila Project. Previously, state leaders, such as Governor George Hunt during the 1920s, encouraged Arizonans to appropriate as much water as possible in order to limit the growth of farming in Mexico. In the 1940s Arizona officials realized that offering Mexico a guaranteed amount of water from the Colorado River could regulate Mexican water use. The actions of Arizona's leaders, though clothed with the language of the Good Neighbor policy, perpetuated a historically strained relationship with Mexico.

In the delta, leaders of the Yuma County Water Users Association (YCWUA) did not so much object to the amount of water that Mexico would receive under the Mexican Water Treaty (1.5 million acre-feet) as they did to the method in which the water would be delivered to Mexico. One of the provisions in the treaty gave Mexico the right to build a dam near the international border. The dam, however, would be located south of Yuma near the site of Hanlon's Heading. The IID had previously built a diversion structure there to divert water into the Alamo Canal, which passed through Mexico on its way to the Imperial Valley. With the completion of the All-American Canal in 1942, the IID no longer relied on the controversial Alamo Canal to carry water from the Colorado River to the Imperial Valley. Yet the Alamo Canal no longer diverted ample water to the Mexicali Valley for irrigation purposes. Therefore, Mexico proposed the new dam as a part of the treaty.

YCWUA leaders feared that the dam would threaten the city of Yuma during flood stages as well as allow water to infiltrate the Yuma Valley's water table, leaving the lands waterlogged and alkaline. At a March 6, 1944, meeting of the YCWUA board of governors, President Henry Frauenfelder reported that L. M. Lawson, chairman of the International Boundary and Water Commission, believed "the cost of a Mexican diversion dam and protective works which would meet American requirements would be so great that it would not be built."[25] Lawson suggested that an alternative source of delivery might be made through the All-American Canal into the Alamo Canal.

Thereafter, YCWUA officials pressed Arizona's U.S. senators to lobby for delivery of water to Mexico through the All-American Canal instead of agreeing to construction of a diversion dam near Yuma. In a letter to Senator Ernest W. McFarland, Frauenfelder emphasized that the proposed dam, if located at Hanlon's Heading, might allow lands to become "seeped in a relatively short time." Such problems could require "years to reclaim and restore them to former productive capacity."[26] Not only could diversion through the All-American Canal avert such seepage problems, but it might also check the IID's arbitrary control of Imperial Dam, where Yuma diverted water to the Arizona side of the river.[27]

While Senators Hayden and McFarland sympathized with the concerns of Yuma Valley farmers, the political urgency of obtaining sufficient water to supply the Central Arizona and Gila Projects kept them from objecting to the dam. Arizona's senators knew that the dam would catch drainage water from the United States and divert it to the Mexicali Valley through the Alamo Canal. They also realized that if the majority of the water destined for Mexico was comprised of return-flow water, larger amounts of cleaner water could be used upstream in developing the Central Arizona Project. During the Senate hearings on the treaty in 1945, Senator Hayden pressed C. M. Ainsworth, engineer for the International Boundary and Water Commission (IBWC), for assurances that the dam would not harm Yuma County farms. Ainsworth observed that the dam would not accelerate seepage or flooding in southwestern Arizona and that it would "assure credit to the United States for the return flow and other flows that will appear in the river."[28] Ainsworth further reminded Hayden that U.S. officials had suggested construction of the dam so that the United States could reduce the amount of stored water destined for Mexico.[29]

Ainsworth's responses alleviated Hayden's fears regarding the threat posed to Yuma Valley lands by the dam. In an effort to protect his decision in favor of the treaty, Hayden added an amendment to the treaty that required Mexico to pay for the construction of levees to protect lands in Yuma and Imperial Counties from any damage the dam might occasion.[30] While Yuma Valley farmers were still apprehensive about the adverse effects of the new dam, the treaty's ominous silence on the quality of water delivered to Mexico assured Arizona's congressional politicians that the United States could largely fulfill its obligations to Mexico with irrigation drainage water that returned to the river. On April 18, 1945, Senators Hayden and McFarland, along with seventy-four other senators, voted in favor of the Mexican Water Treaty. Ostensibly, the 76–10 Senate vote in favor of the treaty sent an overwhelming message of goodwill to Mexico. With the approval of the treaty secure, the Mexican government

Figure 8 Morelos Dam, in the foreground, diverts water to the Mexicali Valley through the Alamo Canal in the lower left. Note the striking irrigated landscape of Yuma Valley in the upper right. (U.S. Bureau of Reclamation photograph)

began planning for construction of the dam that Yuma County farmers feared. The structure, named Morelos Dam, was built at Hanlon's Heading on the Arizona-Mexico boundary. Construction commenced in 1948 and was completed in 1950.

Historians of the Mexicali Valley have written little on the attitudes of local residents toward the Mexican Water Treaty and its perceived benefits for the valley. This probably reflects a consensus of support for the treaty, given the difficulties that the IID had created for farmers in the Mexicali Valley to obtain adequate supplies of water from the Colorado River. With construction of the All-American Canal, the IID had abandoned use of the Alamo Canal, diminishing the flow of water entering the ancient canal on which the Mexicans still depended.[31]

The Mexican Water Treaty provided provisions not only for a set amount of water for the Mexicali Valley from the river (1.5 million acre-

Figure 9 Waterworks in the delta are unique symbols of nationalism. At Morelos Dam, the Mexican government placed a statue of the great Mexican patriot of independence, José María Morelos, the soldier-priest. The base of the statue is inscribed with a statement by Morelos in Spanish: "The land is the nation. Let us cultivate it so it is free." Below it is a statement by Miguel Alemán, Mexican president at the time of the dam's dedication: "Irrigation will make the work of our campesinos fruitful." (U.S. Bureau of Reclamation photograph)

feet per year) but also to break free from the capricious control the IID exercised over Mexico's share of water. Therefore, just as the All-American Canal symbolized the Imperial Valley's "freedom" from reliance on a bina-tional canal for water, Morelos Dam symbolized Mexican independence from asking the United States for water in times of drought. At the dam's inauguration on September 23, 1950, Mexican secretary of hydraulic re-sources Adolfo Orive Alba linked the dam's symbolic purposes with its practical benefits for the valley. With completion of the dam, he noted, the region could support up to 200,000 hectares of agriculture. While Orive Alba lauded U.S. and Mexican efforts to construct the dam, he extolled the structure as a symbol of Mexican independence. He observed, "[José María] Morelos and the no less great [Miguel] Hidalgo are symbols of our independence, and this dam is also a symbol of our country's independence in one of its most remote and distant corners; a symbol of political and economic independence." Orive Alba also recognized that the traditional goals of the Mexican Revolution (namely, free land widely distributed) had slightly changed in Mexico's arid northwest corner. The dam was necessary, he believed, because "the land without water[,] even in the hands of our farmers, does not mean for them 'liberty or personal benefit or benefit for the country' as Morelos wanted."[32]

The security of the Mexican Water Treaty, the onset of the Korean War, and depressed cotton production elsewhere ushered in a golden age of cotton cultivation in the Mexicali Valley. Between 1950 and 1954, prices increased as much as five times on the commodities markets. Rod-rigo Valle, manager of the Mexicali Gin during the 1950s, remembered that the influx of profits contributed to the mechanization of Mexicali Valley farms. Many farmers traded burros and horses for shiny tractors. The newfound prosperity not only expanded the wallets of local farmers with hundreds, thousands, and even millions of pesos but also filled their heads with grand delusions of wealth in the desert. One farmer, after receiving his profits from the harvest, went to a local bar and bought drinks for everyone present as well as pricey watches for the waitresses. Still other farmers hired mariachi bands to enliven the sultry countryside with music or towed their tractors down narrow country roads with wide new Cadillacs.[33]

These opportunities produced plenty of individual stories to corroborate Rodrigo Valle's memories of Mexicali in the 1950s. For example, Juan Buenrostro Guerrero and his wife moved to Mexicali from the state of Jalisco in 1948. Upon their arrival, they found a dusty town with few opportunities for advancement. As a result, they decided to try and earn seven thousand pesos, buy a truck, and return to Jalisco the following year. Buenrostro took out a loan, bought fourteen hectares of land, and started planting cotton. That first year, Buenrostro made between fifteen and sixteen thousand pesos: enough to buy a truck and return to Jalisco but not enough to cure the fever brought on by "white gold." By 1953 Buenrostro had amassed one hundred hectares of private property, buying parcels from neighbors who had little interest in farming. After ten years, he had diversified his production into wheat, cattle, and cotton; had mechanized production; and savored the fruits of earning one million pesos. The desire for additional wealth was incurable: "Instead of saving money or getting drunk," he later remembered, "I bought small pieces of land . . . and we forgot about investing in a truck to return to the interior of Mexico."[34]

Buenrostro's experiences illustrate the ways in which Baja California served as something of the Mexican alternative to California. Like many Mexicali residents who were prospering at the time, Buenrostro felt no desire to migrate to the United States. "No sir," he wryly noted, "I am allergic [to the United States]. Here it was going very well for me, much more so than where I came from and in various places where I have lived." During this time of agricultural growth, the profits from the cotton bonanza financed the construction of stately stone houses on Mexicali's main streets, including the Avenidas Madero and Obregón. In later years, the landscape of the Mexicali Valley would pay a high price for the brief explosion of cotton cultivation in the 1950s.[35]

Mexican Conquest of the Alamo Canal

Despite the construction of Morelos Dam, the Mexican Water Treaty, and high prices for cotton on the world market, increased cultivation and immigration further depleted water resources in the Mexicali Valley. From 1940 to 1950, population increased in the region from 45,569 to 137,200 inhabitants. By 1957, the population had increased by 50 percent over the 1950 figure to 192,500. At the dawn of the Cárdenas revolution in 1937, 54,190 hectares of land were irrigated in the Distrito de Riego del Río Colorado (Colorado River Irrigation District [CRID]). By 1940 that figure had increased to 113,190 hectares. With the completion of Morelos Dam and the initiation of irrigation from deep wells in the region, 145,382 hectares were being farmed. By the end of the 1950s, the amount of acreage irrigated from the Colorado River peaked at 192,612 hectares. Thereafter, dwindling water supplies from the river forced farmers and the Mexican government to pump water from aquifers located beneath the delta's soil.[36]

In terms of water availability in the Mexican delta, 1954 proved to be a critical year. Operation of the Gila Project in Yuma County and plans for construction of Glen Canyon Dam drastically reduced the amount of water that would reach the Alamo Canal thereafter. While the Mexican Water Treaty stipulated that Mexico would receive 1.5 million acre-feet, over 2 million acre-feet had reached Morelos Dam on an annual basis before 1954. The following year, regional irrigation and farming interests convened to discuss plans to offset the reduction in river water. Engineers suggested that deep wells might provide enough water to irrigate a substantial portion of Mexicali fields.[37]

Following the meeting, a coalition of farmers, bankers, workers, and politicians came together to voice their concerns about the decreased water supplies. They were also concerned because the level of cotton production in the Mexicali Valley, stimulated by the Korean War, had increased nearly 400 percent since 1948–49. They informed Mexican president Adolfo Ruíz Cortines that a decrease in water supplies would substantially affect the ad valorem taxes that the government collected as cotton left Baja California destined for world markets. They proposed the construction of a new siphon and canal to better service farms in Mexicali and San Luís Río Colorado. In order to compensate for the over-development of the valley and the reduction in water supplies, they also suggested that the local irrigation district and private interests provide funding for four hundred deep wells in order to sustain present levels of cultivation. This measure would support sixty thousand hectares of arable land and "lead to the complete salvation of the Mexicali and San Luís Río Colorado valleys." The CRID simultaneously decreed a twenty-hectare irrigation rule, effectively limiting the amount of land that could be irrigated on an annual basis with river water. Campesinos loudly complained to President Ruíz Cortines, however, that large farms received water ahead of ejido lands.[38]

Ultimately, then, the construction of Morelos Dam did not extricate Mexicali farmers from dependence on U.S. facilities to provide water for the valley. It only raised water into the Alamo Canal. The roots of dependence on U.S. structures had strong linkages to development initiated at the turn of the century. In 1916 the IID purchased the Alamo Canal and appurtenant waterworks in Mexicali Valley from the Southern Pacific Railroad Corporation, which had obtained the works from the then-defunct California Development Company. The IID-owned Compañía de Terrenos y Aguas de la Baja California, S.A., which had operated the works since 1904, continued to deliver water from the Colorado River to the Alamo Canal and into the lateral canals in the Mexicali Valley.[39] The board of directors of the company, largely comprised of U.S. citizens, received a limited fifty-year concession that would end in 1960 to deliver water from the Colorado River to the Mexicali Valley. Despite the push to "Mexicanize" the agricultural infrastructure in the valley during the Cárdenas administration, the secretary of agriculture and development during the Ávila Camacho administration reaffirmed the company's right to deliver water to Mexicali in 1941.[40]

Ever since the early 1940s, however, Mexican officials had been frustrated by the inability of the canal to provide the volume of water needed by Mexicali farmers to irrigate their crops. Furthermore, valley officials were put off by the IID's unwillingness to allow the CRID to build a temporary dam in the river to lift sufficient water into the canal for delivery to Mexicali farms.[41] Eligio Esquivel Méndez, CRID manager, stated that the new structures were adapted to the Alamo Canal because "your Company was not able to comply with the demands requested by the CRID in order to satisfy its [farmers]."[42]

With the completion of Morelos Dam, the company's dissolution was a fait accompli. The company's attorney in Mexico City, José Barcenas, informed Arturo H. Orcí, company counsel in Mexicali, that with the new dam, "the Company considers that the most appropriate and convenient settlement for both parties would be the purchase by the Government of all the properties of the Company." Barcenas noted that operation of Morelos Dam infringed on the rights of the company. Furthermore, in tandem with Matamoros Check (a structure that guided water from the dam into Alamo Canal), the dam reduced the revenues of delivery by "approximately 25 to 30 per cent."[43] In September 1951, W. K. Bowker, company manager, met with the secretary of hydraulic resources, Orive Alba, to inform him that the company wished to sell its interests in Mexico.[44]

Legal and political considerations also spelled the end of the company's operations in the Mexicali Valley. In 1960, the company's board of directors appealed for a five-year extension of its fifty-year concession to operate in the Mexicali Valley, fearing that if it did not, the company would not be able to complete the sale of the waterworks. The Mexican government denied the company's request but informed the board that the expiration would not affect the liquidation.[45] The terms of the company's concession expired on August 25, 1960.[46]

The Mexican government made the most of the fact that it practically owned Alamo Canal by virtue of its location between Morelos Dam and the lateral canals of the farmers. The new secretary of hydraulic resources, Alfredo del Mazo, informed attorney Orcí that "in private and as a friend he would state that he was not in favor of buying the said assets, advising me that that opinion was not to be taken as that of the Government, nor as final, adding that with a 'much' smaller amount the canals and other works which the Company is selling could be built, all more modern and adaptable to the present, reducing the width of the canals and avoiding the great loss of water by evaporation." While del Mazo's statements had the air of political legerdemain, the CRID was already considering rehabilitation of the local irrigation system. Those plans also included many of the propositions set forth by del Mazo. Del Mazo also emphasized that the government felt no obligation to buy the works "if the price did not suit it."[47] The secretary of hydraulic resources later stressed that the lowest possible price should be assigned to the company's holdings to decide "whether the Government would buy the assets of the Company and in order to be able to take something concrete for the decision of the President of the Republic." He noted that the federal government was presently strapped for funds and that "it would have to be for a very low price (mentioning seven million pesos)."[48] In March 1961, Orcí presented the Department of Hydraulic Resources with an offer of 15 million pesos for company property valued at 49,461,640 pesos.[49] On May 8, 1961, del Mazo made a counterproposal for 4.5 million pesos in three payments. The contract of sale was completed on August 9, 1961.[50]

water and interdependence in the Border oasis

At a time that historians consider one of increased dependence of the Mexican economy on the United States, Mexican water policy in the delta continued to stress the move toward independence. To reach that goal, Mexico had to exert greater control over natural resources, particularly water. The Mexican Water Treaty provided Mexicali farmers with a firm baseline of how much water they could expect on an annual basis. Morelos Dam and the Alamo Canal served as a wholly Mexican conduit for channeling that water onto the valley floor. To be sure, independence was a stated goal; however, some interdependence was inevitable in reaching developmental goals. For example, Morelos Dam, named for the father of Mexican independence, was contracted out to a U.S. transnational, Morrison Knudsen of Sonora. Conversely, the expansion of large, capital-intensive farms in the Imperial and Yuma Valleys was impossible without bracero workers.

Ecologically, delta water relations during the forties and fifties masked the growing dependence of both economies on water from the Colorado River. That dependence became doubly apparent in the Mexicali Valley as hundreds of wells were drilled in order to compensate for the decreased volume of water from the river in order to continue rapid expansion south of the international border. The border and the binational aspects of delta water relations also encouraged farmers, developers, and politicians to worry about what would happen to regional water supplies should development on the other side of the border drastically increase.

Yet a guarded spirit of cooperation provided the foundation for this quest for economic growth throughout the period. Despite tensions between the IID and Mexican officials, periodic emergency arrangements for delivery of water to Mexico were negotiated, and the company never made good on its threat to stop delivery of water to the Mexicali Valley. Additionally, although Mexico exercised some sleight of hand to obtain the holdings of the company, it eventually reached an agreement with its liquidators, even though the concessionary period had expired.

Even if these "good neighbors" were not always the best of friends, they did not let their misunderstandings descend into violence. Yet the joint push to develop the region economically foreshadowed a period of ecological crisis and an impending regionwide realization that the well-being of humans, plants, and animals throughout the delta required restraint and respect for the resources that had made the region so prosperous.

Deltascape Aldo Leopold's Delta

In 1922, pioneering conservationist Aldo Leopold visited the lower delta, a region he later referred to as the Green Lagoons. Canoeing through the region with his brother, Leopold noted the abundance of freshwater and saltwater lagoons and countless streams that ran away from the main body of the Colorado River as it approached the Sea of Cortés. The river shifted and pulsed along the changing contours of the delta floor, built up over thousands of years with rich silt from the river. "The river was nowhere and everywhere," Leopold observed, "for he could not decide which of a hundred green lagoons offered the most pleasant and speedy path to the Gulf . . . he divided and rejoined, he twisted and turned, he meandered in awesome jungles, he all but ran in circles, he dallied with lovely groves, he got lost and was glad of it, and so were we." Leopold also noted the ever-present mesquite trees, flush with dark pods, as well as cachanilla brush, ducks, quails, coyotes, and deer, "all of incredible fatness." Impressed by the abundance of lagoons, Leopold noted that the waters were "of a deep emerald hue, colored by algae . . . but no less green for all that." Farther in the distance, a "wall of mesquite and willow separated the [river] channel from the thorny desert beyond." Mallards, willets, and egrets scattered around the brothers as they made their way through the lagoons. Leopold also commented on the abundance of wildlife in the region. "Families of raccoons waded the shallows, munching water beetles. Coyotes watched us from the inland knolls, waiting to resume their breakfast of mesquite beans, varied, I suppose, by an occasional crippled bird, duck or quail."

The smell of mesquite burning on the campfire lingered in Leopold's nostrils long after he had left the delta. As he wrote *A Sand County Almanac* he reminisced, "Brittle with a hundred frosts, baked by a thousand suns, the gnarled imperishable bones of these ancient trees lie ready-to-hand at every camp, ready to slant blue smoke across the twilight, sing a song of teapots, . . . and warm the shins of man and beast." In his hunger to remember the tastes and smells of the region, he recalled the sensation of feasting on roast goose cooked over a makeshift campfire fueled by delta mesquite.[51]

"All this was far away and long ago," Leopold later noted. "I am told the green lagoons now raise cantaloupes. If so they should not lack flavor." Reflecting on the transformation of the region by irrigation, he lamented, "By this time the Delta has probably been made safe for cows, and forever dull for adventuring hunters. Freedom from fear has arrived, but a glory has departed from the green lagoons."

Leopold ended his reflections on the delta with a more macabre observation. As the Colorado River linked the delta to the agricultural, municipal, and recreational needs of the American West, its beauty and natural abundance declined. "Man always kills the things he loves, and so we the pioneers have killed our wilderness." Somberly, America's pioneering conservationist predicted the decay of this transnational desert paradise.[52]

Saline Solutions

*It is one of the great tragedies of the Southwest. If you want to see
what happens when an area goes dry in the desert, just go to the
Wellton Mohawk Valley.*

—William E. Warne[1]

During the fall of 1961, the U.S. Bureau of Reclamation (USBR) began
draining salt-saturated irrigation water from the Wellton-Mohawk
Valley in eastern Yuma County, Arizona. It was carried through a drainage
channel that emptied into the Gila River. The Gila River then carried the
contaminated water into the Colorado River near Yuma, where the USBR
believed that the river would dilute the high level of salinity before the
water reached the U.S.–Mexican border. Instead, the contaminated water
immediately touched off an ecological crisis, killing crops and damaging
farmland in the Mexicali Valley. The saline water also polluted domestic
water supplies on both sides of the border.[2] Several Mexicali leaders
threatened to boycott California businesses if the U.S. farmers in Arizona
did not curtail their harmful drainage practices. On December 14, 1961,
8,000 Mexicans protested the dumping of toxic waters by marching in
front of the American consulate in Mexicali. Two weeks later, 35,000
people protested in front of the same building. Some participants noted
the disparity between the pollution of the Colorado River and the ideals
of the Alliance for Progress, observing that "polluting the river was not
the way to get a partner in an alliance and certainly was not progress."
Others assigned blame for the debacle closer to home. One of the protesters' signs simply stated, "Arizona—tiene la palabra" (Arizona, you have
the word).[3] Journalist Lenora Werley observed that "Arizona causes the
protests and the Mexican demonstrators are not unaware of this."[4]

That the Mexicali demonstrators protested against the United States *and* Arizona not only reveals the marchers' political astuteness but also identifies an important omission in the historiography of U.S.–Mexican disputes during the 1960s and 1970s over salinity in the Colorado River. The placard "Arizona—tiene la palabra" implies that Arizona officials played a leading role in the environmental imbroglio that eventually soured international relations. Scholars have written extensively about the environmental and diplomatic ramifications of the crisis, but they have not analyzed adequately how Arizona politics made the disaster possible.[5] Although Arizonans did not intend to damage U.S.–Mexican relations, political expediency compelled them to push for authorization of the Wellton-Mohawk division of the Gila Valley Project. Ultimately, the vision of growth through federal largesse set in motion a series of actions that drastically increased the salinity levels of water from the Colorado River destined for Mexico.

Genesis of the Wellton-Mohawk Project

The Mohawk Valley lies in the desolate Sonoran desert thirty miles east of Yuma. Mexican and U.S. farmers, hoping to utilize Gila River water, moved to the region during the late nineteenth century. Irrigation and the cultivation of alfalfa had begun by 1875, and before long the region resembled an agricultural atoll in an arid sea of land.[6] In 1923 farmers organized the Gila Valley Power District and the Mohawk Municipal Water Conservation District, both of which allowed farmers to contract for the electrical power they needed to pump water from underground wells onto valley fields.[7] Initially, farmers raised alfalfa, cotton, and vegetables, placing 6,200 acres of land under cultivation on 81 farms by 1931. After the 1935 completion of Coolidge Dam 250 miles upstream, however, the Gila River failed to carry enough water to replenish wells in the area, causing local farmers to reuse groundwater for irrigation. Without adequate drainage or sufficient rainfall, the increasing level of toxic salts eventually made the recycled groundwater harmful to crops.[8]

To relieve the situation, Hugo Farmer, a tireless Yuma County booster and state senator, launched a campaign in 1941 to incorporate the irrigation needs of Mohawk Valley farmers into the Gila Project, an undertaking

Figure 10 Thousands of protesters, including members of the independent peasant union, the Central Campesino Independiente (CCI), manifest their displeasure with American water policy in the lower delta in front of the American consulate in Mexicali during the summer of 1962. Employing a play on words, one sign reads in Spanish, "First salt us. Dispute later." (Courtesy of the Fondo Martínez Retes, Archivo Museo Universitario, Universidad Autónoma de Baja California)

originally approved in 1935 to develop 150,000 acres of land on the Yuma Mesa. Farmer wanted to rescue farms that had been damaged by saline water and then expand the region's arable acreage. He frequently reminded U.S. senator Carl Hayden of families who were losing their farms in the valley and complained about the paltry appropriation of $500,000 the project received each year. Farmer warned that if the appropriation were not substantially increased, "part of the country will have gone back to the desert, and the people will have had to vacate their homes long before water would reach them."[9] Although many individual families did farm in the Mohawk Valley, evidence suggests that corporate absentee landowners controlled significant portions of the valley.[10] Ultimately, financial difficulties in the form of delinquent taxes and bonded indebtedness on valley farms delayed approval for expanding the Gila Project.

The USBR refused to contract with the Gila Valley Irrigation District for improvements until the land could be financed completely by the federal government.

Farmer and other prominent valley officials also promoted the Gila Project as a potential provider of homesteads for World War II veterans. In a 1944 letter outlining the Gila Project Association's plans, Farmer informed USBR commissioner H. W. Bashore that the project's unredeemed acreage represented "a very substantial area of very excellent land for settlement by our returning soldiers."[11] Leon Jacobs, a Yuma attorney representing the primary bondholder on the project, expressed disbelief that Mexico was able to commit federal funds "to recondition its railroads" while "poor little Arizona [could] not even get a few hundred thousand dollars" to bail out the indebted farmers on a project that would benefit many American veterans.[12] Government buyout of the blighted land would also relieve Jacobs's clients of their cumbersome investment. In the end, the promotion of land for veterans played an integral part in securing approval for improvements in the Mohawk Valley. In 1947, USBR commissioner William Warne observed that "a principal reason" for funding the Mohawk Valley project was to "preserve an existing settlement and enable it to expand through the infiltration of war veterans who are desirous of taking advantage of settlement opportunities in Arizona."[13]

The threat of increased Mexican water usage was another factor that prompted Farmer to push the Mohawk Valley irrigation project. Farmer voiced his concerns throughout the 1940s. "Substantial development is still going forward in the Mexican Delta of the Colorado River," he informed Senator Hayden in 1941. "During the past year some ten thousand acres of new land has been cleared and additional canals have been constructed."[14] If the federal government failed to appropriate money immediately for the Gila Project, he warned, Mexico might "make use of available Colorado River water [and] . . . establish a recognizable prior right therein."[15]

Competition with central Arizona for water projects also influenced Farmer's strategy. Antagonism between Yuma County and the Salt River Valley (metropolitan Phoenix) dated back to the 1920s debates over the Colorado River Compact (CRC).[16] At that time, Yuma officials championed construction of Boulder Canyon Dam (present-day Hoover Dam) to

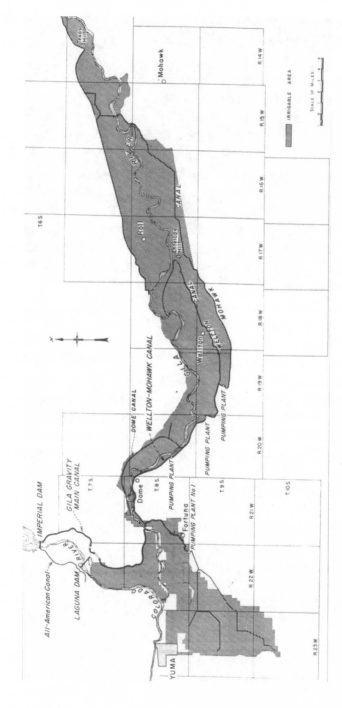

Map 4 The Gila Project, which includes the Wellton-Mohawk Irrigation and Drainage District. (U.S. Bureau of Reclamation map)

protect local farmland from yearly flooding of the Colorado and Gila Rivers. Phoenix leaders, on the other hand, argued that the CRC limited the amount of water Arizona could divert from the river and that Boulder Canyon Dam undercut the state's own plans to develop the river's hydroelectric potential and to transport water to central Arizona. When the CRC was passed (over Arizona's objection), intrastate competition for water from the Colorado River became even keener. Fearing that not enough water would be available to develop all of Arizona's arable land, groups in Yuma County and central Arizona carefully monitored each other's actions. According to political scientist N. D. Houghton, "central Arizona farmers . . . resented prospects for bringing more Yuma County land under competitive cultivation by use of Colorado River water."[17] In 1935, the president of the Salt River Valley Water Users Association, located in the Phoenix area, stated, "I don't want to see another . . . acre of land brought under cultivation in Arizona."[18]

Hugo Farmer feared losing prospective irrigation projects to the state's more populous Salt River Valley. Disgruntled that little headway had been made in obtaining funds to build a canal from the Colorado River to the Wellton-Mohawk Valley, in January 1941 Farmer vented his frustration to Hayden. "While I am sympathetic to any need that may exist for taking some water from the Colorado River to Central Arizona, I do feel that the agricultural future of our state demands lands close to the [river] which can be irrigated at a reasonable cost per acre." These "should be developed as rapidly as possible."[19] Farmer doubted that central Arizona interests would be able to finance the Central Arizona Project (CAP) to carry water across the desert to Phoenix.[20] Meanwhile, Gila Project farmers were cut off from mountain runoff stored in central Arizona reservoirs, "as the dams in Central Arizona prevent any substantial amount of water from coming down the Gila."[21] Finally, at the 1947 hearings over reauthorization of the Gila Project, Farmer lost his patience with committee members who believed that approval should be contingent on meeting the needs of the CAP. "The [CAP] and the Gila Project are not the same thing," Farmer insisted, "but they are separate projects. I do not see why they throw the two of them in here. The bill [under consideration] is the Gila Project bill. We are particularly sympathetic with the Central Arizona situation, but it does not properly belong in this bill."[22]

Farmer did all he could to check the power of water officials in the Salt River Valley. Yet without the support of Senators Hayden and McFarland, his effectiveness would have been limited. Eager to garner votes in Yuma County, both Hayden and McFarland championed the Gila Valley Project as part of Arizona's water policy.[23] Hayden had taken an active interest in securing government assistance for Yuma County farmers since he was elected Arizona's first congressman in 1912. Serving as the consummate steward over Yuma County water interests, he worked closely during the 1920s with officials from the Yuma County Water Users Association (YCWUA) to win federal appropriations for flood protection. Crafting a comprehensive water policy meant more than winning projects and protecting the land from the river's ravages. It also entailed watching over the Siamese twin of water projects: cheap farm labor. When domestic labor was at a premium during World War I, Hayden had lobbied for temporary admission of Mexican laborers to harvest Yuma County crops.[24] A staunch advocate of the bracero program during and after World War II, he continued to assist Yuma County farmers in obtaining Mexican labor. In sum, Hayden energetically served the agricultural community in Yuma during his years in the Senate.

In the 1940s, the USBR commissioned several studies of the Wellton-Mohawk area to ascertain whether assumption of farm debts and construction of a gravity canal from the Colorado River were feasible. Dr. Harlan H. Barrows from the University of Chicago conducted one of the earliest assessments of the problems in eastern Yuma County. Barrows identified key environmental hurdles that faced farmers, suggested solutions, and predicted political attitudes among valley residents over the next forty years. Observing that high levels of salinity affected other areas in Yuma County besides the Mohawk Valley, he offered three solutions to the problem: water could be imported from the Colorado River, farmers could be moved "to the first block of the Yuma Mesa," or the USBR could simply "leave the Mohawk-Roll area to the inevitable conclusion of present trends."[25]

Barrows viewed the second option as a viable alternative in the event that local farmers could not procure water from the Colorado River.[26] His proposal to move the farmers to new lands, however, generated numerous objections. Local officials resolutely dismissed the plan's feasibility, while a University of Arizona official declared his belief that "the settlers would, under no conditions, move to the Yuma Mesa lands from the Mohawk-Roll area." Hugo Farmer concurred, observing, "It would have a very injurious effect upon the whole Gila Project." No one expressed the farm rights argument better than Wellton-Mohawk Irrigation and Drainage District (WMIDD) president Wayne Wright. In a letter to Barrows, Wright wrote, "I believe the farmers of this area would prefer to risk their destiny to their present plight than to the Yuma Mesa. . . . A community that has been able to survive with extremely salty water [at a reasonable cost] . . . certainly should prosper with a good water supply."[27]

Despite their intransigent optimism, Barrows recognized that simply providing better water for salty lands might not resolve farmers' problems. The professor noted that although "some of the farmers feel that it would be [a] simple matter to reclaim the lands if fresh water were obtainable, . . . it does not follow that it would be simple in all cases."[28] Barrows's report nonetheless vividly captured the indomitable spirit of officials and farmers in the Mohawk Valley. For them, there was no alternative to salvaging their lands.

The Mexican Water Treaty (1944) played a significant role in Arizona's push for development of the Gila Project. At the project reauthorization hearings, state attorney Charles Carson elaborated on the state's motivations for supporting the treaty with Mexico. State leaders had watched with trepidation during the 1920s and 1930s as Mexico diverted more and more water from the Colorado River. Prior to the signing of the CRC, Arizona had no legal guarantee of Colorado River water. Carson feared that if Arizona failed to ratify the CRC before a treaty was signed with Mexico, Californians would insist that Mexico be furnished part of the 2.8 million acre-feet of water that the CRC had set aside for Arizona.[29] Essentially, Arizona approved the CRC and supported the Mexican Water Treaty because its leaders wanted to limit the amount of water its southern neighbor could use.[30] Many of Arizona's leaders believed that if Mexico's appropriation of water from the river were not legally limited, sufficient resources would not be available to develop the Gila and Central Arizona Projects. Once Arizona governor Sidney Osborn signed the CRC, Senators Hayden and McFarland rallied supporters behind ratification of the Mexican Water Treaty in the U.S. Senate. Hugo Farmer, in anticipation of congressional approval for the Gila Project, also voiced support for the international accord.[31]

Two sets of hearings were held, in Phoenix and Yuma, to determine Arizona's water needs and the feasibility of the Gila Project. At the 1944 Arizona Water Resources Hearings and the 1947 Reauthorizing Gila Project Hearings, local leaders greeted congressmen, senators, and USBR officials with a well-coordinated campaign on behalf of the Gila Project. Testimony revealed the severity of salinity problems in the Mohawk Valley. Farmer informed committee members that nearly 9,000 acres of land had been cultivated, but that "primarily [because of] the increasing salt content of water more than 3,000 acres have gone back to brush." The salt content of water in the valley ranged from 820 parts of salt per million parts of water (ppm) to 10,000 ppm. Overall, the water averaged 4,500 ppm. Farmer pointed out that 4,500 ppm was equivalent to 265 grains of salt per gallon, whereas in Southern California, "water with a salt content of 10 grains per gallon is considered unfit for irrigation of citrus trees."[32]

Mohawk Valley farmers described their plight to Senator McFarland and USBR commissioner Bashore. Phillip Dunn noted that by 1933 "the supply of water available [from the Gila River] began to decrease and the salt content of the wells began to increase." As a result, Dunn was able to irrigate only sixty acres of his land. L. A. Hicks observed that as the water table decreased, "the salt content has increased until our production is very low." Not only did the salty water limit the number of acres Hicks could farm, but it also dictated the types of crops he could plant. Whereas in the 1920s Hicks had cultivated cotton and vegetables, the high salt content of the water in the 1940s restricted him to growing alfalfa and Bermuda seed. Charles M. Hindman testified that 30 to 40 percent of the land that had been under cultivation in 1930 had been abandoned by 1944. Finally, R. H. McElhaney noted that most Roll-area residents had to import water for domestic use. Apart from people who bought water in Yuma, "[practically] all the drinking water is hauled from three or four wells in the community."[33]

The rationale for bringing water into the Mohawk Valley from the Colorado River was based on recent experience. Ample rains had recently provided the Gila River with sufficient runoff water to recharge the wells in eastern Yuma County. When Commissioner Bashore questioned valley farmers about the practicality of mixing fresh water with the brackish well water, Charles Hindman responded that the additional fresh water had significantly raised production levels during 1942.[34] He predicted that within a year the farmland in Wellton-Mohawk Valley could be re-rehabilitated.[35] Madeline Spain, owner of three Yuma-area ranches, testi-fied that fresh water from the floods in 1941 "sweetened up the land tremendously."[36] Additionally, Harold Woodhouse noted that "the quality of water in the wells improved in 1941 and 1942, especially in '42."[37] William A. Seale recalled: "[I irrigated] out of the river from the flood on 25 acres of my own [land], and I had quite a bit of salt, and those 25 acres, I think I irrigated three times while the river was up and running, and I got a pretty good fair stand on all of those 25 acres from the river water and I had never been able to do it otherwise from the pumps."[38] Finally, Hugo Farmer contended that "the salvation [of] these two magnificent valleys . . . lies in the prompt delivery of Colorado River water, and haste in the development of the Gila Project."[39] This testimony, though largely unscientific in nature, most likely influenced the USBR decision to con-struct a canal to transport water from the Colorado River.

Perhaps the most devastating problem in rehabilitating the Mohawk region involved poor drainage. Unfortunately, the push for development and the preservation of existing property rights obscured more critical questions about the capacity of the land in the Wellton-Mohawk Valley to sustain large-scale agricultural production. Testimony from the 1944 and 1947 hearings reveals little concern about the drainage system. Ike Proebstel, self-professed "oldest man on the Gila River," stated, "[Drain-age] is something that we have nothing to fear from. We have one of the few projects in the United States that don't [have problems]."[40] Farmer noted at the 1947 hearings that "there is an excellent drainage condition under all of that land," regardless of the high salt content of the water table.[41] Recalling the rains of 1941 and the miraculous crop production in 1942, Farmer confidently affirmed that "there [was] no question that the lands are excellently drained."[42] In retrospect, committee members in either hearing devoted little time to the complex issue of drainage ca-pabilities of the valley. Most of the discussion focused on the economic feasibility of lining canals with concrete, rehabilitating damaged farms, and improving water shortages in the lower Colorado River Basin.

Although Hayden and McFarland failed to marshal congressional support for approval of the CAP, they arranged compromises that enabled Arizonans to accommodate both the CAP and the Gila Project under the state's water allotment from the Colorado River.[43] Central Arizona politicians, meanwhile, recognized that the Gila Project (S.R. 1698, H.R. 5434) allowed for future use in central Arizona of greater amounts of Colorado River water. Even CAP proponents graciously endorsed the Gila Project. Arizona congressman John Murdock, chairman of the House Committee on Irrigation and Reclamation, observed, "With the enactment of H.R. 5434, a large part of the Mexican water burden can be met by return flow from Arizona land."[44] Arizona politicians were not alone in their exuberance for the project, as USBR officials also endorsed the Gila Project. Journalist Marc Reisner links Arizona's ambitious plans for water projects with the USBR's agenda for development. He writes, "With the Central Arizona Project deadlocked in Congress, the Bureau of Reclamation was anxious to build something in that state, not only to mollify its citizenry and the increasingly powerful Carl Hayden but also to give its regional office, suffering existential malaise after the completion of Hoover Dam, something new to do."[45]

Following the passage of the Senate and House bills, the federal government purchased indebted land and refinanced tracts for old and new settlers in the Wellton-Mohawk Valley. Once money was appropriated for the Gila Project, the USBR began construction of a gravity canal between the Colorado River and the Wellton-Mohawk Valley that was completed in 1957.[46] Still, poor drainage hampered comprehensive rehabilitation of the land even after the completion of the gravity canal in 1957.[47] In February 1957, USBR commissioner W. A. Dexheimer lamented to Hayden that "with the irrigation of the land under the Gila Project have come drainage problems. In nearly all cases these problems were expected, *but the rapidity with which they developed was not expected.*" Mixing diplomacy and bureaucracy with dynamic environmental conditions made the emerging crisis even more difficult to contain. Dexheimer noted that "the drainage problem in the Yuma area is but one of a group of water management problems [that include] delivery of water to Mexico to meet treaty requirements, *maintenance of salinity balances,* movement of sediment load . . . and others." The commissioner admitted that "nothing more than a general knowledge of local conditions exists with respect to the Wellton Mohawk Valley."[48]

Despite the completion of the canal, conditions in the Mohawk Valley continued to decline. Although comprehensive studies of valley farms do not exist, small-scale crop histories provide vignettes of the struggles of local farmers.[49] William Wooten planted 110 acres of land in Bermuda grass in 1958 and harvested 800 pounds of seed. The following year, he gathered only 310 pounds of seed from the same land. In 1960, the total amount harvested dropped to 85 pounds. By that time, the land was "out of production for all purposes."[50] Salt also damaged the cotton farms. In 1958, Melvin Taylor reaped 1.3 bales of cotton per acre from his 160-acre homestead. The yield dropped to .5 bale per acre two years later. Eighty acres of hegari and maize failed completely. By 1960, "70 acres [were] out of production and grown up in salt cedar." Even persistent Sam Jones could not overcome the laws of nature. In 1958, he harvested 1.5 bales of cotton per acre and 6 tons of alfalfa per acre. By 1960, his cotton production had dropped to .3 bale per acre, and alfalfa production declined to .75 ton per acre. Determined not to be defeated by the toxic groundwater, Jones replanted forty damaged acres in alfalfa, which "did not come up." By February 1961, "sixty acres, over 50 percent of the farm, [was] out of production."[51]

A 1959 USBR report on Gila Project drainage facilities provides a broader overview of valley conditions. The report noted that 50,000 of 75,000 acres were under development. This rapid increase in cultivation, coupled with the valley's poor drainage features, triggered a sharp rise in the water table as water was pumped in from the Colorado River.[52] Bureau officials suggested that $14 million in excess of what was already financed by valley farmers was needed immediately to build the fifty-eight-mile conveyance channel to empty runoff water into the Colorado River. If construction of a drainage channel were delayed, it would hurt area farmers and "[jeopardize] the repayment of the Government's large investment in irrigation works."[53] Completed in 1960, the channel set in motion the salinity crisis in Mexicali the following year.

Ecological problems also aggravated the plight of valley farmers. Each poor crop pushed them deeper into debt. Yuma County supervisor Wilburn J. Brown observed, "It will be very difficult under present curtailed production and economic conditions for lenders to work out sound loans to cover the cost of farm operations." Not only were farmers defaulting on loans, but each year of cultivation meant additional water costs and taxes. Furthermore, farming land with poor drainage caused significant ecological "damage which [would] be expensive to correct." Accordingly, Brown observed that it was in the best interest of the banks and farmers not to "encumber land which would have limited productivity due to ground water damage."[54] The promise of the postwar frontier turned into a trail of salty tears for many Wellton-Mohawk farmers. J. D. Mansfield, a local attorney associated with valley farmers, summed up the feelings of the entire community in a letter to Carl Hayden's assistant, Paul Eaton: "In all the years I've been knocking on your door asking for help," Mansfield observed, "I don't believe I have ever had a tougher one than our drainage problem."[55]

Mohawk Valley farmers, who had looked to the federal government to redeem the project during the 1940s, turned to the government to extricate them from the economic and ecological crises of the late 1950s and 1960s. Hayden remained a conduit for Arizonans to all levels of federal government. Farmer Rollie Keller pleaded with Senator Hayden in 1959: "I have lost 25 acres to seepage. This whole area will be ruined within a short time. Is there any way we farmers can get this area declared a Disaster Area? So we can get some money for the Reclamation here to put in the seep drains. They are surveying and have plans for this now, but say it will take three years to get it done. By this time most of this land will be ruined."[56]

Government bureaucracy exacerbated Keller's sense of victimization.[57] Hayden forwarded Keller's complaint to Acting Secretary of the Interior Fred G. Aandahl, who informed Hayden that he was aware of the valley's drainage problems and that a bypass channel was being constructed to further alleviate the damage. Nevertheless, the acting secretary offered little solace in terms of monetary relief for farmers like Keller. He explained that Mohawk Valley could not be designated a disaster area, because "a major disaster [as defined by Act of President on September 30, 1950] means a flood, drought, fire, hurricane, earthquake, storm or other catastrophe of great severity or magnitude. *We do not believe that a local drainage problem falls in that category.*"[58] Ultimately, many Mohawk

Valley farmers felt that the national government was out of touch with their local concerns.

State leaders addressed the impact of the salinity crisis on the state's water resources. John Haugh, assistant majority leader in the Arizona House of Representatives, expressed the local view to Governor Paul Fannin: "My own concern is not only that of international relations between our country and Mexico, but the possibilities that in the interests of these international relations our own government may take some action which is prejudicial to the position of the state of Arizona. I know that you and the members of our Congressional Delegation do share this concern."[59] Sam Dick, president of the YCWUA, reiterated this position to Hayden, advising the senator that "any attempted revision of Mexican treaty to eliminate credit for return flows [or waters such as those from Wellton-Mohawk] will adversely affect [the] entire state of Arizona."[60]

These concerns were not lost on Hayden, who wielded powerful influence in Congress. Mexican officials also recognized Hayden's authority. While Mexican diplomats opened up a dialogue with State Department officials in Washington, Gustavo Vildosola Almada, senator from Baja California, attempted to influence the diplomatic process by communicating directly with Hayden. He urged the Arizona senator to "consider postponing the [Wellton-Mohawk] project until together we can find a solution which will not jeopardize either valley." Although Vildosola's principal concern was for the long-term welfare of the Mexicali Valley, he also worried about the fast-approaching cotton-planting season. Vildosola's telegram is important because it demonstrates that Baja California and Arizona officials were trying to deal with the salinity problem in the Wellton-Mohawk Valley at the same time that the U.S. and Mexican governments were transforming the regional issue into an international crisis. Vildosola ended his plea by expressing to Hayden his desire that "the spirit of cooperation" would prevail.[61]

Despite these attempts at regional cooperation, Hayden lobbied to safeguard Arizona's water resources. In addition to protecting the Gila Project, he also wanted to assure his constituency that Arizona would have enough water to build the CAP. Hayden emphasized that the United States was not responsible for the "quality of water delivered to Mexico under the Treaty" and reminded his fellow lawmakers that the Mexican

Water Treaty of 1944 stipulated only the quantity, not the quality, of water Mexico received from the United States.[62]

In December 1961, Hayden warned Secretary of State Dean Rusk that granting Mexico any additional water to compensate for the saline runoff dumped into the river by Wellton-Mohawk would establish "a dangerous precedent" that might "diminish the total water supply available to the basin and to Arizona." Hayden argued that farmers in Arizona had used water of a similar quality during previous years and that a decrease in pumping would threaten farmland in the Mohawk Valley. He rejected Mexico's claims of an impending ecological crisis, insisting, "Mexico can solve her own problem if it is in fact a problem."[63] Nevertheless, Hayden extended a tenuous olive branch to Mexican officials. In keeping with his insistence that Mexicali's problems stemmed from a poorly developed irrigation system, he offered to "help our sister nation to the South [through the World Bank or the Alliance for Progress] to develop its agricultural potential on a sound basis."[64] In sum, he vigorously defended Arizona's present and future interests in the Colorado River.

Locally, WMIDD administrators felt victimized by the tendency of national leaders to give precedence to cordial relations with Mexico over the resolution of the valley's environmental and economic problems. In late July 1964, Pete Fishbein, a White House official, toured the Mexicali and Mohawk Valleys with representatives from the International Boundary and Water Commission. William A. Couple, counsel for the WMIDD, lamented the results of the tour. "I gather the impression that he was more sympathetic with the 'poor Mexicans' than with the 'rich Americans,'" he sardonically wrote to Senator Hayden. Couple also despaired that federal money might be used to build a bypass channel that would carry water to a point beyond where Mexico diverted water from the Colorado River rather than using it to increase the amount of tile drainage in the Mohawk Valley. He argued that any effort to complete the bypass should protect the "full entitlement of water from the mainstream of the Colorado [for Mohawk farmers] undiminished by the settlement of any international problems." Finally, Couple suggested that Arizona launch a public relations campaign against Mexicali Valley farmers, who, he had learned from various newspaper reports, were planning to increase their wheat production. Depending on where the wheat would be marketed,

Couple argued, it was quite possible that "better water for Mexico, at the expense of the United States, provides more wheat for Red China."[65]

In 1965, the United States agreed to the conditions of Minute 218, an arrangement drawn up to resolve the salinity crisis. According to the agreement, the United States agreed to construct a thirteen-mile drainage bypass to carry toxic runoff water to a location below Morelos Dam, where Mexicali diverted water from the Colorado River.[66] An alternative solution would have required the United States to install tile drains to improve the recovery rate of saline waters from Wellton-Mohawk farms. Mexican officials opted for the bypass drain because it allowed them to either accept or reject waters from the affected valley.[67]

The actions of President Johnson and the State Department in support of Minute 218 angered officials close to the WMIDD. Exasperated by suggestions that the project curtail its pumping of saline waters, the district's legal counsel lamented, "As always, the Wellton-Mohawk seems to be the goat that everyone picks on because we are the last ones to deliver return flows to the river."[68] The lawyers reminded Hayden that water users throughout the entire Colorado River Basin were to blame for the increase in river salinity. Was not the drainage bypass enough to satisfy the Mexicans? They feared Mexico would press the United States for additional measures to decrease the salinity of Colorado River water. The WMIDD lawyers suspected that President Johnson did not comprehend "some of the problems which we face on the Colorado." They feared that the president would be more receptive to Mexico's complaints than to their domestic concerns in future negotiations with Mexico. In an attempt to curry favor with Mexico, they suggested, Johnson very well might "work a great restriction upon the district." The attorneys implored Hayden to do "anything that would stiffen President Johnson's position" in dealing with the Mexican president.[69] The complaints arising from Yuma County and Arizona lawyers, farmers, and politicians reveal different priorities in dealing with the Mexicans. These differences further exacerbated the sense of political alienation that afflicted Mohawk farmers throughout construction of the project.

The sense of disillusionment experienced by residents in Yuma County during the mid-1960s is also illustrated through the plight of individuals *not* involved with agricultural production. Betty I. Lucas's experience demonstrates that international water politics affected everyone in the delta to one degree or another. Following World War II, Lucas faced the challenge of taking care of two daughters and her husband, who had suffered "an incurable brain injury" during the war. In addition to operating a family campground, Lucas held a second job. The camping area was located adjacent to their house, yet the title to their land allowed the USBR to construct a bypass across their property. Lucas lamented that she had to surrender one third of her property for the construction of the drainage bypass that would carry runoff from the Wellton-Mohawk Valley to a point below Morelos Dam. Her major complaint, however, was the arbitrary manner in which contractors left materials strewn across her property. One morning Lucas arrived home from work at 2:30 a.m. and "had to uncouple three approximately forty-foot lengths of irrigation pipe and drag them in the roadway" so that six campers could enter the campground. In addition to these inconveniences, Lucas complained that the "threat of being dispossessed from our land is exceptionally bad for my husband's health." To add insult to injury, the wife of the local USBR chief telephoned Lucas and told her that if she did not like the bureau's treatment, she could "move to Mexico or Baja California."[70] The USBR commissioner responded to Lucas's claims in a letter to Carl Hayden. He acknowledged that "due to [the] urgency" of resolving problems with Mexico, "misunderstandings may inadvertently have appeared to give cause for alarm that would not have arisen under a more normal pace of construction." The commissioner pledged to provide "intensive surveillance" for Lucas's property in the future. He also informed Hayden that the bureau had made an offer of $1,800 to Lucas for her property, which she accepted on September 23, 1965.[71] Lucas's troubles further illustrate the distance that existed between local and national priorities during the salinity crisis.

Even after construction of the drainage bypass, high salinity levels continued to pollute the Colorado River. As a consequence, political relations between the United States and Mexico remained strained. Candidate Luís Echeverría used inflammatory anti-American rhetoric to kindle nationalist fervor and enhance his 1970 campaign for the Mexican presidency.[72] During a speech to the U.S. Congress in 1972, Echeverría contrasted U.S. actions in Vietnam and in Mexico. "It is impossible to understand," he commented, "why the United States does not use the same

boldness and imagination that it applies to solving complex problems
with its enemies to the solution of simple problems with its friends."[73]
Echeverría successfully transformed a regional issue into an international
platform for Mexican nationalism.[74]

conclusion: The Local consequences of a Binational crisis

Since the beginning of the salinity problem in 1961, protesters in Mexicali
had recognized its regional origin as well as the international platform
upon which the crisis was resolved. Scholars have traditionally emphasized the actors on the diplomatic/international platform. Nevertheless,
the dynamics of Arizona water politics, together with the plans of the
USBR, also played a significant role in inadvertently creating the heated
environmental and political crisis along the U.S.–Mexican border. In addition, the sundry motives of the principal actors contributed to the
complexity of the political process leading to the approval of the Gila
Project. Hugo Farmer was simultaneously motivated by political pressures
within and outside of Arizona—a desire to rescue embattled farmers and a
hope to enhance Yuma County's development through settlement of veterans on the project. But if Carl Hayden had not been amenable to the
project, local agendas probably would not have had international consequences. The subsequent actions of politicians and attorneys only exacerbated local, national, and international tensions.

Ultimately, the catastrophe reflects the complexity of environmental
issues in the delta. Ecology and politics often responded to each other in
disconcerting ways.[75] Because the Colorado River is so intimately tied to
every facet of life in the region, the consequences of controlling its water
spilled over into the political, social, and economic lives of the Mexicans,
Americans, Quechan, and Cocopah who called the delta home. And as
Yuma County illustrates, local environmental politics could be as complicated as relations between the two nations involved in the crisis.

Moreover, the salinity crisis reveals the dichotomy of regional and
national politics in the Colorado River Delta. On the one hand, both
Americans and Mexicans recognized that a river linked their distinctive
and collective fortunes. The "Arizona—tiene la palabra" placard served as

Figure 11 A large public protest on the salinity crisis in Mexicali during the summer of 1962. One banner proclaims, "Salt should not separate two friendly peoples." (Courtesy of the Fondo Martínez Retes, Archivo Museo Universitario, Universidad Autónoma de Baja California)

a reminder of the localized context of critical environmental issues in the region. Yet increased federal control over natural resources on both sides of the border precluded the possibility of a truly regional solution to the problem. As the water supply dwindled throughout the twentieth century, Mexicali Valley and Yuma County farmers were forced to look to their respective national capitals for relief. Even if "la sal no debe separar a dos pueblos amigos" (salt should not separate two friendly peoples), sprawling bureaucracies made regional understanding difficult.[76] Many Mexicali residents felt just as isolated from their national capital as did American farmers in Yuma. Historian Celso Bernal Aguire argues that Mexico's leaders began to aggressively defend their water resources only after extensive protests in Mexicali, a car caravan to Mexico City to raise national awareness of the situation, and mass mailings of informational materials throughout the country.[77]

In the end, the intimate relationship between the environment, politics, and culture on the lower Colorado River assured that any single solution, however well intentioned, could scarcely remedy environmental conflicts that had riddled regional relations since the early 1900s. On the other hand, the crisis was not inevitable. Arizona politicians, the USBR, and farmers throughout the basin, including Mexicali, made certain choices about development that inadvertently created conditions ripe for disaster.

Deltascape The Threat of Salinity

Throughout human history, agrarian societies that relied on irrigation, particularly those located in arid valleys, have fought a losing battle against a most unlikely adversary: salt. On the one hand, salt is a natural constituent of river water. Even at its source, the Colorado River's tributaries lap up salts and minerals from weathered rocks on their way down to the Gulf of California.[78] Furthermore, the delta's valley floors contain an unusually high amount of salts and minerals, a reminder of when the region was covered by the Gulf of California.

Several factors make this battle against salt a nearly impossible challenge to overcome. As water rushes into the calm waters of Lakes Powell, Mead, Havasu, and the other reservoirs on the Colorado River, up to a third of the water evaporates in the hot sun, whose glazing stare lasts nearly the entire year.[79] The remaining water absorbs the salts left over from the evaporated water. Below Hoover Dam, additional water evaporates as it winds through long irrigation canals and waits in stagnant ditches. By the time the remaining water is applied to crops, it deposits the excess salts, acquired over the long journey from the source to the delta, near the roots of the watered plants. Unless additional water (with its own salts) is applied to leach out the excess minerals, the seemingly benign compound of sodium chloride (which, ironically, will later be used by consumers to enhance the flavor of many of these crops) becomes the fatal enemy of nearby plants and kills them upon contact with their roots.

Salt's fatal touch comes not only from aboveground. The greatest challenge for irrigated civilizations in river basins, from the Hohokam in ancient Arizona, to the Sumerians and Mesopotamians in the Middle East, to the Americans and Mexicans in the Colorado River Basin, has been to achieve proper drainage of irrigation water on their respective valley floors.[80] If excess irrigation water is not removed, it will raise the water table. As the water table rises to within four to six feet of the soil, capillaries in the earth wick water upward toward the ground. This process, known as osmosis, threatens the plants from below unless sufficient care is taken to remove excess drainage from the water table with wells or expensive tile drains. Extended contact with the saline groundwater produces the same results as irrigating with hypersaline water: plant growth is impaired or stopped completely.

Farmers in the Wellton-Mohawk Valley faced this second dilemma in the 1940s and 1950s. Unfortunately, sometimes when one region solves its salinity problems, it creates new salinity problems for people downriver. This is what happened in the Mexicali Valley, as drainage from the Wellton-Mohawk project added excess salts to the waters used by Mexicali Valley farmers, whose fields were already laden with salts left by the Gulf of California centuries before.

Water and the Landscapes of Power in the Mexicali Valley

The salinity crisis in the Mexicali Valley represents a unique chapter in Mexico's environmental and diplomatic history. The angry response of many local residents against the Mexican government's reluctance to address their concerns in the face of foreign exploitation of land and water, however, mirrors popular patterns of protest in Mexican history. At the turn of the twentieth century, for example, Emiliano Zapata protested President Porfirio Díaz's complicity in American and European encroachment on Indian lands in the rural state of Morelos. Mobilizing natives and mestizos, Zapata threw off the yoke of the Porfirian-controlled state government and became the voice for land reform during the Mexican Revolution. More recently, the masked Subcomandante Marcos and his EZLN followers have protested the land reforms initiated by the Mexican government during the early 1990s, seizing land, killing Mexican soldiers, and decrying the impact of globalization on native peoples in southern Mexico. In both cases, Zapata and Marcos expressed local outrage at Mexican policies calculated to integrate the southern periphery into the global economy. These episodes also illustrate that residents on Mexico's periphery often view contested landscapes in ways very different from those of national officials.[1]

Such was the case during the salinity crisis as well. Throughout the twentieth century, the Mexicali Valley played a critical role in the struggle between Mexican and U.S. interests for control of land and water in the delta. As the salinity of Colorado River water entering the Mexicali Valley increased in the fall of 1961, the valley once again became an embattled territory. National and state officials from both countries saw the Mexicali Valley as a testing ground for their theories about the cause of the salinity crisis. Not surprisingly, political views and previous experience with irrigation influenced the theoretical questions asked by policy makers and scientists.

For the most part, officials who viewed the Mexicali Valley as an international political landscape, including those from the State Department, the International Boundary and Water Commission (the organization under the State Department responsible for administering border and water issues with Mexico), and the Mexican federal government, did not live there but recognized the centrality of the region in resolving the growing crisis. They also viewed the problem within the broader context of domestic and international politics. However, residents of the Mexicali Valley viewed their home as a local political landscape. For them the salinity crisis was not an abstract issue that could be reduced to statistics or policy positions but instead represented a profound ecological transformation that affected the taste of their drinking water, the fertility of their land, and the bounty of the harvest. Local political organizers such as Alfonzo Garzón, founder of the Liga Agraria Estatal de Baja California (LAE), often had objectives different from those of national officials. In fact, one of the turning points in the salinity crisis occurred in 1964, when the diplomacy-driven perspective of the Mexican government subsumed the agenda of many local residents in the Mexicali Valley. Similarly, as the crisis continued, the Wellton-Mohawk Irrigation and Drainage District (WMIDD) increasingly found local concerns for improving its water resources at odds with the State Department's efforts to improve relations with Mexico.

The Mexicali Valley as an International Political Landscape

During the fall of 1961, as water deliveries to Mexico from the Colorado River declined after summer irrigation, the WMIDD began intensive pumping of its highly saline aquifers in order to create storage space for better quality water from the Colorado River. The drainage waters contained an average salinity of nearly 6,000 ppm as they entered the Gila River, which quickly joins the Colorado River. In November, Assistant Secretary of State Robert F. Woodward observed, "[The] water now being delivered may not be useable in the condition in which it arrives at the Mexican diversion dam."[2] At the same time, the State Department urged the secretary of the interior, Stewart Udall, to find a way to decrease the salinity of water destined for Mexico.[3]

Bill Blackledge, an employee of Anderson-Clayton's agricultural subsidiary in Mexicali, Compañía Industrial Jabonera del Pacífico, noted that since 1956, salinity levels had steadily increased at his company's local experiment station. By mid-October, Blackledge found that the salinity of water deliveries at Morelos Dam averaged 2,690 ppm. The water was unfit not only for irrigation but also for domestic and industrial use. "Practically everyone in the Mexicali Valley drinks water originating from the river," he noted, "and are now complaining that it is no longer potable." Blackledge found it odd that Mexicali farmers would be expected to risk the failure of their crops because of their efforts to remove saline water from drainage wells upstream.[4] The saline water threatened not only the crops but also the soil of many Mexicali Valley farms.[5]

Blackledge conceded that with so much competition for water in the U.S. portion of the Colorado River Basin, Mexican concerns probably would not be adequately addressed. Ultimately, Blackledge hoped that U.S. policy makers would quickly resolve the budding crisis. "If not," he predicted, "it will not only cause dissention among the Mexican farmers and public, but will also be exploited by subversives to further create animosity towards the United States."[6]

The Mexican government quickly responded to the crisis on its northern border, where local discontent was mounting. Mexican ambassador Antonio Carrillo lodged a formal complaint with Secretary of State Dean Rusk on November 9, 1961. His arguments outlined the legal positions the Mexican government would pursue in an effort to win concessions from the United States. First, Carrillo argued that although the Mexican Water Treaty did not explicitly guarantee a certain level of water quality in deliveries to Mexico, poor quality water could not be used for "domestic and municipal uses [and] agriculture and stockraising," a stipulation included in the treaty. The ambassador also expressed frustration that the federal government of the United States was not willing to remedy the problem for fear that American farmers in the region might pursue their own legal cases against the government should those solutions be detrimental to their farms. If the problem were not remedied, Carrillo threatened, Mexico would be forced to take its case to the World Court.[7]

Two organizations within the U.S. government were charged with responding to Carrillo and finding a solution to the crisis: the State Department and the Department of the Interior (DOI). From the outset, the two organizations approached the crisis in very different ways. On the one hand, the DOI had an interest in promoting and protecting the irrigation interests of western farmers through the U.S. Bureau of Reclamation (USBR). Therefore, the DOI viewed the crisis from the local perspective of farmers in the Wellton-Mohawk Valley who felt victimized by the Mexican complaints related to their pumping of saline drainage into the river. On the other hand, the State Department viewed the growing crisis in the Mexicali Valley within the broader context of U.S.–Mexican relations and U.S. foreign policy at large. The Mexicali Valley episode affected not only America's reputation with Mexico but also its image throughout the world. These differing geopolitical agendas clashed throughout the crisis and also conditioned the State Department's responses to Mexican requests for help.

DOI and State Department officials quickly exchanged strategies for solving the salinity crisis. DOI undersecretary James K. Carr observed that the Imperial Irrigation District (IID) would provide Mexicali Valley farmers access to cleaner water through the All-American Canal, but only if Mexico fulfilled its promise to construct adequate water treatment facilities to prevent the emission of raw sewage into the New River, which flowed across the border to Calexico. A second option would have been to limit the pumping of saline groundwater from drainage wells beneath the Wellton-Mohawk Valley. Carr noted that it would be difficult for the WMIDD to substantially decrease the pumping of drainage water from underground aquifers without "jeopardizing a United States investment of approximately $50,000,000 that the project users have contracted to repay." He also pointed out that the option of releasing additional water from dams upstream to dilute deliveries to the Mexicali Valley would generate political fallout in the United States. Snow runoff had been minimal during the fall of 1961, contributing to low levels of water behind Lakes Mead and Mojave.

Carr concluded by suggesting some actions that Mexico could take to remedy the problem. This would become a familiar response from the USBR and western water interests during the salinity crisis. Carr's solutions for Mexico included limiting its irrigation to the available supply of suitable water, using additional groundwater to supplement the winter water supply, and diversifying crop production to better match the water supply. Carr's response reflected the prevailing feeling at the DOI that Mexico needed to deal with a problem of its own making. He finished by noting that Mexico could expect the same quality and quantity of water from the Colorado River during the next few years.[8]

The State Department replied to the Mexican protest on December 20. It initially adopted the defensive approach advocated by the DOI. In its response, the State Department denied that the United States had violated the Mexican Water Treaty. In fact, the State Department refused to admit that the drainage from Wellton-Mohawk Valley polluted the Colorado River. It sidestepped any reference to the treaty's guarantee that water would be fit for domestic and agricultural purposes.[9] In response, Ambassador Carrillo expressed dismay that the United States would not uphold the stipulation to deliver water fit for domestic and agricultural use. He also rejected the DOI's assertion that the federal government could not "compel the Wellton-Mohawk District to cease pumping salty water into the Gila [River] under the Treaty."[10]

The next month, Secretary of State Rusk defended his position in a letter to Ambassador Carrillo. Rusk reminded Carrillo that Mexico had opted not to receive water through the All-American Canal in exchange for completion of the sanitation plant in Mexicali. Furthermore, he noted that State Department and DOI scientists had visited the Mexicali Valley and subsequently reported that the saline waters had not adversely affected crops there. In fact, the scientists recommended that "a reduction in the pumping of drainage waters in the Wellton-Mohawk Division under existing circumstance, as the Ambassador [Carrillo] proposed, would result in substantial injury to that irrigation district." Recognizing that Mexico might periodically receive highly saline waters, Rusk emphasized that efforts be made in the Mexicali Valley to prevent the possibility of further damage. In an effort to assuage Mexican anger and perhaps salve the conscience of many U.S. officials, Secretary Rusk observed, "Water users on the river in the United States are also experiencing the effects of this situation."[11] In response, Ambassador Carrillo continued to insist that releases from dams upstream would completely resolve the salinity crisis.[12]

The State Department and DOI also issued a press release to Mexican newspapers in early 1962 to counteract the public relations disaster created by their refusal to remedy the crisis. In the release, DOI secretary Udall insisted that the two nations work together to resolve the problem. The release also pointed out that Mexico could have scheduled for additional water to have been delivered to the Mexicali Valley during the fall of 1961 but failed to do so "possibly because the degree of salinity was not anticipated by Mexico." The release also made explicit comparisons between what U.S. irrigation districts had done to combat salinity and what Mexican farmers might do to improve drainage in their fields. Suggestions included classifying lands, improving drainage systems, and selecting crops that matched the salt tolerance of available water supplies. Finally, Secretary Udall insisted that the water delivered to Mexicali in 1961 was "usable on a short term basis for irrigation of crops such as wheat, alfalfa, and cotton under the proper drainage practices."[13]

Local officials in the Mexicali Valley issued a swift and stinging response to the press release. Rafael Martínez Retes, representative of the Comité General de la Defensa del Valle de Mexicali, took issue with the tone and content of the release. He singled out Secretary Udall, whose ties to Arizona made him an easy target for such an attack. Martínez condemned the United States for not resolving a crisis it had helped create as well as for its audacity to suggest that Mexico was entirely responsible for the problem.[14]

Pressure to resolve the crisis also came from the academic community in the United States. Sidney L. Gulick, dean of arts and sciences at San Diego State College, informed Secretary Rusk, "With our interest in Latin-American affairs, we know that what happens here can ruin every billion spent on the Alliance for Progress." He also expressed fear that radical groups in the Mexicali Valley might resort to terrorist activities because of U.S. unwillingness to resolve the problem. Gulick conjured up images of an "embittered and ruined Mexican hothead" using a tractor to cut through the dikes in Mexican territory that protected the Imperial Valley from the waters of the Colorado River. "By morning the salt torrents would bear down on El Centro," he warned, "[and] the Salton Sea would no longer lie 287 feet below sea level." With reference to the 1905 flood, the dean queried, "When these waters last came in, U.S. Army engineers helped the Mexican government plug the holes; would we be invited in again? If not, would we go in by force? That would be an act of war, from which we could not recover in a century." The macabre Gulick closed his letter with a more practical consideration. He observed that the United States would be best served by not adding additional farming acres in its portion of the Colorado River Basin. This would at least stabilize water quality in the delta.[15]

In March 1962, Arizona senator Carl Hayden met with DOI and State Department officials to further discuss avenues for solving the crisis. The meeting reflected a new trend during the salinity crisis: the State Department and the International Boundary and Water Commission (IBWC) tended to stress U.S. responsibility for the problem, while the USBR tended to stress what Mexico needed to do in order to alleviate the salinity issue. U.S. ambassador to Mexico Dean Mann opened the meeting, noting that the Mexican government was willing to improve drainage works in the Mexicali Valley. However, with the onset of the salinity crisis, Mexican officials were reluctant to make an investment that might be rendered worthless with continued deliveries of poor quality water. Desirous for the USBR to generate a solution to the problem, Mann reaffirmed his conviction that the United States would lose any case taken to the World Court.

In response, USBR officials maintained a defensive posture. They mentioned that conditions at Wellton-Mohawk were normal in terms of its return flows to the river. The chief of the USBR's Irrigation Division, Maurice Langley, observed that the salinity of deliveries during the past winter (averaging about 1,700 ppm) were usable. He also argued that farmers in the Imperial Valley had faced similar challenges in previous years and as a result had elected to install expensive tile drains on their farms. Finally, Langley stressed that the salt in the Mexicali Valley represented "the accumulation of previous years and not the result of the use of salt this year." While Langley was indeed correct that accumulated salts in the soils inhibited normal plant growth, he did not address the impact of salt applied from the top in the form of saline water from the Colorado River.

A. B. West, regional director of the USBR at Boulder City, Nevada, also confirmed the "normality" of operations at Wellton-Mohawk. He reiterated that the project must continue pumping drainage water from its wells. West also revealed that the WMIDD was unwilling to install tile drains because it wanted to "create an underground reservoir of better water for future use." Once the saline water was removed, pristine Colorado River water would be pumped into the wells for storage and later use. Langley also objected to the option of installing tile drains in the Wellton-Mohawk Valley, noting that it would "take four or five years to get an appropriation and install them, i.e., about half the period during which it was expected there would be a salinity problem." West went on to state how important it was for Mexico to install a drainage system, for without it the "Mexicali Valley was doomed." He refused to speak for the WMIDD when Ambassador Mann asked if it would install drains if the Mexican government installed them in the Mexicali Valley.

Ultimately, the meeting did not generate a concrete plan of action. In an effort to break the political logjam, Ambassador Mann suggested that a joint study be carried out through the IBWC and its Mexican counterpart, the Comisión Internacional de Límites y Aguas (CILA), in order to arrive at a single set of facts from which both nations could work. Mann advocated a balanced approach to resolving the crisis. He thought the study should focus on adequate drainage and the quality of water Mexico could use. He pointed out that even if the technicians were not able to agree on everything, "it might remove some of the misunderstanding."[16]

science, politics, and environmental Diplomacy

Science and international politics lay at the center of the salinity crisis and helped define the positions taken by each nation between 1961 and 1974. Scientific studies in the Mexicali Valley served as fodder for legitimizing positions on both sides of the border. However, while cynics might contend that the contradictory conclusions reached by scientists on both sides of the border were merely the result of political calculation, one must look at the questions they asked to find the differentiating factor in the results they obtained. The numerous studies contained in State Department records reflect the focus of U.S. policy makers and scientists on the quality of land in the Mexicali Valley. Scientists for the USBR were heavily influenced by experiences with saline farmlands in the Wellton-Mohawk Valley. As a result, they focused on the poor drainage qualities evident in the Mexicali Valley. Through this approach, many U.S. policy makers insisted that Mexico was responsible for the saline quality of the soils in the Mexicali Valley.

In contrast, Mexican scientists and policy makers focused on the quality of water being delivered to the Mexicali Valley at Morelos Dam. In spite of the misperceptions of U.S. policy makers, the Mexican government had done a great deal of research on the drainage problems of soils with elevated salinity in the Mexicali Valley, beginning as early as 1954. In fact, on the eve of the salinity crisis, plans had been outlined to improve the drainage capacity of lands that were part of the Colorado River Irrigation District (CRID). The saline waters introduced in 1961 added an additional variable that harmed fields already tottering on the verge of infertility. Accordingly, it is not surprising that Mexican diplomats, scientists, and politicians stressed the poor quality of the water delivered to the valley in establishing the cause of the crisis.

Scientists, government agencies, and private corporations issued studies related to the crisis. Dr. Leon Bernstein, from the U.S. Salinity Lab in Riverside, California, and IBWC engineer Joseph Friedkin toured the Wellton-Mohawk and Mexicali Valleys in November 1961. At the time, they noted a sharp increase in the salinity of water from the Colorado River. The report also provided a standard for measuring acceptable water quality. Bernstein and Friedkin noted, for example, that in 1958 the World Health Organization set 1,500 ppm as the level of "excessive" salinity for potable water. Bernstein and Friedkin observed that Mexicali's domestic water supply, with a salinity of 2,500 ppm, grossly violated this standard.

The scientists concluded that both nations must work toward a remedy for the salinity problem. Bernstein noted that prevailing irrigation practices, as well as the saline waters, contributed to the poor cotton harvests in the Mexicali Valley. However, he also observed that wheat seedlings irrigated with saline waters had reached two inches in height and appeared to be healthy. Wheat and alfalfa proved more resistant to salt toxicity than cotton. Despite the current success of heartier crops, Bernstein noted that the failure of crops during 1961 could be compared with better harvests the previous year, when higher quality water was available. The evidence appeared conclusive enough to implicate U.S. water users as contributors to the salinity crisis. Bernstein suggested that the salinity of irrigation water should be limited at least to 1,800 ppm, additional water should be applied to crops to properly leach out excess salt, and intensive soil testing should be conducted.[17]

In February 1962, the Mexican Ministry of Agriculture and Livestock issued its own study of the salinity problem. It suggested that salinity levels had remained acceptable until November 1961, when they increased to 2,900 ppm. The report insisted that excess drainage pumped from the wells in the Wellton-Mohawk Valley was not runoff (an allowance permitted under the 1944 treaty) but instead an artificial substitution for natural drainage. In an effort to emphasize this critical point, the ministry asserted, "This is not return flow, any more than if the U.S. government was to decide to divert water from the Salton Sea into the Colorado River to substitute it for natural Colorado River water to be delivered to Mexico." Finally, the report contended that since the U.S. government had authorized the dumping of drainage waters into the Colorado River without consulting Mexico, it must find a solution to the problem.[18]

At the same time, Bill Blackledge, the Anderson-Clayton scientist at the experiment station in Mexicali, reviewed current conditions in the valley. His 1962 study suggested that both nations contributed to the problem. Blackledge noted that while the CRID was in the process of improving irrigation techniques on local farms, the potential for crop and soil damage with the use of hypersaline water remained probable. He observed that during 1961, "the amount of salt deposited per acre was nearly double that which would have been applied with natural Colorado River water." He attributed the failure of cotton grown on marginal lands to saline irrigation water. While he believed it was too soon to know how much damage the saline water would inflict on the current wheat crop, Blackledge provided vignettes of farmers in the valley who were uneasy about using the water. For example, Federico Rioseco planted 125 acres of wheat, a portion of which was irrigated with good water and another section with "relatively high" saline waters. The section irrigated with high quality water produced a healthy stand of wheat, while the latter section had to be replanted. From these results, Rioseco concluded that "the part irrigated with the uncontaminated Colorado River water looks good, while that irrigated with water containing the salts from Wellton-Mohawk looks bad." Blackledge's interaction with Rioseco was "representative of various experiences with other thinking farmers in this Valley."[19]

In accord with Ambassador Mann's desire for both nations to conduct a joint study, the IBWC and CILA commissioned their scientists to study conditions in the Wellton-Mohawk and Mexicali Valleys. During the early stages of the study, the U.S. panel of scientists arrived at some startling conclusions. They noted that salinity levels in water delivered to Mexicali Valley farmers during the fall of 1961 "seriously aggravated the problem and created an emergency." "[The] salt content of water delivery by the United States since October 1961 [was] so high," they observed, "that agricultural production in the Valley [would] probably have to be largely abandoned unless there is a reduction in salts." Well water at Wellton-Mohawk contained between 2,500 and 18,000 ppm of salt. As a result, the WMIDD received about one ton of salt per acre-foot of water taken in from the Colorado River. In contrast, the irrigation district pumped between eight and nine tons of salt per acre-foot of water into the Gila and Colorado Rivers.[20] Despite the fact that many of the conclusions of U.S. scientists bolstered the Mexican position, the Mexican government roundly refused to let its scientists sign off on the studies because American policy makers continued to insist that poor soil and inadequate drainage facilities in the Mexicali Valley had precipitated the crisis.[21]

After reviewing the results of the joint study by the United States and Mexico in 1962, the Department of Health, Education, and Welfare (HEW) concluded that the saline waters dumped into the Colorado River could be considered "pollution." As a result, the HEW argued that the only way to effectively end the crisis would be for the DOI to retire all or part of the WMIDD from agricultural production. The memo advised against a plan to increase WMIDD pumping during the summer because such an action would increase the mineral content of Mexicali Valley water by about 50 percent. Furthermore, increased pumping would make it practically impossible, in the estimation of the HEW, to maintain an annual average salinity of 1,400 ppm. The department concluded its study by recommending the installation of a subsurface drainage system in the Wellton-Mohawk Valley.[22]

Western politicians and USBR officials rejected the State Department–sponsored study. DOI secretary Udall and USBR officials questioned whether the U.S. government should do anything to relieve the water quality problem "unless [it had] a commitment from the Mexican government that it plans to undertake a complementary program in the Mexicali Valley."[23] Members of Congress from the Colorado River Basin states later proposed a moratorium on further scientific investigations of the problem, demanding that no federal money be spent to study any proposal that would grant additional water to Mexico without charge.[24] They also refused to fund any proposal to build a bypass drain from the Wellton-Mohawk Valley to a point below Morelos Dam that did not include the runoff in Mexico's annual water total. Arizona officials continued to insist that no action be taken until the WMIDD could be assured it would receive credit for all water pumped out of its wells.

Unsatisfied with the joint study, the USBR released its own study of the salinity issue in February 1963. The report contended that the poor harvests in the Mexicali Valley resulted from poorly drained farmlands and not recent applications of saline river water. The report saddled Mexico with the burden of resolving the issue. "If Mexico carries out accepted irrigation and leaching procedures," the study proclaimed, "the salt concentrations will not be detrimental to the crops that are presently being grown."[25] The USBR vowed to continue pumping drainage water out of the WMIDD. Ironically, the report stated that salinity levels of river water would be decreased from somewhere in the 2,000-ppm range to 1,700 ppm "as refreshing of the Wellton-Mohawk aquifer took place."[26]

Release of the USBR report provoked a strong reaction from Mexican ambassador Carrillo, who blasted the study for exonerating the USBR from any wrongdoing. Such hubris, the ambassador noted, "departs from all rules of international law, which in no way and under no circumstances can conceive of a State's not being responsible for its own acts which may in any way affect another State of the international community." With reference to water quality, Carrillo disputed the report's suggestion that

Mexico would have to adapt its crop regime to waters with salinity between 1,800 and 2,000 ppm. He pointed out that U.S. farmers would not accept water of a similar quality. Observing that the USBR's only active solution set forth in the report entailed salvaging additional water from the Wellton-Mohawk Valley by adding additional drainage wells, Carrillo contended that the USBR heartlessly placed Mexican farmers, their lands, and their water in constant peril.[27]

On the other side of the diplomatic table, Carrillo's counterpart, Ambassador Mann, continued to press for U.S. projects, particularly the WMIDD, to achieve salt balance. Mann stressed that the issue remained the most important short-term problem in binational relations. With the United States yet to take any action, Mann noted, "we should expect Mexico to move toward actions which can only be harmful to our national interests." Further inaction, in Mann's estimation, would probably lead the Mexican government to remove its muzzle from the national press. At that point, the ambassador observed, "communists and opportunists will take every advantage of this opportunity to attack us on legal and moral grounds, raising issues on which they will be joined by many other Mexicans, even those who are anti-Communist and normally friendly to us." Mann stressed that "the Wellton-Mohawk salinity problem was not created by an act of God." Instead, he noted, "it was deliberately created by us on the theory that . . . the 1944 Colorado Water Treaty is silent on the issues of salinity." As a result, Mann asserted that USBR officials fallaciously reasoned they were "free to dump [salty drainage water] on the Mexicali Valley . . . and gradually replace those underground waters with water of a better quality from the Imperial Dam so that the Wellton-Mohawk could have a useable underground reserve supply available for its crops in addition to its allotted share of water."[28]

In 1964, the salinity crisis dragged into its third year. Mexicans were shocked by the assassination of John F. Kennedy, who had promised to end the elevated salinity levels in the Colorado River. Furthermore, economic conditions in the valley were tinged with uncertainty induced by the salinity. Anderson-Clayton temporarily stopped financing the farmlands of many valley farmers because they could no longer meet their financial obligations growing crops with saline water on marginal lands. While the affected fields represented only a small portion of valley lands,

Bill Blackledge believed that the damaged fields represented the proverbial tip of the iceberg. The deterioration of lands would accelerate if water quality did not improve. "Even if the contamination were discontinued this very instant," he opined, "the reclamation of the damaged soils will be a major problem for years to come."[29]

Ambassador Carrillo continued to protest salinity levels that approached 2,000 ppm during the winter of 1964.[30] He also reminded State Department officials of the deteriorating condition of fields in the Mexicali Valley as well as the growing strength of radical groups such as the Central Campesino Independiente (CCI).[31] Nevertheless, the USBR continued to stall. In March 1964, a USBR official stated that he was well aware of the increased salinity and "expected it to go higher as Wellton-Mohawk pumps the higher saline wells . . . and increases overall pumping to compensate for overall reductions during the winter." The State Department expressed its disapproval of this plan, which was calculated to promote local interests in the West at the expense of binational relations. Foreign Service officer Robert Sayre noted, "Reclamation takes the position that it has no commitment to do anything," ignoring President Kennedy's 1963 pledge that the problem would not recur.[32] A month later, IBWC commissioner Friedkin similarly noted that delay tactics undermined the adoption of a permanent resolution. He also sensed a lack of concern on the part of the USBR for upholding the good faith of the United States in maintaining salinity levels below 1,500 ppm.[33]

The Mexicali Valley as a Local Political Landscape

Differences in the political structures of the two nations were a critical determinant of the degree to which local politics influenced environmental diplomacy in the delta. Farmers in the WMIDD and surrounding irrigation districts enjoyed the benefits of a legislative process highly responsive to effective local organizers. In the western United States, where water and political power were closely linked, local farmers found their interests well represented at the highest levels of government. In April 1962, IBWC commissioner Friedkin requested that the seven states of the Colorado River Basin select two representatives for the Committee of Fourteen, an organization that would advise the State Department on its position on the salinity crisis. While the committee was helpful to the interests of the individual states, it approached the type of nonelected power described by political scientist Karl Wittfogel in *Oriental Despotism* and more recently by historian Donald Worster in his critique of U.S. water policy in the American West, *Rivers of Empire*. In effect, the committee further weakened the ability of the State Department to formulate a constructive solution to the problem. Its initial concerns were to protect the water rights of the basin states, not surrender additional water to Mexico, and to protect the WMIDD from dissolution. The committee arrogantly announced that any solution to the crisis "must be without detriment to the joint and separate interest of the concerned entities within the seven Colorado River Basin States."[34]

In contrast, the Mexican government did not provide an official place at the bargaining table for local groups in the Mexican delta. Nevertheless, grassroots organizations manifested their discontent with U.S. and Mexican policies through letter-writing campaigns, an auto caravan to Mexico City, and organized marches. During the early period of the crisis (1961–65), several groups mobilized political support in the Mexicali Valley. The first, supported by the Mexicali Chamber of Commerce, was the Comité Coordinador de la Iniciativa Privada de Mexicali, which was comprised of industrial, agricultural, and commercial organizations in the valley. It organized protests in front of the U.S. consulate in Mexicali; encouraged Mexicans not to shop in Calexico or El Centro, California; and lobbied government officials of both nations to remedy the problems occasioned by the excess salt.[35] Public protesting ebbed and flowed with the increase and decrease of salinity in water deliveries from the Colorado River. On December 14, 1961, James Boyd, American consul in Mexicali, estimated that between eight and ten thousand protesters had marched in the rain. The following day, Ambassador Mann informed Secretary Rusk that an estimated twenty thousand people had protested in front of the U.S. consulate in Mexicali the same day.[36] Mann feared that "Communist and Nationalist elements may now be seizing upon [the] problem for purposes . . . against us."[37]

The manifestations of December 14 and 15 vividly displayed the impressive manner of political mobilization achieved by local groups. Businesses were asked to close at noon. Thousands of rain-soaked protesters marched past the U.S. consulate, bearing banners with slogans such as "world peace will only be possible when the weak receive from the strong just and equitable treatment." Later on, during a speech before the governor of northern Baja California, Aurelio Flores Valenzuela, local president of the Unión Agrícola Regional, asked the governor to petition federal officials to resolve the crisis. While these events could be counted as a success by organizers, members of the northern Baja California legislature did not take advantage of an opportunity to talk with the American consul. Consul Boyd commented that only one member of the legislature stopped by to talk with him about the salinity.[38]

Until 1958, ejidatarios and agricultural workers in the Mexicali Valley had associated themselves with the Liga de Comunidades Agraria y Sindicatos Campesinos, a local branch of the Confederación Nacional Campesina, a peasant union tied to the powerful PRI that ruled Mexico. However, several of the members of the existing organization, including Alfonso Garzón, were not satisfied with the organization's leadership. As a result, they created the LAE in 1958. Their initial efforts included protesting the low prices paid for cotton commodities. The LAE also encouraged independent political organization in the Mexicali Valley during the early 1960s, achieving renown not only on the local level but also on the national stage. Finally, the LAE helped farmers to trade their private property for ejido lands. President Adolfo López Mateos created the Ejido Sombrete for these new campesinos in May 1961.[39]

Garzón, a fervent nationalist, hoped to defend the rights of the campesinos not only against the transgressions of their neighbors in the Wellton-Mohawk Valley but also against the wealthier colonos in the Mexicali Valley. Garzón believed that the colonos, in league with officials from the CRID, were habitually undermining the promises of land and water that the Constitution of 1917 offered to the landless and oppressed. CRID officials often gave preferential treatment in the distribution of water to colonos. For ejidatarios, protests and organized manifestations before Mexican and U.S. officials offered at least the semblance of recognition of their demands. Garzón noted that outside of the manifestations "the farmers of the Mexicali Valley had no other way of expressing their feelings for urgency in a solution of the problem."[40]

Garzón creatively used the salinity crisis to achieve his broader agenda of land and water reform. Consul Boyd observed that on December 13, 1961, Garzón and the LAE held their own demonstration in front of his office with approximately four hundred protesters.[41] On December 18, 1961, Boyd reported that three to four hundred members of the LAE again protested in front of his office, intent on remaining "until assurance [of receiving a favorable response] from U.S. Ambassador [related to resolution of the] saline water problem." Ambassador Mann suggested that Boyd avert problems in the local area by working with local leaders to assure them of "efforts being made by [the] U.S. to resolve [the] problem." Boyd later reported that he had spoken with members of Garzón's movement. While the protesters remained friendly, they refused to disband.[42] The protesters were still in front of the consulate on December 20, 1961.[43]

Garzón eventually abandoned the demonstrations in front of the U.S. consulate. He then turned his attention to the national stage by leading a caravan of forty automobiles and two buses from Mexicali to Mexico City to request help from the federal government.[44] By mid-February, the caravan had arrived in Mexico City with some 220 protesters. Garzón met with Alfredo del Mazo, the secretary of hydraulic resources; Foreign Minister Manuel Tello; and the CILA commissioner, David Herrera Jordán. Despite Garzón's energetic appeals, the federal government continued to preach patience in reaching a tenable solution. Del Mazo promised that the federal government would begin the much anticipated rehabilitation project of the Mexicali Valley, pending approval from the World Bank.[45] The same day, in an interview with a prominent Mexican magazine, Hoy, President López Mateos confirmed that the government was moving ahead with a billion-peso plan to rehabilitate the drainage system in the Mexicali Valley.[46]

Garzón, more than any other local leader, encouraged regional discord when the Mexican government appeared unwilling to press the United States for immediate improvements in water quality. In February 1962, he complained, "Our government is not doing everything possible . . . to help [the] people of Mexicali."[47] Despite Garzón's zeal, it was evident that his methods were not effective in winning over federal officials to his platform for immediate action. Even though he had successfully led the caravan of cars to Mexico City, he failed to gain audiences with either Mexican president Adolfo López Mateos or U.S. ambassador Mann. Garzón's brash demands that reparations be paid to farmers in the Mexicali Valley fell on deaf ears.[48]

Garzón subsequently turned his attention to matters related to the limited water supply in the Mexicali Valley. Because the irrigation district had not accepted large amounts of saline water in 1961, shortages forced districtwide rationing of water in the spring of 1962. While irrigated acreage had been cut back to fourteen hectares per farmer, colonos were permitted to use their private wells to irrigate land above the fourteen-hectare limit. Garzón and representatives from fifty-seven ejidos set up a permanent protest in front of the CRID headquarters, demanding that water be shared equally among valley farmers.

Unlike his failed attempts to meet with federal officials during the "salt caravan" to Mexico City, Garzón's actions quickly gained the attention of the subsecretary of agriculture, Jorge Patino Navarette, who came to Mexicali to hear the LAE's complaints. Garzón successfully lobbied for the revocation of the colonos' right to use their private wells for acreage above the fourteen-hectare limit. Well water would instead be used for the benefit of all the valley's farmers. Garzón cited Article 75 of the Agrarian Code from the Mexican Constitution of 1917, which stipulated that ejido lands should be provided with water before private lands. If the water rights to such lands were not honored, Garzón contended, the ejidatarios legally held the right to take over the irrigation district.[49] Later that year, Garzón compiled a list of nearly three hundred farmers who had allegedly not been complying with the water agreements reached in March 1962.[50] Garzón's efforts to enforce the precarious social legacy of the Mexican Revolution demonstrated the distance between the legal rights and historic treatment of ejidatarios in general throughout Mexico.

The following year, Garzón allied the LAE with a national independent peasant's union, the Central Campesino Independiente (CCI). Because of its ties to the nationalist Movimiento de Liberación Nacional, the CCI was linked to Communism in the minds of many U.S. officials. Garzón was appointed one of the organization's three general secretaries but continued to champion land and water reform in the Mexicali Valley. In 1963, he took the lead in combating increases in the price of irrigation water. Garzón pleaded with northern Baja California governor Esquivel Méndez to act in behalf of ejidatarios before federal officials in Mexico

City. Garzón feared that not only would the price of water be raised but all users would also be required to pay for the water in advance, a requirement that did not bode well for ejidatarios who were strapped for cash. By February 18, 1963, the LAE contingent was again camped in front of the CRID office. The ejidatarios focused their frustrations on district manager Oscar González Lugo, who had allegedly refused to speak with them about their concerns. As a result, requests for lower water prices were also accompanied by calls for Lugo's removal as district manager.[51]

On March 9, 1963, Garzón reached his zenith of power. Luís Echeverría, the future Mexican president who was then undersecretary of government, and Alfredo Colin Varela, undersecretary of hydraulic resources, met with Garzón and other ejido leaders to hear their complaints. In exchange for an agreement to stop protests in front of CRID headquarters, federal and state officials agreed to allow greater ejidatario representation on the Comité Directivo Agrícola. Mexicali Valley farmers also received a guarantee that water prices would not be raised until after a committee that included ejidatario representatives had studied the issue.[52] Furthermore, Juan Muñoz Martínez replaced González Lugo as CRID manager.[53]

Alfonso Garzón continued to ride a wave of popularity in the Mexicali Valley in 1964. Mexican ambassador Freeman noted, for example, that during a recent survey conducted in Mexicali, those polled expressed "overwhelming support for far-leftist CCI leader Alfonso Garzón, among both rural and urban residents of the area." In addition to participating in protests throughout the year, the organization mounted a vigorous letter-writing campaign that resorted to extreme measures to gain the attention of private and public officials in Mexico and around the globe. The letter was sent to "make known to all the unmerciful aggression that Mexico is suffering at the hands of the United States." Copies of the letter were intended for all members of the United Nations, Mexican governors, national deputies, chambers of commerce, labor organizations, peasant unions, industrial groups, and banking groups. Often given to bombast and shock, the letter compared the salinity crisis to the United States building a nuclear plant and shipping its waste into Mexican waters. A stamp that read "Genocide. The USA contaminates the waters of the Colorado River, annihilates 300,000 human beings in the Mexicali Valley" was printed on each copy of the letter.[54] Equally as shocking, the CCI-affiliated Federación Estatal Campesina de Sonora petitioned President Johnson on the salinity issue, comparing the damage in the Mexicali Valley to the atomic destruction of Hiroshima and Nagasaki. The federation appealed to Johnson to "avoid the misery and exodus of all the people of a region always promising great agricultural production and the men and women forged in that work."[55]

Garzón's Decline from Power

Strong prospects for imminent resolution of the salinity crisis prompted national officials to turn their brief support for Garzón toward a rejuvenated Comité General de la Defensa del Valle de Mexicali. By March 1964 it was rumored that CILA commissioner David Herrera Jordán had worked through the Asociación Algodonera del Valle de Mexicali, A.C., in an effort to revive the more politically conservative Comité General and take momentum away from Garzón.[56] The committee reorganized itself on March 22, 1964, providing the Mexican government with greater assurances that public protests would not adversely impact international negotiations. Despite the national infiltration of local politics, federal officials remained leery of the impact of public protests on negotiations, except when it was in the strategic interest of the Mexican government to use protest as a tool to manipulate the opinion of the American public and its policy makers.[57]

In May 1964, some of the more creative manifestations during the crisis took place in Mexicali. The Comité General used a large flatbed truck accompanied by about four hundred protesters and marched from the Chamber of Commerce to the U.S. consulate. The trailer carried a coffin filled with salt, figuratively representing northern Baja California. Consul Boyd noted that "representatives of each group took turns standing honor guard over the coffin." Each group carried signs with slogans. The CCI and LAE mounted a banner that read, "Mr. Johnson, your [Texas] ranch is irrigated with virgin waters from Mexico. We demand virgin water from the Colorado." Another read, "Salt us first—talk to us later." The Comité General also hung a sign on a building located across the street from the U.S. consulate that read, "Enough salinity already." Organizers intended to leave it there for Consul Boyd to see until the problem was resolved.[58]

Ordered protests continued during the summer. By August, however, the federal government requested that the Comité General call off its demonstrations, as it believed a solution to the salinity problem was imminent. The Comité General immediately communicated the request to its members.[59] The sudden announcement came as a shock to the CCI. Garzón notified Aurelio Flores Valenzuela, general coordinator of the Comité General, that his group had already organized protests in approximately thirty cities throughout Mexico.[60] By the fall, continued whisperings of resolution weakened the ability of popular organizations to mobilize popular support in Mexicali and largely did away with large-scale demonstrations.[61]

Anticipation of a solution to the salinity problem dragged on into 1965. For that reason, the announcement of Minute 218 in 1965 received a lukewarm reception in the Mexicali Valley. The agreement required the United States to build a drainage channel from Wellton-Mohawk to Morelos Dam. Mexico could then decide whether or not it wanted to mix the effluent with better water from the river. In either case, Mexico would still be charged for water that was either used or wasted into the Gulf of California. The agreement would be effective for five years beginning on January 1, 1966. At the end of five years, it would be reviewed by both nations to assess its efficacy.

A PRI-sponsored rally of appreciation for President Díaz Ordaz's efforts to secure Minute 218 attracted only five hundred participants. The incoming U.S. consul in Mexicali, Arthur Feldman, attributed the lukewarm reaction to "the long awaited and frequently promised solution which took over a year to become a fact." Additionally, many Mexicans felt that the solution was not just, because Mexico would still be charged for the saline water it chose not to accept. Furthermore, continued efforts to rehabilitate farmlands in the Mexicali Valley reinforced the idea that Minute 218 was only a temporary solution.[62]

conclusion: pollution, power, and protest

In 1964, an upset Mexicali resident, Humberto Hernández, fired off a four-page letter to Senator William Fulbright, chairman of the Foreign Relations Committee. Quoting a Fulbright speech, Hernández wrote, "We are confronted with a complex and fluid world situation—and we are not adapting ourselves to it. We are clinging to old myths in the face of new realities." Hernández then lamented the plodding nature of resolution of the salinity crisis, observing that Mexicali's local problems were "buried under the lengthy, slow and deliberate proceedings of a rigid and prejudiced international policy, influenced by the selfishness and arrogance of a few."[63]

Hernández's remarks spoke for thousands of Mexicali residents. His insight and new historical evidence from the salinity crisis suggest the need to reassess the nature of the dilemma and its resolution. The tangled approach of the State Department and the DOI suggests that there were at least four identifiable political entities dealing with each other: the U.S. government; the American West, composed of a linkage between western legislators and the USBR; the Mexican government; and local organizers in the Mexicali Valley. Personalities played a tremendous role in the dynamics of the crisis. Conflicts of interest within the DOI as well as the constraints of checks and balances (for example, all executive treaties in the United States had to be approved by the Senate, in which the West exercised great power on water issues) presented as much of a challenge to the State Department as did complaints from Mexico. It cannot be claimed that the West, the Sagebrush Rebellion notwithstanding, was a powerless "colony." Its leaders possessed the leverage to hold international treaties captive.

For the most part, State Department officials were sympathetic to Mexican claims, yet the existing water rights of western farmers and the plans of the USBR limited their authority to act. Ambassador Mann privately encouraged irrigation districts in the United States to balance the amount of salts taken in from and returned to the river. The U.S. consuls in Mexicali also had an interest in seeing the issue resolved judiciously. Inaction was the very condition that facilitated the rise of organizer Alfonso Garzón. Once an international solution to the crisis was close at hand in 1965, however, Garzón's influence declined. Garzón was co-opted by the ruling party and eventually became a federal deputy.

The first four years of the salinity crisis also illuminated distinctive attitudes toward ownership of natural resources. Farmers in the Wellton-Mohawk Valley used an accessible legislative apparatus to protect their interests. On the other hand, the legacy of the Mexican Revolution and uncertain circumstances demanded that ejidatarios and colonos share water resources during the salinity episode. Even if such efforts at sharing resources failed or were subverted, the fact that such mechanisms existed for times of crisis reflected differing attitudes toward land and water resources.

As scientific data from both sides of the border attested, the salinity crisis was neither an act of genocide nor a figment of the "Communist" imagination. In truth, the salinity crisis was a legitimate problem with various solutions. Several incidents corroborate this assertion. Most telling, perhaps, were the complaints from people in the U.S. delta who noticed a decline in water quality for domestic and agricultural uses. For example, Thomas Allt, a representative for the city of Yuma, Arizona, testified at the Colorado River Salinity Control Act (1974) hearings that prior to the fall of 1961 the city had taken its drinking water directly from the Colorado River. After the release of toxic drainage from Wellton-Mohawk, however, the city reached an agreement with the Yuma County Water Users Association to receive water from the Yuma Canal, which was connected directly to Imperial Dam.[64] Second, a study completed after the salinity crisis calculated that Colorado River water with salts totaling 1,400 ppm in the Imperial Valley could cause $74,568 worth of damage. While these statistics were not calculated for the Mexicali Valley, the contiguous nature of the two regions and similar geological properties makes a rough comparison possible.[65]

Furthermore, agricultural economists estimated that the salinity of "pristine" waters in the Colorado River at Imperial Dam nearly tripled between 1926 and 1965 (383 ppm to 839 ppm).[66] IBWC data related to salinity differentials of Colorado River water between Imperial Dam and the Mexican border also shed light on the extent of the problem. In 1960, water at the international boundary contained an average of only 33 ppm of salt more than water at Imperial Dam. The following year, however, salinity differentials at the border increased 1,636 percent over the previous year, to 540 ppm.[67]

Ultimately, the first four years of the salinity crisis witnessed a profound transformation in the ecology of the lower delta. The uncertainty of increased volumes of salinity on both the national and local levels not only increased tensions between the United States and Mexico but also made it possible for local tensions to elicit national and international attention. The desire on the part of both national governments to minimize uncertainty during the negotiation process contributed to the decline of local political flame-throwers like Alfonzo Garzón. As a result, by 1965 policy makers largely examined the political terrain of the Mexicali Valley from afar—in Washington, D.C., and Mexico City.

Garzón's efforts to mobilize protesters in Mexicali and throughout the country on behalf of discontented Mexicali residents illustrate the early attempts of local organizers in post–World War II Mexico to voice their discontent with federal policy related to natural resource allocation in Mexico. The uprisings in Chiapas in the 1990s, for example, reflect a much more dramatic manifestation of local dissatisfaction with national land policies. Yet both instances highlight the contrasting ways in which federal governments and local residents have viewed the contested lands and resources of distinctive Mexican landscapes. And while Garzón's automobile caravan to Mexico City had little of the dramatic flair of Subcomandante Marcos's historic entry into Mexico City's main plaza in March 2001, both episodes illustrate grassroots efforts to mobilize public support outside of the electoral process. With little political capital beyond the power to mobilize the support of the masses, Mexican farmers and laborers have cultivated a unique political tool that dramatically reflects local responses to national policies.[68]

Deltascape The Mexican Delta *Fradkin at the mouth of the River*

In November 1980, author Philip Fradkin and lawyer Gary Weatherford visited the Mexican delta. At the time, Fradkin was writing a book entitled *A River No More: The Colorado River and the West,* which chronicled the decline of the Colorado River from its headwaters to its mouth.

One foggy morning at dawn, Fradkin reported, "Coyotes were all around us, yapping and howling to an extent neither my companion nor I had ever heard before." Additionally, "avian noises of every description added to the cacophony."[69] Enshrouded by fog,

Figure 12 Mudflats in the lower delta beside the Colorado. Note the flatness of the delta plain as well as the cracked, alkaline texture of the mudflats in the foreground. (U.S. Bureau of Reclamation photograph)

Fradkin launched his kayak into the river. Like earlier travelers to the delta, Fradkin experienced a sense of disorientation encouraged by the capriciousness of the river: "The problem was that we did not know where we were on the river. . . . There was no high ground to reconnoiter from, nor any tree strong enough to support our climbing it for a view." He later elaborated on his feelings of disorientation: "[Constant] uncertainty in a strange land was what we experienced the whole ten days spent either paddling down the river or up the northern extremity of the gulf."[70]

During their week and a half in the delta, Fradkin and Weatherford ran into bottle hunters from Los Angeles who had adapted trail bikes to handle the terrain of the dry delta. Near the northernmost point of the Gulf of California, Fradkin described the landscape of the region: "The land—actually I never had the feeling that it was quite solid enough under my feet to refer to it in such a definite way—was absolutely flat and completely devoid of vegetation. Small pieces of driftwood and wooden crates resembled trees or structures shimmering in the distance above the surface of a glass lake. Rowboats improbably sat in the middle of this ultimate desert. . . . The debris was scattered about with the randomness of an old graveyard. The scene was sepulchral."[71]

Fradkin and Weatherford slopped across the lower delta in search of the abandoned Port Isabel, a repair station for steamboats headed up the Colorado River during the late nineteenth century. "Huge gobs of mud, feeling like weights," he later wrote, "formed on the bottom of the cleated soles and had to be knocked off every few minutes at a rest stop." The hulls of ships, hemp ropes, and iron remnants lay encased in the dry riverbed. The silt of the Colorado had buried yet another speculative heyday in its relatively recent encounter with human civilizations.

Fradkin and Weatherford continued their November journey by kayak down the remnants of the Colorado River's main channel. Below the final diversion canal, which carried water to the Laguna Salada, Fradkin tossed a stick into the stream. The stick returned upstream under the pull of the canal's headgate. They then continued toward the point where the river evaporated under the ninety-degree November sun: "The end of the river was now all too apparent. The mystery was gone, and I felt deflated. I walked downstream on cracked mudflats beside the remnant of a river for about half a mile. It became shallower and wider, a sure sign of quick death in that evaporation-prone climate."[72]

Fradkin then felt an impulse to walk across the river. "It was something I hadn't had the chance to do since jumping across the freshets at the beginning of the four tributaries, and not too many can boast of having walked across the main stem of the Colorado." He reconsidered his fantasy as his knees quickly sank into the ooze of the deceptively firm riverbed. "I had gone far enough in my quest for the end of the river," he later recalled. "I did not want to see something once grand suffer the ultimate despoliation."[73]

5

Salt of the River, Salt of the Earth

Debates over water quality lay at the heart of the thirteen-year salinity disputes between the United States and Mexico. In many ways, they also reflected the shortsighted nature of decisions made on each side of the border. During Senate debates over the 1944 Mexican Water Treaty, for example, Arizona politicians with the most to gain in the short term by leaving out any provisions for water quality argued that *any* water given to Mexico would be acceptable. This regional policy had less to do with watching out for Mexico's welfare than it did with realizing the dream of building the Central Arizona Project. To be sure, Mexican officials softened their rhetoric when the United States offered them 1.5 million acre-feet from the Colorado River. Understandably gratified at this prospect, as the United States had continually rejected any Mexican requests for a similar quantity of water, Mexican politicians knew that if they pressed for a standard of water quality, then the quantity would surely be reduced. Put another way, those with the most to lose economically and politically insisted on letting the next generation grapple with issues related to water quality. Leaving these questions unanswered, however, only opened a larger Pandora's box when saline water spilled into the Alamo Canal from the Colorado River in the fall of 1961. While the Mexican Water Treaty cannot be classified as a "paper tiger," its inability to resolve central issues related to water quality in the river basin left the door open for more rancorous conflicts as the balance of the twentieth century unfolded. As a result, the sudden rise of salinity in the Colorado River in 1961 presented an unexpected challenge to Mexicali Valley residents and federal officials in their century-long quest to better control their water resources. As the previous chapter illustrated, some Mexicans were as unhappy with their own government's inability to improve water quality as they were with the United States for creating the debacle.

The announcement of Minute 218 in 1965 brought some hope for improvement in the quality of water entering the valley. The U.S. Bureau of Reclamation (USBR) constructed a bypass canal to carry drainage from the deep wells in the Wellton-Mohawk Valley to a point in the river near Morelos Dam. At that juncture, the Colorado River Irrigation District (CRID), the Mexicali Valley's government-controlled irrigation district, could decide whether or not it wanted to accept the water for use on valley farms. One of the new problems created by this measure centered on the fact that whether Mexican farmers accepted the saline drainage from the Wellton-Mohawk Valley or not, it would be charged to them as part of their normal delivery under the 1944 treaty. And while some national officials in Mexico found this compromise acceptable, many Mexicali residents believed that it was merely a new form of imperialism. This would ignite a whole new wave of Mexican nationalism, strong enough to draw both nations back to the bargaining table during the early 1970s.

To be sure, Minute 218 did improve water quality in the lower delta incrementally during the first five years of the agreement (January 1966–December 1971). But the inability of Mexican and U.S. diplomats and politicians to make immediate sacrifices for the long-term benefit of residents and landscapes on both sides of the border rendered the solution a half-solution, much like the 1944 treaty.

In retrospect, Minute 218 teaches us that political remedies to social, economic, and environmental problems are sometimes important not so much for what they accomplish but for the way they influence subsequent actions. First, the Department of the Interior announced that it would drill new wells on Yuma Mesa, close to the Mexican border. This, coupled with the timing of the announcement (almost simultaneous with Minute 218), brought the salinity crisis to a new impasse that would transform the dimensions of the debate. Mexico responded by threatening to rescind bans on new wells in the valley. Increased Mexican pumping could attract water from U.S. portions of the aquifer beneath the delta.

Groundwater issues injected a new variable into the salinity crisis. Ironically, even in the wake of resolution of the salinity crisis in 1974, officials in both nations were less than eager to approve plans for comprehensive regional water management. While they agreed on measures to improve the quality of water flowing into the Mexicali Valley from the river, they postponed any firm decisions on pumping limits in the binational water aquifers. The contested aquifers represented another aquatic source of trouble that would have to be dealt with in the future.

War of the Wells

The salinity crisis significantly increased the reliance of Mexicali Valley farmers on well water. The premium quality waters provided 40 percent of the valley's water and irrigated 50 percent of its crops.[1] Well water was mixed with water from the Colorado River in order to reach an acceptable salinity level for irrigating cotton, alfalfa, and wheat. Announcement of new wells in Yuma County in 1965 only intensified interest in developing subterranean water resources in the Mexicali Valley and San Luís Río Colorado, Sonora. In October the Comité General de la Defensa del Valle de Mexicali petitioned President Díaz Ordaz to study the geohydrological tendencies of the aquifers that lay beneath the binational delta. Stressing the demographic explosion occurring in the southwestern United States, the committee noted that the population of the region would likely increase from 10.5 million to 30 million by the year 2000. If implemented, schemes such as the Pacific Southwest Water Plan would utilize drainage wells in the Yuma Valley to fulfill their obligations under the Mexican Water Treaty, while more pristine waters upstream would be used for the anticipated growth in the United States. The committee feared that such actions would harm the agricultural industry of the Mexicali Valley. It disputed International Boundary and Water Commission (IBWC) claims that the new pumps on Yuma Mesa would not affect the subterranean flow of water to Mexicali Valley wells. Changes in pressure from the new wells, the committee believed, might alter the direction of existing flows.[2]

Mexicali newspapers featured the well issue on their front pages. *El Mexicano* claimed that fifty wells had been drilled on Yuma Mesa and commented on the negative effect decreased amounts of well water could have on Mexicali's economy. The newspaper also reported that the wells would be used to extract 271 million cubic meters of water each year, "so as to obtain . . . [the United States'] full share of the water." *El Mexicano* also noted that the wells would interfere with geohydrological studies that the Mexican Departamento de Recursos Hidráulicos (DRH) had to conduct prior to initiating the rehabilitation program. The newspaper also conveyed regional fears of an imminent well-pumping war. Subsequently, local papers urged the Mexican government to press the U.S. government to prohibit use of the new Arizona wells. They also called for a groundwater treaty.

The U.S. consul in Mexicali, Arthur Feldman, also noticed a flurry of political organization. The Baja California branch of the Confederación Revolucionaria Obrero Campesina (CROC), a national labor union, announced its intent to collaborate with organized labor in the United States in order to protest the Pacific Southwest Water Plan and its appropriations to drill additional wells in Arizona near the border. Campesinos also manifested a renewed willingness to protest. Yet government officials effectively contained any unrest. Feldman noted, "The agriculturists of this area do not seem to have any dull moments. If it isn't salinity, or rehabilitation with enforced relocation of farms which will not be serviced with irrigation under the proposed plans, then it is the Yuma wells and the pink boll weevil." "Unfortunately," he concluded, "in all these issues the U.S. seems to be involved either directly or indirectly and the temptation to take pot shots at the neighbor to the north is rarely overlooked."[3]

Ostensibly, the new wells in Yuma County were installed to pump excess groundwater beneath farms in the Yuma Valley and on Yuma Mesa. Politicians also had other reasons for promoting the installation of the wells. Senator Hayden hoped that as much as 200,000 acre-feet of water could be salvaged by the wells and delivered to Mexico at the border in fulfillment of U.S. obligations under the 1944 treaty. Better water upstream could then be assigned to the Central Arizona Project. In the final analysis, Hayden believed that operation of seventeen new wells in Yuma Valley would only create a "slight diminution of present ground water flow to Mexico."[4]

The State Department gave conditional approval of the new well schemes. While it agreed with the Department of the Interior (DOI) that drainage water was a natural part of irrigation, it counseled the USBR to drill wells in places that would not significantly affect aquifer flows into

Mexico. By making this demand, Foreign Service officer Robert Sayre asserted, the State Department could "minimize the possibility of a quarrel with Mexico on the quality issue." The State Department also disagreed with the DOI's plans to install wells for groundwater recovery in locations where irrigation was not taking place. Sayre noted, "We doubt that the United States has the right to pump waters which are not clearly 'waters of the Colorado River' and deliver them to Mexico." Furthermore, Sayre believed that DOI secretary Udall had a responsibility to "treat equally all water users in the same relative geographic location on the river." "Any other policy," he observed, "will keep us in perpetual difficulty with Mexico."[5]

In June 1966, the IBWC took an inventory of drainage wells on Yuma Mesa. At the time, there were sixty-one private and federal wells there, yet only twenty-nine were in operation, ten for irrigation and nineteen for domestic and industrial purposes. It was estimated that the operating wells collectively extracted 8,000 acre-feet of water per year. IBWC commissioner Friedkin believed that such pumping "would not have any significant effect upon the groundwater basin underlying the Mexicali Valley." He calculated that only 2,000 acre-feet of this total would have moved "westward towards Mexico." If all the wells were operating, he observed, they would only extract about 26,000 acre-feet per year from the delta aquifer. He did point out, however, that if plans to irrigate 40,000 new acres of the mesa were carried out, "the total net withdrawal would amount to about 145,000 acre feet." This would diminish Mexicali groundwater flows by approximately 30,000 acre-feet per year. On the other hand, Friedkin noted that Mexico pumped 600,000 acre-feet per year. He further noted that the private wells in the United States did not return water to the river but reused the salvaged resources in Arizona.[6]

On May 26, 1967, Secretary Udall met with Mexican secretary of hydraulic resources Hernández to assure him that the new drainage wells on Yuma Mesa would not significantly affect the quality of water delivered to Mexico at San Luís Río Colorado or flowing into the Mexican portion of the aquifer. Despite the assurances, Hernández was not satisfied with Udall's commitments. Hernández was troubled not only by wells in Yuma Valley but also by drainage wells in South Gila Valley that he believed had augmented salinity levels of the Colorado River. Hernández requested that all of Mexico's river water be delivered in the summer. Such a request, however, would have meant a substantial loss of water for U.S. users. Udall tried to reassure Hernández that a practical instead of legal solution to the crisis was in the best interests of both countries.[7]

The Mexicali press continued to protest the new wells being drilled in Arizona. *La Voz de la Frontera* consulted lawyers to assess how a groundwater treaty might be drawn up between the two nations. It subsequently called for a treaty limiting pumping to the number of wells already sunk in the delta. This arrangement would have favored Mexico, which had about six hundred wells in the Mexicali Valley versus the sixty-one wells near Yuma. The *Unión Agrícola Regional* suggested that Secretary Hernández revoke the prohibition against drilling wells in the Mexicali Valley "so that should an agreement be reached between the U.S. and Mexico on the use of the subterranean waters, Mexico will continue to have the advantage in the number of wells." Arthur Feldman astutely noted that Mexicali residents were concerned about the well situation for several reasons. First, the best crop yields came from farms irrigated with well water. Second, farmers with wells were, for the most part, exempt from irrigation limitations imposed by the CRID in the Mexicali Valley.[8]

As early as 1960, Mexican engineers saw the potential for a pumping war on San Luís Mesa (contiguous with Yuma Mesa). Antonio Coria, chief of technical consultation for the DRH, expressed a desire to renegotiate the 1944 water treaty in order to define Mexico's groundwater rights in the delta. In light of a ban on drilling new wells in the Mexicali Valley, Coria felt that failure to include groundwater rights in the 1944 treaty would allow farmers in Arizona to drain the aquifer. Coria's sensationalistic comments were generated partly as a commentary on the current ban on new wells in the Mexicali Valley. On the one hand, he felt that the ban was needed, particularly in light of massive overdraft pumping in Mexico. On the other hand, though, he feared that uncontrolled pumping in the United States might prejudice users in Mexico.[9] By 1968, the ban on new wells on San Luís Mesa near San Luís Río Colorado was a relic of the past. DRH engineers planned to install new wells in order to compensate for overdraft pumping in the Mexicali Valley.[10] Mexican officials felt that too much water was flowing past valley wells without being used. Engineers suggested that the San Luís wells not only extract groundwater beneath Mexico but also entice water across the border from the United States.[11]

In February 1970, the IBWC and USBR presented their findings on groundwater flows near the border region of the delta. They stressed that water flows across the border did not occur naturally. Instead, operation of wells in Mexico drew percolating irrigation water across the border. The study calculated that 60,000 acre-feet per year crossed into the Mexicali Valley region, and 27,000 acre-feet per year went across the Arizona border into the aquifers beneath San Luís Mesa. Friedkin stressed that any pumping in the United States had a sound legal foundation, since the waters being pumped originated on U.S. farms. Friedkin hoped that this study would avert serious conflict with Mexico over the groundwater issue. He also had no reservations about U.S. farmers exercising their right to "increase pumping in the Yuma Mesa to recover [their] own irrigation percolating waters for use in the country, rather than let them be drawn westward by Mexican pumping."[12]

Two years later, Mexican president Luís Echeverría agreed to double the amount of water pumped from the wells on the San Luís Mesa.[13] These measures were taken as a temporary strategy to replace saline water from the Colorado River until the CRID's rehabilitation program was finished.[14] In July 1972, Echeverría approved the construction of one hundred additional wells near San Luís.[15] Thereafter, U.S. officials grew increasingly concerned with Mexican plans to pump approximately 320,000 acre-feet of water per year from the San Luís Mesa. Engineers from both nations met in Phoenix on December 12, 1972, to discuss these plans. The U.S. team stressed that flows in the aquifer were man-made. Mexican pumping at a rate of 160,000 acre-feet per year would draw 465,000 acre-feet from the United States between 1972 and 1982. If Mexico increased pumping to 320,000 acre-feet per year, the ten-year drawdown from the aquifers would approach 720,000 acre-feet. Friedkin noted that "all such waters are needed and can be used by the United States interests, and their withdrawal by Mexico will create a serious political problem for the United States." Ultimately, Friedkin hoped that the exchange of demands between the two countries would not lead to a pumping war. "There should be a better way," he observed, "and we should seek one, but it may be too late."[16]

Toward a Solution

While Minute 218 made a modest improvement in water quality during the five-year period of the agreement, water quality problems persisted. Even Mexicali soft-drink bottlers protested poor water quality, writing letters of complaint to American officials.[17] In December 1966, the secretary of hydraulic resources returned from talks with Secretary Udall, pessimistic about the possibility for better water from the Colorado River and noting that during the previous year deliveries had been "unusable."[18]

Official and unofficial threats of pursuing claims for damages hung like a dark cloud over the heads of U.S. officials during the crisis. Some of the threats came from nongovernmental sources, such as the Liga Agraria Estatal de Baja California (LAE). The threat of litigation for damages appeared most frequently when Mexico desired additional action from the U.S. government. The Central Campesino Independiente (CCI) demanded reparations for damages after the announcement of Minute 218. The Confederación Nacional Campesina (CNC) threatened to "demand [that the] U.S. pay for damages done by salinity."[19] Additionally, Comité General president Aurelio Flores Valenzuela contended that eleven thousand Mexicali farmers were losing 75 million pesos each year "as a result of increasing infertility of land."[20] Often these demands were based on impressionistic evidence. For example, wheat growers demanded reparations for wheat that allegedly failed to mature due to the salinity of irrigation water. Additional observations, however, undermined the validity of the initial claims of land infertility. Francisco Díaz Echerivel, general secretary of the LAE, observed that upon further investigation, the wheat "was developing normally."[21]

The Mexican government generally did not use exact figures for damages but retained the threat of presenting claims as a bargaining tool. After the announcement of Minute 218, Foreign Secretary Antonio Flores Carrillo asserted, "The rights of the affected farmers remain for them to assert in the manner they consider appropriate." He also noted that his office would study their claims if asked. U.S. officials in Mexico City viewed the revival of damage claims as a result of the poor reception of Minute 218. Ambassador Freeman also noted that candidates in state and local elections in northern Baja California discussed solutions to the salinity crisis as part of their platforms.[22]

As early as 1965, the Mexican desk at the State Department and Ambassador Freeman contemplated providing Mexico with a favorably financed loan for the rehabilitation of the Mexicali Valley in exchange for an agreement to drop the damage claims.[23] Freeman continued to push the idea, noting that the loan would have to come from U.S. sources, apart from the World Bank, to which Mexico already enjoyed access. Senator Hayden also desired to obtain attractive financing for the Mexicali rehabilitation plan. He even volunteered to sponsor a bill supporting the loan in Congress.[24] Secretary Rusk stated that the United States would cast a positive vote for Mexico if it needed financing from the International Development Bank to carry out a feasibility study for the program.[25]

As time passed, Consul Feldman sensed that Mexicali residents were more and more dissatisfied with Minute 218. The Mexican government, on the other hand, expressed a favorable opinion of Minute 218, in part due to yearly improvements in water quality. This was most evident when Secretary Hernández visited Mexicali to implement the rehabilitation plan. He spoke highly of the agreement, noting it had alleviated the salinity problem. A local journalist took issue with the secretary, pointing out that large amounts of water had been wasted through the drainage canal from Wellton-Mohawk. Feldman believed that the latter position represented conventional wisdom amongst technicians and officials in the valley. Whether the Mexican government listened to the local authorities or not, Feldman predicted, "Act 218 will encounter some rough sledding when the U.S. and Mexican officials meet . . . to evaluate the results and to make plans for the future."[26]

Local opposition to Minute 218 continued when the Comité General de la Defensa del Valle de Mexicali resumed its meetings in 1969. *El Mexicano* reported that the Comité General firmly opposed renewal of the agreement when it expired at the end of 1970. Engineer Martínez del Campo suggested that Mexico demand water equal in quality to that used by U.S. farmers in the Imperial Valley. The chemistry department at the Universidad Autónoma de Baja California also expressed interest in studying the local effects of the salinity crisis in hopes of assessing the extent of damage to valley fields. Over time, participation in the Comité General ebbed and flowed. "Some elements of the community will continue to beat the drums," Consul Feldman noted, "and the more need for a diversionary tactic, the louder the drums will beat."[27]

Ironically, the Imperial Irrigation District (IID) provided support for Mexican claims of salinity damage from Colorado River water. Its officials protested that "the increasing salinity of the Colorado River irrigation water . . . [damaged] the agricultural productivity of the region." The IID complained that water released from Imperial Dam had an average salinity of 838 ppm in 1968, but in 1969 the average salinity had risen to 908 ppm. The IID's public information officer noted, "When water with this high a salinity count is used in land like the [Imperial] Valley's, there's a good chance crops won't grow at all." The statement did not arouse much sympathy from Mexicali officials but did raise questions related to the legitimacy of Mexican complaints regarding the poor quality of water Mexico received from the Colorado River. One Mexicali farmer noted that "evidently what is considered to be good for the Mexicans is not as acceptable by the Americans even to a lesser degree."[28] At the same time, federal opinions attesting to Minute 218's effectiveness continued to emanate from the Mexican government. Near the end of President Gustavo Díaz Ordaz's presidency, Mexican officials approved a temporary extension of Minute 218 that would allow the new president to negotiate a permanent settlement the following year.[29]

Despite Mexico's apparent vote of confidence for Minute 218, the IBWC and USBR grappled with the limited effectiveness of the 1965 accord. Commissioner Friedkin somberly reported to the Office of Mexican Affairs that the USBR would not be able to carry out the improvements in water quality slated for 1969. USBR officials would be lucky to reach an improvement of 10 ppm, much less the promised improvement of 12–15 ppm. The commissioner explained that given the dynamism of the river and the limited avenues for improving water quality, USBR efforts to reduce salinity had reached a point of diminishing returns. Friedkin feared that the 1969 results stacked the odds even more heavily against Minute 218 as a permanent solution to the crisis.

Mexican scientists made their own evaluation of Minute 218. Enjoining science in the service of diplomacy, the Mexican government set up the Mexican Commission of Salinity Studies, composed of scientists, engineers, and lawyers from the DRH and the office of the secretary of foreign relations. The commission concluded that the salinity of Colorado River water delivered to Mexico between November 1965 and November 1969 averaged 1,050 ppm. At the same time, it noted that Minute 218 had been effective in stabilizing levels of salt pollution.[30] Similar to the conclusions reached by IBWC commissioner Friedkin, the commission asserted that the complexity of agricultural production in the Mexicali Valley made it difficult to pinpoint an overriding factor responsible for local farming problems. Instead, "all agricultural production is exposed to diverse factors that can affect it, technological, ecological, entomological, financial, mercantile, social, political, etc." Yet the commission still ranked salinity as the primary factor affecting agricultural production in the valley. Elevated salinity levels in irrigation water forced farmers to increase the amount of water applied to each acre of farmland. The CRID was also forced to decrease total farm acreage in the Mexicali Valley to compensate for water not accepted from the Wellton-Mohawk drain.[31] As a result, the CRID had wasted approximately 3 percent of its water into the Gulf of California each year.

The commission suggested that the DRH counter U.S. intentions to increase pumping in Yuma Valley by expanding Mexican pumping on the San Luís Mesa. In the process, Mexico might develop rights to water currently flowing toward the Gulf of California. The report also encouraged the DRH to pump "an annual volume greater than that which actually flows, with the object of exploiting the underground storage" in order to offset future American pumping that might divert the aquifer flow away from Mexico.[32] The commission also felt that enough water could be saved through the rehabilitation program to "cover the needs of the District" in the near future. In fact, the rehabilitation plan, which included improved drainage, compacted farmlands, and more efficient canals, might save enough water to "send to the sea all the drainage from the WMIDD, without greatly affecting the established perspectives in the study of facts."[33] The commission determined that if the salinity of Wellton-Mohawk drainage water continued to decline, "[Mexicans] will be able to . . . utilize some of the volumes from this Canal for mixing them, and obtain greater availability of water."[34] In conclusion, the commission urged the Mexican government to sign an extension of Minute 218, as it would not have sufficient data to reach an informed decision on Minute 218's effectiveness until 1974.[35]

The commission's recommendation to extend Minute 218 dovetailed with Mexico's political transition in 1970. During the last few months of the Díaz Ordaz administration, Mexico's course of action with the salinity crisis appeared uncertain. Initially, Foreign Secretary Carrillo hoped that an extension of Minute 218 could be arranged until the next president decided how he wanted to proceed with the matter. Carrillo made this proposition contingent on the ability of the United States to provide Mexico with a full allotment of usable water, perhaps by using well water from Yuma Mesa in place of drainage from Wellton-Mohawk.[36]

IBWC commissioner Friedkin hoped that this concession would provide the basis for an extension of Minute 218.[37] Carrillo and Hernández agreed that the offer to replace 60 million cubic meters of Wellton-Mohawk drainage water with better water from Yuma Mesa would be an improvement. They also agreed that pumping on Yuma Mesa would not damage the flow of water to the Mexicali Valley.[38] However, outgoing Mexican president Díaz Ordaz did not press for replacement water from U.S. wells and instead approved an interim extension of Minute 218, leaving the matter in the hands of the new president, Luis Echeverría.[39]

Continued pressure from Mexicali interest groups probably influenced President Díaz Ordaz's decision not to renew Minute 218 for five more years. Foreign Service officer Robert McBride, recently returned from Mexicali, attested to local hostility toward Minute 218. "I can only concur with Carrillo's view that inhabitants of Mexicali Valley are totally irrational on this subject," he noted, "and they were extremely discourteous to me personally because obviously I could not solve their problem." Looking into the future, McBride observed, "I feel sorry for anyone who has to deal with these people on any sort of regular basis."[40] Díaz Ordaz also continued to feel pressure from Mexicali groups to resolve the crisis. The Comité General de la Defensa del Valle de Mexicali, for example, sent Díaz Ordaz a letter demanding three things from the Mexican government: first, that Minute 218 not be renewed; second, that the Mexican government take the case before the World Court; and finally, that Mexico's rights to underground waters be protected in any agreement between the two nations.[41] Fifty-one ejidal commissioners, under the banner of the CNC, demanded that Díaz Ordaz broker a permanent solution to the crisis that included completion of a canal to drain 100 percent of Wellton-Mohawk drainage to the Gulf of California.[42]

Luís Echeverría, the salinity crisis, and Mexican Nationalism

With the changing of the Mexican president imminent, new individuals entered the stage of international politics in the delta. A friend of PRI candidate Luís Echeverría Álvarez, Milton Castellanos, gained influence with Mexicali's campesinos and students because of his radical position on the salinity issue. Castellanos had been a justice on the Baja California Supreme Court. He feared that continued acceptance and use of water from the United States would serve as an admission of usability. He contended that Mexico should refuse all water from the Colorado River in order to strengthen its claims of hardship should the case be taken before the World Court. Such a position would also improve the claims of farmers seeking reparations for lost crops and allegedly damaged farmland. To compensate for water losses, Castellanos advocated the drilling of additional wells in the Mexicali Valley and/or on San Luís Mesa. He also pressed the Mexican government to simultaneously complete the rehabilitation program in three, instead of seven, years and decrease the amount of acreage under cultivation in the valley.[43]

During a prepresidential visit in December 1969, Luís Echeverría held a twelve-hour meeting with Mexicali cotton farmers. Local water policy was a prominent topic discussed at the meeting. Two opposing viewpoints on regional water policy emerged from the meeting. First, David Herrera Jordán, commissioner of the Comisión Internacional de Límites y Aguas (CILA), the Mexican equivalent of the IBWC, defended the effectiveness of Minute 218 and argued that the drop in crop productivity could not solely be attributed to saline irrigation water. Second, Alfonso Garzón and CNC officials attacked Herrera Jordán's position. Promoting the ideas of Milton Castellanos, CNC officials argued that Mexico should only accept virgin water from the Imperial Dam and that water should be delivered to the Mexicali Valley through the All-American Canal. These differences of opinion reflected growing tensions between exasperated local farmers and scientifically informed national officials. While Herrera Jordán was armed with scientific data to demonstrate the various factors associated with decreased crop yields, such explanations could not sufficiently persuade farmers who had spent nearly a decade wondering when the salinity issue would be resolved.

During his Mexicali visit, Echeverría also spent time at the Baja California Asamblea Popular de Desarrollo Estatal, where he heard comments from his close friend (and later governor of Baja California) Milton Castellanos. Castellanos reinforced the idea that the saline waters from the United States should not be used at all but instead drained into the Gulf of California. He also emphasized the historical aspects of water politics in the delta and contended that with the construction of the All-American Canal and Hoover Dam, the fate of the Mexicali Valley was set. Together, both structures provided the United States with nearly total control over the river. He praised President Díaz Ordaz for signing Minute 218 but also stressed the need to push for better water.

In defense of his position, Castellanos cited water historian Norris Hundley Jr., who had written, "It is almost assured that no Tribunal of Arbitration will support the United States as long as it looks to fulfill the treaty giving Mexico unusable water." For Castellanos, the origin of the Wellton-Mohawk waters remained the central issue. Since it did not qualify as a natural source of water for the Colorado River, it represented a violation of the 1944 treaty. Castellanos urged Mexican officials, including the next president, to pursue a tougher position with the United States and carry their grievances before the World Court if necessary.[44]

Luís Echeverría's ascendancy to the Mexican presidency in 1970 changed the dynamics of the salinity problem. The new president saw the salinity crisis as a useful tool to promote Mexican nationalism and enhance Mexico's role as a leader against imperial aggression in the Third World. As Consul Feldman observed: "It is interesting to note that whereas in the past, officials, organizations, and farmers in Baja California mainly complained about salinity and limited their activity to passing resolutions, a new note has been struck in that concrete proposals concerning

Figure 13 Mexicali farmer Gilberto Buitierrez Banaga laments the salinity that has overtaken his field. This Charles O'Rear image graced the pages of *National Geographic* in May 1973 and proclaimed the plight of Mexicali farmers to the American public and the world. (National Archives and Records Administration photograph)

the issue are being offered for consideration by the U.S. and the [government of Mexico]. This would seem to reflect the policy of President Echeverría in setting up dialogues with his people and stimulating them to give voice to their problems and possible solutions thereto."[45] Part of this new momentum could also be attributed to the new foreign secretary, Emilio Rabasa, who was much more confrontational than his predecessor, Antonio Flores Carrillo.

As soon as Echeverría took office, the U.S. negotiating team continued to press for the extension of Minute 218. One of the features of the revamped Minute 218 was a pledge by the United States to attain "salt balance [of U.S.] operations within three years." Some Mexican specialists in the State Department, however, were skeptical of the salt balance promise. Chris Petrow, country director for Mexico, noted, "If this increase [in salt] continued at the recent rate, the water delivered to Mexico would in a few decades be unusable by almost any standard, and salt balance would be almost meaningless." Feldman also pointed out that offering salt balance "tended to emphasize the fact of our noncompliance with the concept at Wellton-Mohawk for some ten years." He warned that little improvement would be made without prohibitions on new projects in the river basin.[46]

Concurrently, Mexico's new secretary of hydraulic resources, Leandro Rovirosa Wade, outlined measures to counteract water shortages incurred by the salinity crisis. He announced that Mexico would drill ten wells on the San Luís Mesa, beginning in 1971. These waters would be used to dilute the highly saline drainage deliveries from the Yuma Valley at the international border "to some 1450 ppm, with consequent benefit for Sonoran farmers in the District irrigated from [the] Colorado River." U.S. officials saw this as a potentially important concession for negotiation. McBride noted, "Admission of usability of 1450 ppm water for irrigation purposes could be useful in further discussions with [Mexico]." IBWC commissioner Friedkin noted that such actions would "essentially draw on [the] U.S. Yuma Mesa Reservoir," but he did not know how long such reserves would last, particularly if they were "subject to [the] U.S. pumping its Mesa waters at source."[47]

By the summer of 1971 some American officials had begun to consider construction of a desalinization plant as a possible solution to the crisis. On July 16, 1971, DOI secretary Roger Morton responded to Secretary of State Rogers's request for solutions to the crisis. Morton suggested several long-term solutions, including "augmentation of Colorado River flows through desalting sea water, saline groundwater, and geothermal brines; weather modification; and waste water reclamation." Morton observed that a desalinization plant would reduce the impact of the Wellton-Mohawk problem as well as have "immediate high visibility." He outlined construction of a multistage desalinization plant that would eventually produce 150 million gallons of fresh water per day and could be completed by March 1975.[48]

In response to Morton's recommendations, IBWC commissioner Friedkin discouraged studies for a desalinization plant at Wellton-Mohawk. First, such a measure would complicate the negotiation process, especially the U.S. plan to extend Minute 218. Second, a desalinization plant would provide Mexico with water of 1,000 ppm, a quality superior to standards requested by Mexico. Furthermore, Friedkin pointed out, "it would directly support Mexico's contention that it does not have to accept any drainage flows as a part of the Treaty deliveries, which, if sustained, would result in doubling the desalinization works or require other measures by the United States to further improve the salinity of waters to Mexico."

Well aware of the calculus of water politics in the West, Friedkin noted that a desalinization plant would create a loss of 50,000 acre-feet of water per year (concentrated brine left over from the desalinization process) to U.S. water users on the lower river. Additionally, the cost would be prohibitive with existing technology. Friedkin did not believe that western politicians would "do more for Mexico than they believe [they] are required to do." Instead, U.S. politicians would rather clean up other sources of salinity along the course of the Colorado River. Friedkin encouraged USBR officials in Denver to wait until Mexico had rejected or accepted the modified treaty before pressing ahead with desalinization projects.[49]

By September 1971, prospects for resolution of the crisis outside of a legal tribunal waned. Foreign Secretary Rabasa informed Robert McBride that President Echeverría had rejected Minute 218 as a long-term solution and instead wanted legal advisors from both nations to examine the issue. If an understanding between them could not be reached, then it might be submitted to the Organization for American States or the World Court for resolution.[50]

The State Department saw Mexico's shift toward a legal solution as a crucial turning point in U.S.–Mexican relations. T. R. Martin stressed that in the past, problems between the United States and Mexico had largely been resolved through bilateral talks and not adjudication. The gains made through agreements over such issues as El Chamizal, a disputed island in the middle of the Rio Grande between El Paso and Ciudad Juárez, could be lost if the water issue were dragged into court. Martin suggested that the two nations reach an operational agreement before the case went to court. If not, he warned, western states would probably be very reluctant to "agree to a continuation of the present agreement."[51]

As negotiations stalled, environmental groups from the United States also took up the cause of Mexicali farmers. The Natural Resource Defense Fund (NRDF) pressed local officials to take action against the United States in U.S. courts. "They seem to be showing little interest in withholding their fire," Feldman noted of the groups, "until both governments have a chance to resolve the issue in a case which is of deep concern to both the U.S. and Mexican governments [and which] could cause embarrassment to both governments." The NRDF had enlisted the help of James Stone, a U.S. expatriate who had settled in Mexicali and managed Anderson-Clayton's interests there. Even after some prodding, however, Stone was reluctant to aid the NRDF's cause. Attorney Ignacio Guajardo had an equally difficult time finding Mexicali farmers who would serve as test cases. Guajardo doubted if any of the farmers affected "would have the temerity to do so without the encouragement of the [Mexican government]." Feldman believed that the impact of the environmental groups would be negative: "The advocacy of action and intervention by volatile U.S. groups interested in ecology will not serve as a mollifying influence on the Mexican position," he noted, "and we can expect more fireworks in the future if an agreement between the U.S. and Mexico is not quickly reached in the resolution of the salinity problem." Feldman believed they were more interested in promoting their own agenda and had "little or no consideration of the international repercussions involved which may only result in hindering [the United States] in bringing about an improved ecology for the world."[52]

In 1971, the U.S. negotiating team felt that conditions were ripe for a long-term agreement on Minute 218, yet they remained leery of the unpredictability of Rabasa and Echeverría. At talks in November 1971 in Mexico City, Rabasa continued to insist on leaving a legal door open for Mexico in case the bilateral negotiations did not provide an agreeable solution. With characteristic cleverness, Rabasa cited a U.S.–Canadian transboundary water dispute in which the United States had pressed not only for a redrafting of the 1909 treaty between the two nations regarding binational waters but also for the payment of damages. Negotiations ended in a renewal of Minute 218 for another year.[53]

Two weeks later, Cervantes del Río, secretary general of the presidency, met with State Department officials in Mexico City to discuss the salinity issue. Cervantes del Río pointed out that it was hard for Mexicans to understand "how a country which can put a man on the moon can fail to find the means to reduce effectively the salinity of waters in a given river basin." Similarly, he suggested that with the wealth and power the United States commanded, "this was really a minor problem." In sum, "he questioned the wisdom of paying the political costs to our foreign policy which arise from letting it drag on year after year."[54]

As tensions sharpened between the United States and Mexico, Mexican politicians and labor leaders increased their calls for reparations from the United States. Baja California governor Milton Castellanos led the charge on the state level, suggesting that any reparations be used for the rehabilitation program in the valley. Federal deputy Alfonso Garzón hoped that the settlement would be shared among the affected farmers. He claimed that the United States owed valley farmers approximately one billion dollars.[55] Finally, scholars at the Universidad Nacional Autónoma de México Center for International Relations discussed the Wellton-Mohawk case with McBride and informed him that Mexico would easily win a case against the United States in the World Court for the damages incurred during the crisis. McBride found it ironic that these intellectuals supported the Mexican government so vigorously, noting that "intellectuals in Mexico . . . are not noted for their support of their own government's position."[56]

Despite American promises to maintain the salt balance within U.S. projects, Mexico again rejected a long-term extension of Minute 218 in November 1971, opting instead for another twelve-month extension.[57] The State Department remained baffled by the chameleon-like position of Mexican officials on the issue, especially since Rabasa had hinted at acceptance of a six-year deal that included well water in place of Wellton-Mohawk drainage. Mexico experts at the State Department also noted that it would be even more difficult for Mexico to obtain better quality water during 1972, an election year in the United States when western politicians would be less likely to make water concessions to Mexico.[58] Hopeful officials in Mexicali were under the impression that the crisis would be successfully resolved by November 15, 1971, yet were disheartened when an extension of Minute 218 was announced.[59]

conclusion: Salinity and U.s.–Mexican Relations

In September 1972, Foreign Service officer Robert McBride reflected at length on the impact of the salinity crisis on U.S.–Mexican relations from his post at the U.S. embassy in Mexico City. He observed that failure to resolve the issue would seriously affect binational relations. He noted, however, that water was only one of many issues of mutual interest to Mexico and the United States. He wrote, "The adverse or favorable repercussions would primarily affect the climate of our relations and the large amount of mutual daily cooperation, particularly along the border. We do not see how success or failure in these negotiations would have much effect on the other major problems between our two countries largely because these problems are to a considerable extent beyond the control of the two governments." The salinity crisis would have little impact on larger issues, including dealing with illegal immigrants and border crossings. Negotiations related to binational trade also depended on completely different factors. Concurrent with the salinity crisis, McBride observed, President Echeverría was assisting with the U.S. antidrug campaign. Yet McBride pointed out that the salinity crisis could set important precedents for water disputes between the two nations, including those in the Rio Grande watershed.[60] McBride's insights illustrate the potential impact that the salinity crisis posed for those living in the border region. For them, it was a daily issue. For diplomatic negotiators, however, water disputes might impact other issues along the border region but would probably not irreparably damage relations between the two nations.

Mexican officials welcomed President Nixon's appointment of former attorney general Herbert Brownell as special ambassador to resolve the salinity crisis. Rabasa and Echeverría temporarily tabled their legal reservations and waited to see what solution Brownell would present. Brownell began by making visits to the Wellton-Mohawk Valley, the Mexicali Valley, and Mexico City. He visited Mexicali in November 1972, where he met with Governor Castellanos and local farmers.[61]

Brownell's appointment appeared to strike a compromise between the international focus of Mexican and American diplomats and the more regional focus of western leaders. His interactions with local and national officials on both sides of the border allowed him to craft a quasi-regional solution to a problem that had been approached primarily from an international perspective. His visits to the Mexicali Valley allowed him to see the damage the excess salt had caused during the previous eleven years. Likewise, the unwillingness of western politicians, as voiced through the Committee of Fourteen, to part with water in order to solve the problem encouraged Brownell to turn to a desalinization plant in order to resolve the crisis.

Deltascape The Mirage Culture

To this point we have examined the influence of binational agricultural development in the delta on the decline of water resources in the region.[62] Urban growth, industrial development, and the expansion of tourism throughout the broader Colorado River Basin also led to the desiccation of the delta. The next chapter explores contests over water in the delta within the broader context of western water politics. The following description of Las Vegas in

Figure 14 Fountains are cultural fixtures in the arid West. They conjure up illusions of oases and are a hallmark of the West's mirage culture. Note the Colorado River in the background of this photo taken by Charles O'Rear at Lake Havasu City. (National Archives and Records Administration photograph)

the late twentieth century illustrates one of the great paradoxes of the Pacific Southwest: the cultural celebration of water (the mirage culture) at the expense of the region's natural paradisiacal settings, including the delta.

The Mirage Resort in Las Vegas helped to define the mirage culture in the late twentieth century. Catering to tourists looking for the most appealing sensory stimulation, its owners and developers created a South Seas environment complete with dolphins swimming in a 1.5-million-gallon pool and a rainforest theme lobby with an exotic aquarium behind the registration desk. Its architects perpetuated the mirage culture by making it "acceptable to completely ignore the natural setting." "The contrast with reality," they rightly believed, "[made] the fantasy stronger."[63]

In order to maintain the illusionistic culture of the South Seas at the Mirage, the hotel's extensive horticulture department sought to fulfill its objective to "dispense with the guests' belief that they are in the middle of a desert." There are seven acres of outdoor landscapes, 17,000 square feet of interior plant space, and an extensive atrium covered with palm trees and exotic flowers. In addition to the grounds, the staff maintains a "jungle" landscape for Siegfried and Roy's tigers. The signature volcano outside the hotel rests inside a 2-million-gallon pond, with a waterfall that uses 47,000 gallons of water per minute. This marriage of technology and exotic flora remains one of the most striking examples of a paradise in the desert.[64]

Another Las Vegas hotel, the Bellagio, not only boasts a collection of art worth $300 million but also has one of the most technologically advanced fountain shows in the world. An eight-acre artificial lake with hundreds of fountains choreographed to music fronts the hotel. The 40-million-dollar extravaganza mixes technology and ornamentation to a level only Las Vegas tourists and developers can appreciate. Computer programs determine how much water each stream will carry and how high each stream will go during the show. The large computer that runs the fountains fills several eight-foot-tall containers behind the lake and underneath the hotel. The impact of this natural manifestation of water has not been lost on spectators, who consider it to be the grandest water show in the city.[65]

Bellagio is also home to Cirque du Soleil's exclusive production entitled O—an Americanized translation of the French word for water, eau. In short, the production and the stage are the zenith of water worship. The 1.4-million-gallon water stage permits the actors, dressed in costumes that range from clowns to penguins, to perform death-defying feats in an aquatic setting. The soundtrack includes songs entitled "Terre Aride," "Desert," "O," "Jeux d'Eau," and "Mer Noire."[66]

Journalist Robert Hughes noted of these facets of the mirage culture: "The key to all this is water, whose conspicuous display and consumption is as important a sign of luxury, of control over

Nature, to Vegas entrepreneurs as it was to Umayyad caliphs who began building the fountains of the Alhambra on a dry hillside near Granada 12 centuries ago. . . . To install performing dolphins in huge saltwater tanks in a hotel in the Nevada desert seems, on the face of it, about as rational as filling a cruise ship with sand and camels."[67]

"The Politics of Place"

The tragedy . . . [of the Colorado River Delta] is not just that local populations with the greatest stake in local ecosystems are politically marginalized in [the] process of globalization, but that natural resources are managed not as constituent parts of an ecosystem but as so many separate assets by a host of agencies[, distant communities, and interests].
—James B. Greenberg[1]

M ost Mexicans and Americans associate the process of globalization with cultural borderlands located at great distances from where they live. For many American tourists in Mexico City, for example, globalization means being able to munch on a Big Mac while looking out on the Zócalo (the main plaza in the capital city), site of the National Palace, the Metropolitan Cathedral, and a Mexican flag so big it never completely unfurls in the wind. Equally, for Mexicans in the United States, globalization means being able to walk into a *tortillería* on Chicago's Westside just down the street from a Polish American shopping enclave and buy dozens of corn tortillas, still warm from the oven.

Distance, however, is not the defining characteristic of globalization. Even in the delta, the same cultural interactions that take place on the hemispheric stage transpire on a regional scale. In Mexicali, you can eat a Big Mac and *papitas fritas* at a McDonald's located between two distinctively Mexican landscapes, the Plaza la Cachanilla, a massive shopping mall named for the scrubby grass that flourishes in the lower delta, and La Avenida Adolfo López Mateos, a thoroughfare named for one of Mexico's former presidents. Across the border in El Centro, Spanish culture has affected not only the food served in local restaurants but also religious life, the community's social structure, and prevailing language dynamics. Mexican television channels pervade the airwaves, and Mexican radio stations blare Spanish and English songs to youth on both sides of the border.

Thus, the essence of globalization has more to do with the strength of connections between communities than it does with the distance between those places. The relationships between localities on a regional level are just as complex as on the global scale. This is as true for the ways in which changes in the environment affect the relationship between communities as it is for the process of cultural diffusion. Henry David Thoreau probably found as many ecological connections between flora, fauna, and human landscapes at Walden Pond as did environmental historian Alfred Crosby Jr. when he wrote about the global dimensions of the Colombian Exchange.

In the Colorado River Delta the salinity crisis served as the catalyst for reordering the political, economic, and ecological relationships between human and nonhuman communities throughout the river basin. As diplomats prepared to negotiate a political solution to the crisis in 1973, politicians throughout the U.S. portion of the Colorado River Basin saw resolution of the crisis as an opportunity to resolve their concerns over an ever-shrinking water supply and continued economic and demographic growth in the region.

In August 1973, Special Ambassador Herbert Brownell and Mexican foreign secretary Emilio Rabasa brought a sense of closure to twelve years of contentious binational disputes over salinity levels in the Colorado River by drawing up Minute 242 of the Mexican Water Treaty. Minute 242 called for a "permanent solution" to the salinity problem. It also promised U.S. technical and financial assistance during the rehabilitation of farms in the Mexicali Valley. Brownell guaranteed that the United States would take steps to purify the drainage water through the construction of a desalinization plant in Yuma County, Arizona. The United States also agreed to build a drainage channel to carry water from the Wellton-Mohawk Valley to the Gulf of California, where it would not be able to contaminate Mexican diversions from the Colorado River.

During the ensuing year, the Nixon administration, the State Department, Ambassador Brownell, and a legion of local interests in the Colorado River Basin expressed differing priorities in drafting legislation to carry out the salinity control program. While President Nixon and the State Department simply wanted appropriations to build the desalinization plant, western leaders used the opportunity to press for additional salinity control measures that would help conserve the Colorado River Basin's ever-shrinking water supply. Closer to the border, farmers, municipal leaders, and Native Americans had more precise reasons for supporting or opposing the desalinization plant.[2]

The complexity manifest during deliberations over the Colorado River Salinity Control Act illustrates that as one moves from the international to the local level, priorities become more difficult to negotiate on the international level. Furthermore, local and international priorities are often more at odds with each other than the priorities on any other two levels of government. Daniel Kemmis summarized this political reality best when he wrote, "[The] political culture of a place is not something apart from the place itself."[3]

The "Western" Diplomat:
Herbert Brownell and Minute 242

In hindsight, Richard M. Nixon's appointee to negotiate a solution to the crisis, Herbert Brownell, proved to be an appropriate choice for the job. A successful lawyer in international business, Brownell was appointed by Dwight D. Eisenhower to serve as attorney general in 1953. His experience in natural resource litigation as attorney general allowed him to work closely with—and against—western leaders. He observed that during the Eisenhower administration, "states' rights were giving way to the assumption by the federal government of preeminence in [the] field" of natural resources.[4] Brownell noted that this was most evident in water law, as "Congress had not yet enacted comprehensive federal environmental laws, and the states in the Western part of the country still fought for exclusive control of water rights."[5] Brownell gained most of his knowledge of western water politics while he worked on the *Arizona vs. California* case. This landmark case divided disputed water from the Colorado River between Arizona, California, and the native tribes along the river.

Brownell's legal background provided him with immeasurable experience, yet his western roots, fascination with technology, and faith in progress help explain the course he pursued in dealing with western leaders and with the Mexican government. Brownell grew up in rural Nebraska. His exposure to a modern agricultural society attuned him to the mentality that prevailed among western farmers. At the House hearings, Brownell confessed, "It is a temptation, of course, for me, being interested as I always have since my early days in the development of the West, the Middle West, where I came from, to urge the most prompt action in any area that will assist development of the natural resources there."[6] This mentality ultimately benefited western water officials and Mexicans. They were all dealing with a man who believed in large-scale agricultural development.

Brownell's interest in using science to promote natural resource development also played a critical role in the scope of the agreement reached between the two countries. While he consulted with an expert "task force" throughout the negotiations, Brownell's personal fascination with technology likely played a role in crafting the solution envisioned in Minute 242. In his memoirs he remembered the scientific perspective that his father had instilled in him at an early age: "Through my high school and college years, my father taught me at home and in the class room the importance of respecting 'the scientific method' when pursuing the mysteries of life and of the universe in the laboratory and observatory."[7] The desalinization plant proposed for construction in Yuma subtly blended Brownell's love of technology with his understanding of western water politics. Since the plant would purify wastewater without the use of large volumes of additional water, farmers and communities throughout the West would not have to worry about curtailing diversions from the river. Representatives from the desalinization industry also received a financial boost from Brownell's faith in technology. The cost of the plant would escalate from an estimated $120 million in 1974 to $260 million (not including operation costs) by the time of its completion in 1993.[8]

The River before Watergate: Nixon, the State Department, and Minute 242

By 1974, American leaders had begun to feel pressure to end the embarrassing debacle. William Bowdler, deputy assistant secretary of state for inter-American affairs, reflected on his uncomfortable trips to Mexico on official business. "Whenever an issue arose in our relations with Mexico, whenever opportunities appeared for cooperation between the two governments, when our parliamentarians met in joint meetings," Bowdler remembered, "the salinity problem invariably confronted our spokesmen."[9] Arizona congressman Morris Udall marveled at the general knowledge of the problem throughout Mexico. "I was amazed when I first got there," he recalled. "I thought this was probably a grievance in Baja California, and Sonora, perhaps; but you talk to some fellow from Guadalajara or Yucatán and this is the first thing they bring up."[10] Udall also noted the abundance of complaints concerning the quality of water that the United States had delivered to Mexico during the three previous decades. Mexicans complained that the United States had allowed "raw sewage, industrial wastes, hydrochloric acid and whatever" to be included as part of the 1.5-million-acre-feet contract. As these statements illustrate, the crisis had transformed "good neighbors" into reticent strangers. "There has been, over the years, some insensitivity," Udall observed, "in the way we have handled this with our neighbors."[11]

Given the level of U.S. involvement in Southeast Asia, it is not surprising that President Nixon and the State Department adopted a minimalist approach in resolving the salinity crisis. The administration and the State Department advocated H.R. 12,384 and S.R. 3094 in order to keep the cost as economical as possible. The Department of the Interior and the Environmental Protection Agency also endorsed the administration's bills, yet for different reasons. Neither organization had completed its own full-scale study of salinity in the West and did not want to apply for appropriations until those investigations had been completed.[12]

"Total Shutdown": The Environmental Response to Colorado River Salinity

Perhaps no event better represented the monumental transitions in western water politics than the debate over the Colorado River Salinity Control Act. For more than fifty years, congressional hearings dealing with water projects in the delta mainly attracted the attention of those who had the most to gain from them, namely, western farmers, municipal leaders, their congressional representatives, and well-paid lobbyists. In addition to these groups, environmental organizations participated in the Colorado River Salinity Control Act hearings. Eschewing the tactics of radical environmental groups, the Sierra Club and national think tanks sent representatives to Washington to deal within the political system to bring about change.[13]

In contrast to the pragmatic approach of western leaders and the administration, Brent Blackwelder of the Environmental Policy Center and John McComb of the Sierra Club objected to the developmental nature of the Salinity Control Act. Blackwelder contended that those who would benefit from the project should "shoulder a major share of the costs of cleanup."[14] Blackwelder and McComb also advocated the dissolution of the Wellton-Mohawk project. Not only would this be the most environmentally sound method to solve the problem, it would also apply the brakes to runaway federal spending meant to prime the pump of commercial agriculture. Blackwelder claimed that only $1 million of the $50 million owed by the farmers in the Wellton-Mohawk region had been repaid to the government. "It seems incredible that the taxpayers of the Nation are now being asked to spend many millions more, possibly as much as $200 million in the long run," Blackwelder observed, "to remedy the problems occasioned by this district."[15]

Blackwelder and McComb also urged House leaders to examine the project's track record. In suggesting the partial or total shutdown of the Wellton-Mohawk Irrigation and Drainage District (WMIDD), McComb appealed to the past performance of the district. "The irrigation project has been plagued by problems from its very inception," he observed, "and we seriously question the wisdom of any further unnecessary expenditures of federal funds in order to keep it in operation." McComb objected to the wasteful amount of energy that would be necessary to run the desalinization plant. He suggested that the U.S. Bureau of Reclamation (USBR) utilize more prudent methods of reducing salinity, such as "limiting further water resource development."[16]

Environmentalists and western officials did agree on one crucial aspect: the need for increased salinity control throughout the basin. They were divided, however, on which sources should be eliminated. Western farmers wanted to remove natural salt sources. In contrast, the Sierra Club wanted to cut back on "man caused increases in salt load."[17] This would include farms operating in locations such as the Wellton-Mohawk Valley, where poor drainage conditions exacerbated salinity levels in the river. McComb also posited the aesthetic value of several locations targeted for containment under Title II of the proposed legislation. Blue Spring, Colorado, was "an integral part of the Grand Canyon in addition to being spectacular in its own right."[18]

He also reminded the committee that the area served as a religious site for Indian tribes along the river. Environmental and cultural preservation were two of the main goals of the Sierra Club. Two decades earlier, the organization had scored a major victory in its quest to preserve Echo Park in Utah's Dinosaur National Monument. When the USBR announced that a dam would be built there, Sierra Club president David Brower creatively galvanized public support against the project. A relentless ad campaign sponsored by the Sierra Club in the *New York Times* not only prevented construction of a dam that would have inundated part of the Grand Canyon but also invoked the wrath of the federal government against the organization.[19] The idea of natural preservation for the sake of beauty reflected a growing desire for the preservation of natural settings as an escape from industrial society.[20]

McComb believed that members of the general public would be open to cuts in water usage throughout the Colorado River Basin, yet such changes were not politically feasible. He was much more realistic in his assumption that any limitations of western water consumption would be considered "heresy or a denial of some absolute right by the water resource development agencies."[21] The binational nature of the current diplomatic predicament gave western interests political leverage that the USBR never had in fighting against the Sierra Club over Echo Park Dam. Brownell and the administration were working under a time limit. The legislation had to be approved by July 1, 1974. Western politicians could attempt to block passage of Title I until their demands for salinity control were met.

"We Can Make Money from It": The Desalinization Industry and Minute 242

Numerous avenues for reaching a permanent solution to the salinity crisis were explored. Possibilities included building a desalinization plant, seeding clouds, buying out the land of farmers in the Wellton-Mohawk District, or substituting better water from the Imperial Dam.[22] So why did Congress approve the most costly solution? As the cold war heated up in the early 1950s, Congress passed the Saline Water Act in 1952 "to provide for the development of practicable low cost means of producing from seawater, or from other saline waters, water of a quality suitable for agriculture, industrial, municipal, and other beneficial consumptive uses."[23] While the Office of Saline Water (OSW) would function as a part of the Department of the Interior, the 1952 act also called for cooperation with the Department of Defense. After 1952, corporations and labs traditionally associated with the military-industrial complex received contracts to develop desalinization techniques and oversee construction of plants domestically and throughout the world. Spiraling energy costs, however, constantly plagued the OSW's quest to achieve aquatic alchemy. Most importantly, the tantalizing promise of virtually free power from nuclear desalinization plants never materialized. After several proposed plants in the Pacific Southwest were not built, the OSW considered the Colorado River salinity crisis as an appropriate case to test the merits of its new "reverse osmosis" filtration system, a desalinization method that ran saline water through a series of membranes that blocked salt from passing through the cells. In sum, expediency and extensive investments over the course of two decades explain much of the decision to build a desalinization plant in the middle of the Sonoran desert.

In May 1975, editor Ken Lucas wrote a scathing article about the proposed desalinization plant for the *Arizona Farmer-Ranchman*. He argued that little planning had gone into the decision to build the plant. In support of his assumption, Lucas alleged that USBR officials only realized that Yuma and the Imperial Valley lay near the San Andreas Fault line *after* appropriations for the plant had been approved.[24] In reality, however, policy makers knew that the plant lay near the fault prior to the siting announcement. A joint U.S.–Mexican commission had previously explored the possibility of constructing a binational nuclear desalinization plant near the Gulf of Santa Clara (near San Luís Río Colorado, Sonora, Mexico) in the late 1960s only to discover its proximity to the fault.[25] Subsequently, the Yuma site was selected by the USBR and the OSW as a safer location for construction of a nonnuclear desalinization plant.

Lucas also claimed that the plant was an unnecessary project conceived merely to assist the fledgling desalinization industry. If the plant was successful, he argued, American firms could tap into water-starved Arab markets. Yet immediate economic considerations, he noted, also motivated the desalinization industry. Companies like Universal Oil Products stood to gain a great deal through government contracts on the Yuma plant.[26] Brownell concurred with this interpretation when he observed: "[The] construction of the world's largest desalting plant, provides a decided boost to desalting technology which cannot but have significant effect elsewhere in the United States and, indeed, in the world."[27] These linkages between private industry and the government were not lost on developers of desalinization technology. William Warne, former assistant commissioner of the USBR, represented the National Water Supply Improvement Association at the House hearings. Warne gave the association's definitive stamp of approval for the plant during his presentation to the committee.[28] Desalinization companies were the biggest economic winners from the Colorado River Salinity Control Act.

"Charity Begins at Home": Western Interests and Mexican Diplomacy

If 1890 marked the end of the territorial frontier of the United States, then 1968 signaled the close of a more fluid frontier in the Colorado River Basin. During that year, Congress approved the Central Arizona Project. With that project approved, all the surface water in the lower basin of the river was legally apportioned to interests within the different states and Mexico. The growing threat of high levels of salinity forced western politicians to devise a program that would ensure a sufficient water supply to meet those needs without having to sacrifice fresh water to dilute saline river flows. The proposed Colorado River Salinity Control Act provided a new approach to maximizing the annual water supply throughout the basin. Cleaning up natural salinity sources throughout the upper basin would not only appease Mexican interests at the river's "drain" but also protect the needs of water users throughout the basin. A representative from the Imperial Irrigation District (IID) summed up this political transformation when he observed, "Environmental concerns impel us toward greater efficiencies in the use of our water supplies, toward reclamation reuse of water in order to extend the supplies, and toward conjunctive management of surface and ground waters."[29]

The new sensitivity of westerners to environmental issues had less to do with a newfound enthusiasm for environmentalism than with the need to preserve large-scale agribusiness and municipal growth in the arid Pacific Southwest. Nothing attests to the developmental nature of these proposed "environmental" measures better than the plans made for curtailing salt diffusion from the Crystal Geyser near Green River, Utah. Instead of capping the geyser, western officials proposed that a dike be constructed to contain the effluent. Officials assured the Senate committee that the dike would "blend with the exposed sandstone for esthetic purposes." Always sensitive to the demands of tourism, officials boasted: "Because of the return of a portion of the erupted water to the geyser, the interval between eruptions would be reduced from 5–6 hours to 2–3 hours, increasing its value as a tourist attraction."[30] Manipulating nature in an effort to "purify" the river ultimately served more than one economic interest.

With a wide spectrum of developmental priorities throughout the basin, almost all the western interests involved in the debate over the Salinity Control Act recognized that maximizing river resources demanded greater unity among regional officials than had prevailed in the past. California senator John Tunney acknowledged the linkages between greater cooperation and regional water politics. "There has been an unprecedented era of cooperation and mutual effort among the seven states," he noted, "following more than half a century of controversy and bitterness. This bill represents one more step in this new approach along the Colorado, and I am delighted to be able to cooperate in that effort."[31] Tunney's remarks are even more remarkable, considering that only ten years earlier Arizona and California had ended a bitter battle over apportionment of water in the lower basin. California lost a significant amount of surplus water to Arizona in that decision. Western leaders adjusted to shifting circumstances in an effort to protect their existing (and future) interests within the context of regional, national, and international relations.

In addition to adapting their political approach to the constraints of shrinking natural resources in the basin, western politicians also abandoned their traditionally antagonistic attitude toward Mexico's water rights in the Colorado River Basin. Neil M. Cline of the Orange County Water District expressed "sympathy with our good neighbors in the Mexicali Valley." Noting a precipitous rise in salinity in his own water district, Cline observed, "We know what they have been suffering because our situation is much the same as theirs."[32] A similar tenor marked the rhetoric of Arizona governor John Richard Williams. Traditionally, Arizona had cast an imperious shadow over Sonora and Baja California. On this occasion, however, Williams implied that geographic proximity encouraged a close relationship with Mexico. "I lived right next to the great nation of Mexico as a neighbor," he intoned, "and the solution of course, is very pleasing to our neighbor."[33] Finally, the San Diego Water Authority cited "our continuing and close relations with the Republic of Mexico" as the reason why Titles I and II should be approved.[34]

Context, however, further illuminates the varied motives of western leaders championing the act. Cline's water district relied on the Colorado River for 70 percent of its municipal water supply. He observed, "Our district serves about 1,500,000 people in the rapidly urbanizing Orange County." The salinity project would offset the expenses that consumers were currently paying to control salinity in the water supply.[35] In Williams's case, reference to the "neighborly" nature of border relations was couched within a request for greater federal help for the western states. With the Mexican issue solved by Title I, it was "up to those who created the solution to find some relief for the seven states that are threatened."[36] Likewise, the city of San Diego pushed for passage of Title II as part of a "permanent solution to the salinity problem with Mexico." Ironically, the city's letter in favor of the bill dealt almost entirely with the benefits that the proposed legislation would provide for San Diego.[37]

Whether they would admit it or not, western leaders had much in common with Mexican officials in terms of their relationship with Washington. They were all dependent on federal assistance for development of projects that would improve water quality throughout the watershed. Western politicians exploited their self-imposed identity as "second-class" Americans in seeking approval for Title II salt control. California congressman Craig Hosmer cited the government's treatment of the Colorado River Basin during negotiation of the Mexican Water Treaty in the

1940s as an example of federal neglect. Hosmer claimed that President Franklin Roosevelt "got a big concession on the Rio Grande out of the Mexicans and he gave away the Colorado River water to the Mexicans in quantity." "There was not really much attention paid to the Colorado River at that time," he complained. "It was in a peripheral way." Past presidents, he argued, did not understand the value of water in the West. Hosmer particularly despised "the high-handed way in which Presidents seem to go down [to Mexico] and get an 'embracio' and then come back and give away some of the West's water to somebody. That is not exactly something that to my mind is a bargaining chip."[38]

Senator Bible from Nevada also felt there was a critical need for federal help in the West. "I think it is our responsibility to take care of those people in the West that have the same salinity problem that is inherent in the international phase of it," he opined. "I have always felt that charity begins at home."[39] Arizona senator Paul Fannin expressed similar ideas. Taking care of Mexico only alleviated half the problem. "I don't see that we should have irreparable damage come about for U.S. citizens," he observed, "just to allow the citizens of Mexico to benefit by it."[40] Congressman Towell from Nevada encouraged the committee to "live up to [its] obligations of our own individual states" as well as satisfy the various treaties with Mexico.[41] Some westerners pledged their support for the salinity plant only if "something is done on behalf of our own water users."[42] Evoking memories of an old-fashioned stagecoach holdup, Congressman Johnson of California took issue with the State Department's objections to Title II: "It is not our intention to try to hold up anything or hold anybody at gunpoint. We would, however, like to have consideration and recognition given to our problems. We will try and perfect you a good Title I to take care of the international problem, and we would like to have a Title II in the bill that would help give us a little boost on the problems of the American side of the border."[43]

Other western leaders cited the interdependent nature of relations between Mexico and the western United States in their arguments for the Salinity Control Act. They insisted that if Title II were not adopted, the impact could be "as injurious to Mexican as it is to United States water users."[44] Wesley Steiner, chairman of the powerful Committee of Fourteen, a group of western leaders who advised Brownell during the crisis, linked the fortunes of Mexico to both the lower and upper basin in the United States. Steiner warned the committee of the potential costs of a narrow approach to the salinity crisis: "Without the control of upstream salinity, the U.S. will be faced with a new salinity problem in Mexico as salinity levels increase with continued development; and water users in the United States will suffer significant economic impacts, with impacts estimated to reach $80 million annually by the year 2000."[45]

Western leaders also continued their historic pattern of federal dependence by insisting that the government pay for 75 percent of the Title II program. This strategy, in reality, was an effort to turn recent legal decisions concerning jurisdiction over waters of the Colorado River to the advantage of the western states. Through a series of court decisions during the mid–twentieth century, the states failed to gain control of the riverbed passing through their states.[46] While this served as a blow to the cause of western "independence," it proved to be a powerful tool in arguing for federal funding of the Salinity Control Act. Steiner argued that the federal government was the only organization involved "in all major aspects of the salinity problem." Therefore, he reasoned, it should "finance the salinity control project and . . . bear a major share of the repayment responsibility."[47] Other organizations felt that the federal government should shoulder a major portion of the project since many western organizations had already spent millions of dollars combating river salinity. Northcutt Ely, attorney for the IID, stated, "We feel it is appropriate, as well as timely, for the United States to do its part to reduce salinity of the waters reaching us."[48]

Numerous interests throughout the basin clamored for federally funded salinity control projects. The Committee of Fourteen warned that the initiation of large-scale oil shale projects would further exacerbate the salinity crisis. Chairman Steiner pointed to the environmental impact statement drawn up for the shale operations as a precedent for federal help in controlling salinity levels.[49] Other organizations testified to the harmful effects of saline water that could occur in their communities. Farmers in San Diego County cultivated crops that were highly sensitive to saline water. "If the salinity in the Colorado River water rises significantly," officials noted, "the Authority's farmers will find it difficult to continue in production." Saline water from the Colorado River was already beginning to take its toll on homes and the sewer system in San Diego. "Current estimates of the cost due to excessive levels of corrosion in water heaters and other plumbing facilities," the San Diego Water Authority estimated, "range from $10 million to $20 million per year for San Diego water users."[50] In sum, numerous western interests viewed Minute 242 as an opportunity to win approval for a comprehensive plan that would provide greater protection for further development in the Southwest.

Understanding the nature of water politics in the Colorado River Basin is best accomplished by tossing a stone into a placid body of water. The stone enters the water, creating concentric ripples that move away from the point of contact. Each new ripple is generated with a different level of force and velocity. While the point of contact and the series of ripples are related, they are unique in that specific properties generate each new impression. In water politics, a problem such as the salinity crisis serves as the stone. Its impact on the local level (Yuma County), throughout the Colorado River Basin, and in international relations generates unique yet interrelated problems. Yet the crisis, like the splash of the stone, creates its most jarring effects closest to the point of contact. Ironically, the complexity of Yuma County water relations made the process of finding a simple solution to basinwide concerns more difficult. What would be best for Mexico or the State Department was not necessarily the ideal arrangement for Yuma County farmers or the Cocopah. Members of the WMIDD, the Yuma County Water Users Association, the city of Yuma, and the Cocopah tribe expressed their support or disapproval of the bills based on their individual priorities. Their varied approaches to development of the delta region demonstrated the complexity of local relations in coming to terms with an international problem.

Reconstructing Wellton-Mohawk

Farmers and officials in the Wellton-Mohawk Valley felt they had the most to lose through the Colorado River Salinity Control Act. While environmentalists urged the House and Senate committees to completely dismantle the WMIDD, more conservative voices prevailed. Led by the Committee of Fourteen, which included Tom Choules, a member of the WMIDD, western farm interests rallied to protect the embattled project. The words of Herbert Brownell encouraged western politicos. He assured the House committee that "water users in the U.S. would not suffer from the results of this legislation."[51] Yet the bill provided for the retirement of 10,000 acres of unproductive land on the project. Recognizing the necessity for compromise, WMIDD leaders worked to preserve the water rights they had been granted for 75,000 acres of land, even though the project would only include 65,000 acres after approval of the bill. Choules noted, "We are using about 300,000 acre-feet of water . . . at the present time to irrigate less than 65,000 acres."[52] He suggested that the language of the bill should protect the water rights of the district. C. C. Tabor, WMIDD manager, also presented this request to the Senate Subcommittee on Water and Power Resources.[53]

The long-term effects of the crisis took their toll on the leaders of the WMIDD. Intense international, domestic, and state scrutiny contributed to a feeling of victimization. Choules feared that the Salinity Control Act would endanger his district. "We could end up not only at the tail-end of the ditch," he observed, "but getting worse water and worse treatment as a result." Skeptical about the effectiveness of the desalinization plant, Choules quipped, "We are going to be the guinea pig under the act through the means of sizing the desalting plant."[54] He suggested that if WMIDD drainage water had not been dumped into the Colorado River about the same time water delivery to Mexico had been reduced in the 1950s, responsibility for the crisis would have been more evenly distributed throughout the basin. "It just happened that those two coincided, and we, being at the tail-end of the ditch, and near as well [as] having been there at that particular time, the finger is pointed at us."[55]

Tabor expressed similar feelings the following year as liquidation of the 10,000 designated acres took place. Tabor continued to believe that the solution for the problem lay in rehabilitating run-down fields and irrigation systems in the Mexicali Valley, not building a desalinization plant near Yuma. Although the WMIDD retained the rights to 300,000 acre-feet of water, Tabor complained that the new Central Arizona Project would demand that the WMIDD not exceed that total, as it had in previous years. Finally, Tabor lamented the continued presence of government employees on the project. "No pleasure is derived from being swarmed over by federal employees," he lamented.[56]

Domestic Use and Human Consumption:
Yuma City Water Woes

What had been a time of frustration for some was a time of opportunity for others. Even in the staid confines of a congressional hearing room, something of a boomtown mentality prevailed amongst the western participants. Except for a few organizations, namely, the WMIDD, most westerners and Mexicans stood to gain from construction of the desalinization plant and implementation of a comprehensive control project. Not the least of these groups was the city of Yuma. Its struggles during the crisis have generally been overlooked as historians have focused almost exclusively on the impact of the salinity crisis in Mexicali. Yuma's domestic water supply, like that of Mexicali, had been contaminated by saline water from the Wellton-Mohawk Valley in 1961. Journalist Lenora Werley observed that Yuma residents "found that the water [was] not pleasant to drink, that it [was] harmful to lawns and garden and that it [damaged] air conditioning pumps and industrial machinery." Werley perspicuously noted that the city's water woes predated the salinity crisis in 1961. Due to the increased use of water throughout the entire Colorado River Basin, the river carried only "a small amount of water when it [got] to the most southwestern city in Arizona." The contaminated runoff from Wellton-Mohawk aggravated the poor quality of the water supply. Werley emphasized the irony of the situation. Yumans, like residents of Mexicali, were incensed by the increased salinity. Geographic isolation, however, made it more difficult for Yumans to vent their complaints. Werley observed, "Some Yumans have thought of marching on somebody like their suffering Mexican counterparts. But who do you march on? The nearest U.S. Consulate is 54 miles away in salty Mexicali."[57]

Thomas Allt, a representative from Yuma, appeared before the House committee. He noted that Yuma had taken its water directly from the river from 1892 until 1961. In 1961, the saline drainage water from the Wellton-Mohawk area infiltrated the city's intake system and contaminated the water "to the point where it could not be used for domestic purposes and human consumption."[58] In an effort to find a better source for water, the city bought water from the Yuma County Water Users Association (YCWUA). YCWUA farmers used water that was released from

Imperial Dam and then transported to Yuma Valley via a siphon that ran beneath the riverbed of the Colorado River from California to Arizona. However, the cost of obtaining water from the siphon vis-à-vis the original intake system was prohibitive. Faced with few options, Allt quipped, "We right now are in a position where they own the taxi and we want a ride, we've got to pay the bill." The city's predicament illustrated how a regional crisis, though international in its implications, produced peculiar problems on the local level.[59]

Allt contended that the city of Yuma was not responsible for the recent crisis, which had been "imposed on them by circumstances beyond their control." He expressed resentment toward the USBR for its failed attempts to reduce salinity in the Wellton-Mohawk region. Nevertheless, "what was of great benefit to the Wellton Mohawk area," Allt observed, "was economically detrimental to the city of Yuma, in the added cost to acquire raw water."[60] He also contrasted federal treatment of Yuma County and the Mexicali Valley during the crisis. Allt argued that while little had been done to improve the domestic water situation in Yuma, the State Department was feverishly working to resolve similar complaints in Mexicali.[61] Pleading for equal treatment, Allt asserted, "We are disturbed that the people of Yuma should bear a disproportionate part of the burden when the very cause which creates a problem for Mexico also caused an economic problem for the city of Yuma."[62]

YCWUA and the Binational Aquifer

YCWUA leaders developed an interest in the Salinity Control Act because of chronic drainage problems that had threatened the Yuma Valley since the second decade of the twentieth century. A rising water table underneath the valley floor caused by poor drainage conditions and intensive irrigation periodically threatened local agricultural production. As early as 1912, drainage pipes and wells had been installed in the valley. Wastewater was sold to Mexican interests at the international boundary near San Luís Río Colorado. The Mexican Water Treaty of 1944, however, raised the prospect of increased drainage problems. The Mexican government successfully petitioned to build a diversion dam at the international border adjacent to the Yuma Valley. President Henry Frauenfelder and other members of the YCWUA board of governors vigorously protested construction of the dam because they felt it would contribute to their drainage problem.[63]

YCWUA leaders miscalculated the impact of Morelos Dam. The International Boundary and Water Commission (IBWC) took great care to protect the Yuma Valley from any problems Morelos Dam might have caused. Yet similar precautions were not taken with the construction of the Gila Project, which linked the Colorado River to Yuma Mesa and the Wellton-Mohawk region. Irrigation of Yuma Mesa began in the early 1950s, and excess water seeped into the aquifer beneath the Yuma Valley. At a special hearing on Yuma's drainage problems in 1956, Ernest Johannsen, president of the YCWUA, argued that the valley's drainage problems did not begin until water was delivered to Yuma Mesa. A special report prepared to assess the Yuma Valley's drainage situation concluded that "the problem cannot be confined to a limited area. It has a regional aspect. The hydrological region now involved and to be involved to a greater extent in the future includes the Wellton Mohawk area to the east, the South Gila area, the Yuma Mesa, the Yuma Valley, and Mexico. . . . Most of this region is underlain by a highly transmissive coarse-gravel aquifer. . . . It is believed that this aquifer is a controlling factor in the underground hydrology of the region."[64]

From the 1950s until passage of the Colorado River Salinity Control Act, leaders from the YCWUA argued that the federal government was responsible for drainage problems in the valley. Johannsen testified at the 1956 hearings that local farmers refused to take out loans to alleviate the groundwater problem because "it [was] not caused by irrigation operations in this district."[65] He dramatized the severity of the problem, claiming that groundwater was "boiling up under our feet." YCWUA leaders expressed their belief that the government should pay for the installation of drainage wells in the eastern section of the valley to prevent further infiltration of the valley aquifer by seepage from farms on Yuma Mesa. At the time, neither the USBR nor members of the committee believed that the drainage problems merited federal help. Engineer C. E. Jacobs contended that more studies were needed prior to approving federal aid to bail out farmers. Charles Maierhoffer, USBR chief drainage and groundwater engineer, conceded that water was affecting certain areas of the valley, yet "the evidence [did] not indicate that there has been significant net aggravation of the overall drainage problems nor impaired productivity of lands."[66] Although salt levels in valley waters—a sign of rising groundwater—increased after the 1930s, Maierhoffer pointed out that the number of acres taken out of production "decreased to zero in 1953."[67]

YCWUA leaders viewed the salinity crisis of 1961 as an opportunity to obtain federal help. Initially, though, YCWUA president Sam Dick believed that the "international" problem would retard resolution of the Yuma Valley situation. Furthermore, USBR officials wanted to wait and solve Yuma's drainage problems after the Supreme Court ruled on the *Arizona vs. California* case over contested water from the Colorado River. Dick lamented the exorbitant costs incurred by the existing drainage system, which had been paid for by the farmers. He also enumerated the benefits Mexico reaped from valley efforts to regulate the water table. In 1961, for example, the YCWUA delivered 133,000 acre-feet of water to Mexico. The Mexican government paid a paltry $4,000 for the benefits. "The Association thus finds itself in the position of having, at its own cost and expense," he noted, "delivered to Mexico in 1961 as a credit to the Mexican Treaty almost 10% of the amount required to be delivered to Mexico under the terms of that Treaty." Dick felt that his association should be reimbursed for past expenses related to services rendered in fulfillment of the treaty. He argued that the expenses qualified for reimbursement under the Colorado River Front Work and Levee Systems Act, which provided for "constructing, improving, extending, operating and maintaining protection and drainage works and systems along the Colorado River."[68] In a February 6, 1963, meeting with USBR commissioner Floyd Dominy, Dick discussed two plans for alleviating the drainage problems. The more extensive plan called for adding sixty additional wells at a cost of $22 million. The "reduced" plan called for eighteen wells and was projected to cost between $8 and $9 million. Commissioner Dominy preferred the more modest plan, noting, however, that it "could be expanded later."[69]

Despite the loud approval of YCWUA leaders for the drainage wells, some local residents questioned the large amount of money required for such an undertaking. Local resident H. M. Corey refuted the need for "the big eight and a half million dollar boondoggle drainage plan." He believed that the YCWUA board of governors was merely holding out on completing immediate drainage projects in the valley so that the federal government would pay for a bigger project. "It is the opinion of our board of governors and the president," Corey noted, "that they would rather wait on this eight and one half million of non-reimbursable money which would cause us not to spend our own sixty-one thousand." Instead, Corey felt that if the association would expend $60,000 to drain one specific portion of the valley, its problems would be solved "for a long time to come." Corey also astutely perceived the political forces at play with the proposed drainage project. "The [USBR] is overstaffed," he wryly noted, "and they have to find projects to work on." Corey found it ironic that despite nearly twenty years of lobbying for relief from the water table, Yuma farmers "[seemed] to be farming . . . regardless."[70]

Despite these complaints, rumors of intensive groundwater pumping on the Mexican side of the border provided Yuma leaders with an argument that helped them obtain the needed drainage system. In the 1950s Congressman Clinton Anderson of New Mexico did not believe the YCWUA merited federal assistance for the drainage problems until he learned that Mexico might capture the underground flows of water. At the Yuma groundwater hearings, Congressman Anderson asked Engineer Maierhoffer: "If you do not pump these large quantities of water from the lower gravel strata . . . would there not be a tendency that that water, if not intercepted, would just naturally flow into Mexico and you would get no credit for it under the treaty?" Maierhoffer responded, "Very definitely." Anderson believed that in such a situation, "the United States government might be able to pick up some of this excess water" to satisfy the Mexican Water Treaty.[71] In the West, water was not simply a resource, it was the fundamental tool for growth during the twentieth century.

By 1963, local, state, and national leaders had emphasized the strategic importance of Yuma's drainage problems. The attention of the state's congressional delegation brought federal assistance a step closer to reality. In a confidential memo to Arizona's congressional representatives, W. S. Gookin, Arizona state water engineer, apprised state leaders of the need to support funding measures for a drainage project similar to that discussed by USBR commissioner Dominy a year earlier in Yuma. Mexican farmers, he noted, "[were] rapidly and aggressively increasing their pumping through the drilling of new wells and subjugation of new land." If nothing were done to combat the new pumping, he feared that Mexican farmers might pump up to 1.5 million acre-feet of water per year. Instead of allowing Mexico to proceed unchallenged, the state water engineer believed that the water should be "pumped by the U.S. and delivered to Mexico as surface water in satisfaction of the Mexican [treaty]." Gookin warned that state and national interests would probably clash in the process of seeking approval for additional drainage wells. "It is my understanding," Gookin wrote, "that the State Department is unsympathetic with western water problems and seeks to assist agricultural interests in Mexico." He also feared that Secretary of State Dean Rusk and President Johnson would canvass support for "non-interference with Mexican agricultural [interests]." Ever mindful of how such developments might threaten Arizona, Gookin urged state representatives to fully support the project.[72]

Arizona's congressional representatives successfully pushed legislation through Congress that authorized funds for the installation of seventeen drainage wells. Winning approval of the funds, however, did not simplify the complexities of water politics in Yuma County. International diplomacy infringed on local prerogatives in implementing the groundwater program. A confidential memo in Carl Hayden's papers warned that placing all the wells in the valley would increase the salinity level of the river to levels greater than they had been prior to installation of the wells.[73] The USDS had pledged to minimize salinity levels of water destined for Mexico. In light of that directive, USBR officials realized that it would be most effective to place eleven of the wells on Yuma Mesa and only six in the Yuma Valley.

The Colorado River Salinity Control Act provided the YCWUA with another opportunity to obtain additional wells. Herbert Brownell attached a nonbinding article to Minute 242 that limited groundwater pumping by either nation in the aquifer near Yuma/San Luís Río Colorado to 160,000 acre-feet of water. While this article was intended to place a limit on overdraft pumping, it actually had the reverse effect. As a part of Title II, western leaders proposed that an extensive groundwater well field be constructed on a five-mile strip in Yuma County adjoining the Mexican border. Obtaining regional support was not difficult, since every acre-foot of water pumped from below the ground freed up an equal amount of water in the upper or lower basin for use elsewhere. Archie Mellon, president of the YCWUA, also asked the Senate committee to reimburse the YCWUA for its previous expenses in operating the boundary pumping plant and drainage system. He reiterated that drainage from adjoining reclamation projects in Yuma County had caused the problems.[74]

YCWUA's support for Title II of the Colorado River Salinity Control Act developed over the course of three decades. During that time a domestic problem with drainage patterns threatened to trigger an international pumping war. While the organization did not receive compensation for past expenses, the well field was constructed on five miles of land in southern Yuma County. Ironically, as pumping increased during the early 1970s, YCWUA leaders were concerned that too much water was being extracted from the binational aquifer. International concerns over excessive pumping continued until the early 1980s. Since the article of the treaty that was related to groundwater pumping was nonbinding, it did nothing but send a tremor of fear through regional farmers regarding the extent of the aquifer's water reserves and what would happen if Mexico drained them. In retrospect, perhaps no other facet of the Colorado River Salinity Control Act illustrates how well local leaders adapted a recurring problem to regional and national concerns.

First in Time, Last in Line:
Water on the Cocopah Reservation

The proposed desalinization plant threatened the economic interests of many delta natives. The Cocopah were among the first inhabitants of the region, migrating to the area around a.d. 1000 and establishing settlements near the mouth of the Colorado River.[75] Although the Cocopah were organized as a tribe by the U.S. government in 1917, they continued to cross the U.S.–Mexican border to interact with Cocopah in the Mexican delta. During the early 1900s, members of the Cocopah tribe provided much of the backbreaking manual labor needed to construct irrigation ditches, canals, and dams in the Imperial and Yuma Valleys. Unfortunately, they did not benefit from the rush to develop the land. The farming and irrigation bonanza of the early twentieth century left them nearly destitute of arable land.

By 1974, economic development on the Cocopah reservation lagged far behind even the most modest standards realized throughout the rest of Yuma County. In a letter to Stan Womer, federal cochairman of the Four Corners Regional Commission, Hawley Atkinson, special assistant to tribal chairman Robert S. Barley, pointed out that not only was the tribe "destitute" but "[it] has been passed and forgotten for nearly a 100 years." Atkinson claimed that unemployment levels on the reservation were as high as 75 percent. He went on to describe existing living conditions: "The people live in substandard housing; have substandard water supplies; no adequate sanitation facilities; poor health; lack of educational facilities; and the epitome of substandard facilities. The only new facilities is the 'Cry House'—at least their 'wailing wall' is modern. Their evidence of deep abiding faith in God is reflected in this priority."[76] To add insult to injury, prayer was about the only type of long-distance communication feasible on the reservation. The East Cocopah tribal community lacked telephone service. Chairman Barley lamented the fact that "there is only one pay-phone for all the families that live on the East reservation."[77]

Despite these challenges, Barley hoped to achieve new levels of economic development on the reservation. In addition to importuning Arizona governor Williams for assistance in obtaining essential services for tribal members, Barley hoped to develop recently acquired land for agricultural production. The tribe also planned to create a recreation site on tribal lands located directly on the Colorado River. However, the canal designated to transport rejected saline water from Wellton-Mohawk to the Gulf of California intersected the reservation "on a line roughly parallel to the Colorado River." Barley apprised the Senate committee that the canal would not only "deprive the Tribe of desperately needed acreage, but it will pose a formidable barrier, dividing the main portion of the Reservation from the accreted lands that have just recently been won in court." Barley worried that the desalinization plant might curtail the flow of water through the river's main channel throughout the year. He concluded that the proposed recreation site would be "diminished, and probably eliminated, if the river no longer flows by the Reservation."[78]

Barley's testimony illustrated the battle that Native Americans faced as they attempted to develop their communities in a postindustrial economy. He noted that the tribe had fought for ten years to acquire an additional eight hundred acres. Barley recognized that the recent triumph was a Pyrrhic victory, because the tract included "a railroad levy and a floodplain levy." Barley demanded that if the wastewater canal could not be moved, the tribe be compensated for the fragmentation of its land. He also argued that the tribe's land could not be used without its consent. Barley contended, "The United States government should not attempt to meet its treaty obligations to Mexico by ignoring its trusteeships to the Cocopah Tribe." In exchange for the land where the canal would intersect tribal lands, Barley suggested that 720 acres of federal land to the south of the reservation be transferred to the tribe.[79] In addition to the land, the tribe asked that three bridges be built "over the portion of the reject stream [that] crosses the Reservation of the Cocopah Tribe of Indians." The Cocopah felt these measures would "constitute full and just payment . . . for the rights of way required for construction of the reject brine channel and appurtenant electrical transmission lines."[80]

Barley's testimony epitomized the local complexity of the Salinity Control Act as well as a new age in Native American efforts to achieve a self-determined destiny instead of being wards of Congress. Some tribes threatened to use the courts as a way to defend and augment their resources. As a result of its protest, the Cocopah tribe was given alternative government lands. The DOI also built the three bridges that the tribe had requested. For once, the Cocopah's voices were not ignored.

conclusion: International Decisions, Local Consequences

Chaos theorists often cite the "butterfly effect" as an example of how small changes can exercise a disproportionate influence throughout an entire system. In the late 1950s, such an event took place in the Wellton-Mohawk Valley as a new canal transporting water to the salt-laden fields exacerbated drainage problems on the project. USBR commissioner W. A. Dexheimer had noted the deficiencies of the drainage system in Wellton-Mohawk as early as 1957. "Correction of the drainage system is extremely complex," he confided to Senator Hayden, "[and] the drainage problem in the Yuma area is but one of a number of water management problems." He recognized that a sense of ecological order existed, but he pointed out that the USBR did not understand the relationships between the various components well enough to combat the problems that were quickly multiplying. "With the irrigation of land under the Gila Project have come drainage problems. In nearly all cases these problems were expected," Dexheimer continued, "but the rapidity with which they developed was not expected."[81]

By 1961 the drainage water had exacerbated already increasing levels of salt pollution in the main channel of the Colorado River. The emissions not only damaged water quality in the United States but also endangered the well-being of farmers and citizens in the Mexicali Valley. Politically, the event reverberated throughout the basin on both sides of the border and grabbed the attention of national leaders. Over time, the issue played a significant role in the nature of U.S.–Mexican relations.

Efforts to resolve the crisis also underscored the complexity of politics in the binational basin. Numerous political, economic, and ecological variables affected decisions made throughout the region. Furthermore, human agency and deep historic relations between the United States and Mexico provided room for variation, creation, and conflict. Slight changes in any variable could greatly influence diplomatic relations between the two countries. For example, approval of the Central Arizona Project in 1968 altered the perspective of western politicians toward Mexico and the rest of the basin. This accounted for the unprecedented sense of harmony displayed by community and state leaders throughout the basin.

Overwhelming congressional approval of Minute 242 brought the salinity crisis to a point of diplomatic closure on June 11, 1974.[82] Nevertheless, Minute 242 did not blot out the memories of how irrigated agribusiness had gone awry in the Wellton-Mohawk Valley during the 1950s. For many, the 260-million-dollar desalinization plant embodied the cardinal defects of a growth-driven generation. With the added programs of the Salinity Control Act, the total cost approached a billion dollars. Ironically, scientist W. E. Martin noted that better water management in Yuma County alone might have dropped the salinity content of local return

Figure 15 Construction of the Wellton-Mohawk bypass canal unexpectedly created a vibrant swamp oasis for wildlife and birds in the Ciénaga de Santa Clara at the edge of the delta and the Gran Desierto of Sonora. These lush waterways depend, ironically, on drainage from the Wellton-Mohawk Irrigation and Drainage District. (U.S. Bureau of Reclamation photograph)

flows by at least 40 percent. He also observed that buying out the lands in question would be more economical after a decade than operating the plant.[83]

Despite overwhelming congressional approval for the Salinity Control Act, construction of the desalinization plant faced numerous hurdles. Originally set to go on line in 1981, rising costs, funding problems, and design reviews pushed the completion back more than a decade. The complex was finally completed in 1992. By that time, the concrete-lined canal that carried drainage waters from the Wellton-Mohawk Valley to the Sea of Cortés (another component of Minute 242) had unexpectedly rejuvenated the marshlands of the Ciénaga de Santa Clara in the Mexican delta by bringing new supplies of water to the region.[84] Environmentalists noted that operation of the desalinization plant would replace those saline flows with hypersaline waters, posing a threat to waterfowl migrating on the Pacific Flyway. Between passage of the Salinity Control Act, and completion of the plant, increases in precipitation and water flows in the Colorado River decreased the salinity level of water reaching Mexico and diluted the runoff from Wellton-Mohawk. In the face of chronic budget restraints, the USBR welcomed this natural solution to the salinity crisis. Improved desalinization techniques are tested there today, and limited quantities of treated water are offered for sale on the plant's Internet site.[85]

The salinity crisis and the Salinity Control Act reflect the inherent complexity found at each political level in the Colorado River Basin. Delta politics were just as complicated as national and international politics. Furthermore, the "commoditization" of the delta placed local communities and ecosystems at the mercy of distant interests that had a greater concern in continued use of the river for development than in the well-being of the region.[86] Thus, the Salinity Control Act ultimately underscores the challenges that face present-day policy makers who must create basinwide initiatives that balance diplomatic, national, regional, and local priorities within the river basin.

Deltascape The Yuma Desalinization Plant

If you travel west of Yuma five miles, you'll eventually find the turnoff for the USBR's Yuma office, fittingly located on Calle Agua Salada (Street of Salty Water). The adjacent desalinization plant, built under provisions included in Minute 242 to the Mexican Water Treaty, sits on sixty acres of alkali land and is the second largest reverse osmosis desalinization plant in the world. Running at full capacity, the plant can transform 102.7 million gallons of highly saline drainage water into 72.4 million gallons of water fit for drinking.

Water flows into the treatment plant via a concrete-lined canal from the Wellton-Mohawk Valley. Before treatment, small screens block solids, algae, and tree limbs from passing into the treatment area. A barrage of chemicals is applied to the water, beginning with chlorine, to stunt the growth of algae and microorganisms that might pollute the expensive system of nine thousand plastic membranes that desalinize the drainage water.

Pretreatment consists of running the polluted water through a series of pipes, basins, and chemical applications. This process helps separate solids and sludge from the water prior to desalinization. A large, rectangular sedimentation basin slows the speed of the incoming water, allowing gravity to draw solid particles to the bottom of the basin, where automated rakes push the sediment to the sides. Next, three circular basins, measuring 185 feet across and 26 feet deep, mix lime and ferric sulfate with up to 4.71 million gallons of water to remove suspended particles. Visible from the air, when filled with water these basins sometimes resemble gigantic swimming pools.

The sludge then prepares for a journey of its own. After being scraped to the center of the circular basin, the sludge is pumped through a twenty-two-mile-long underground pipeline that deposits it southeast of Yuma in a series of evaporation ponds. Each pond, which measures an acre, fills with solid waste and blends into the desert landscape near the Mexican border. Over time, the sludge ponds harden into limestone deposits.

Back at the desalinization plant, the drainage water continues its miraculous makeover. Sulfuric acid lowers the water's pH number from 10 to 7.5. A flush through a field of anthracite coal and sand filters removes any additional solids. The water and salt then wait for their impending separation in a storage well underneath the desalting facility. From this point, the saline water will be shot through the reverse osmosis membranes.

The water enters the vessels at an average pressure of 362 pounds per square inch. Here the process of reverse osmosis, or the separation of two parts of a solution, takes place. The walls of the membranes are lined with cellulose acetate, which prevents approximately 97 percent of the salt from passing through to the posttreatment stage. The high water pressure from the fourteen pumps forces the water toward the center of the tube and encourages separation from the salts.

During normal operations, the treated drainage water then

flows about half a mile to the Colorado River and enters Morelos Dam for use in the Mexicali Valley. Back in the Wellton-Mohawk Valley, untreated drainage water is also shipped south to Mexico but in a fifty-nine-mile-long canal that carries the rejected water to the rejuvenated Ciénaga de Santa Clara in Sonora.[87]

Epilogue

Beyond the Border Oasis

To this point, we have explored the union of water, soil, and international politics in the delta, focusing particularly on the ways in which U.S.-Mexican relations affected the pace and intensity of development there between 1940 and 1975. During that time, two separate yet interconnected (financially, ecologically, socially, and diplomatically) agricultural revolutions competed and coexisted. Strong governmental interest, abundant capital, and ample links to the world economy insured rapid development of the Imperial and Yuma Valleys during the first third of the twentieth century. By 1935, Lázaro Cárdenas had set in motion a semirevolutionary economic program in the Mexicali Valley intended to link the economy of Baja California with Mexico's interior and wean the peninsula from dependence on American capital. This program sparked a flurry of agricultural development and immigration to the delta and placed *mexicanos* and *norteamericanos* in competition for precious natural resources. The complex web of struggles for water and power in the delta region led to the decline of water quality during the salinity crisis of the 1960s and early 1970s.

To better frame our understanding of this union of land and water and the binational competition for those resources, we must place the delta in a global context, comparing the marriage of land, water, and politics to similar challenges in other arid landscapes. Looking beyond the border oasis offers us an opportunity to place the region's problems in perspective vis-à-vis the dilemmas faced in other arid watersheds around the world.

The Rio Grande Basin offers the closest point of comparison and contrast with the Colorado River Basin. One of the critical differences between the regions relates to the geographical orientation of the rivers and their tributaries. In the Colorado River Basin, the regulation of flows from tributaries occurs completely in the United States. Accordingly, the delivery of water to Mexico takes place only at the border near Yuma, where the IBWC can regulate apportionment of the water. In contrast, numerous tributaries in the Rio Grande Basin along both sides of the border, particularly below El Paso, make river regulation more difficult. Furthermore, water amounts assigned by the 1944 Mexican Water Treaty to each nation in the lower and middle Rio Grande regions were awarded largely on the percentage of river flows, while the treaty for the Colorado River Basin stipulated set amounts.[1]

The upper Rio Grande Basin is composed of three American states— Colorado, New Mexico, and Texas—that signed a treaty similar to the Colorado River Compact. The 1938 treaty apportioned water from the upper Colorado River between them. A 1906 agreement between the United States and Mexico also stipulated that the United States deliver 60,000 acre-feet to Mexico near Ciudad Juárez from the upper Rio Grande. This arrangement has often complicated binational relations, particularly when Colorado has not delivered water downstream, prompting Texas to short-change Mexico.[2] At the same time, new water structures in Mexico, such as El Cuchillo Dam, a structure intended to supply Monterrey, Nuevo León, with water, have decreased water levels upstream on the San Juan River and the Rio Grande.[3]

The Rio Grande Basin has experienced some of the same challenges related to water management and water quality as the lower Colorado River Basin. During the 1950s and 1960s, for example, Mexican irrigation above Mission, Texas, returned highly saline water to the Rio Grande, which harmed the fields of U.S. citrus farmers downriver. Mexico refused to build a conveyance drain for the saline waters until the United States resolved the Colorado River salinity problem. U.S. officials voiced complaints similar to those expressed by Mexican leaders who were concerned about the salinity problem in the Colorado River Basin: "We believe, under international law, that we have the right to object to the harmful salinity [allegedly, three times the normal level] since it is more than that normally necessary for successful irrigation of areas reasonably susceptible of reclamation." With the passage of Minute 218 in 1965, the Mexican government agreed to construct Morrillo Drain on the lower Rio Grande, with each nation contributing 50 percent of the funds for construction of the drain. This episode not only illustrates the way the two river basins have been politically and diplomatically linked but also how both nations reacted in similar ways to unilateral actions taken by the other nation.[4]

Both regions have also experienced tremendous demographic and economic growth since World War II. With the implementation of the *maquiladora* program in the 1960s and PRONAF, a federal initiative to make the border region more attractive to tourists, Ciudad Juárez emerged in the 1970s as the largest industrial center on the border. Approval of NAFTA only intensified regional emphasis on manufacturing.

In the wake of intensive industrial and agricultural expansion, water quality declined. As Hector Fuentes, associate professor at the University of Texas–El Paso, noted, "In bringing industrialization to the border, we are also in the process of creating the longest Love Canal and Superfund site on planet Earth."[5] Recent conditions, including the long drought during the 1990s, suggest the seriousness of environmental degradation in the face of demographic, industrial, and agricultural growth. Declining water quality and additional dams on Rio Grande tributaries have contributed to the decline of numerous species along the river as well. Together, these conditions suggest that the two watersheds on the U.S.–Mexican border face similar challenges, even if the severity of individual problems differs from place to place.[6]

Groundwater issues have perhaps been of even more importance along the Rio Grande, particularly in the El Paso/Ciudad Juárez metropolitan area, than in the Colorado River Delta. Overdraft pumping of aquifers beneath the two cities poses a greater problem in the upper Rio Grande area than in the Colorado River Delta due to exponential growth in the Ciudad Juárez region. Furthermore, the El Paso/Ciudad Juárez metropolitan area is almost completely dependent on groundwater supplies, while inhabitants of other areas of the Rio Grande and Colorado River Basins can at least count on some surface water to meet their needs. The Hueco Bolsón, an aquifer located beneath El Paso and Juárez, remains the most depleted groundwater source in the region. From 1903 to 1976, the aquifer declined by seventy-three feet below El Paso and eighty-five feet below Ciudad Juárez. Extensive overdraft of the aquifer has also compromised the quality of remaining reserves as saline water has been drawn into the aquifer by the intensive operation of ground wells. Differences in groundwater rights have also hampered efforts to reach binational pumping accords. Mexican groundwater rights are vested in the federal government. Local U.S. officials have resisted any type of groundwater regulation, arguing that such actions would infringe on their water rights, which were granted by the state of Texas.[7]

The Aral Sea region in the former Soviet Union provides the best cautionary tale for unchecked development of scarce water resources in arid landscapes. At about the same time that the USBR completed the Wellton-Mohawk canal, the former Soviet government was placing stringent demands on Kazakhstan, Uzbekistan, and Turkistan to increase cotton production. In the process, government engineers and farmers diverted most of the water from the Syr Darya and the Amu Darya (the two main tributaries to the Aral Sea) to farmlands far removed from the drainage basins of the respective rivers. Large canals, including the Kara Kum (850 miles long), diverted water from the Amu Darya, denying return flows to the shrinking river. While cotton cultivation had traditionally been a proud symbol of the region's agricultural community, heavy pressure to increase yields, with a corresponding increase in the use of herbicides and pesticides, pushed the region to the ecological breaking point, adversely affecting not only the lake's rich flora and fauna but also the health of humans who lived nearby. By 1993, the lake had shrunk by 60 percent. Twenty of the twenty-four species of the lake's indigenous fish were extinct. Throat cancer had increased by 500 percent. Typhoid and hepatitis increased dramatically.[8]

Journalist Otkir Hashimov lamented, "Why is the sea disappearing? Quite frankly, the cotton plan has been increased to the heavens, new lands have been brought under cultivation, reservoirs have been poorly constructed and many industrial enterprises have been erected on the banks of local rivers."[9] Soviet leaders were "obsessed with becoming independent of other nations in cotton production, [and] political leaders in Moscow declared pursuit of that goal to be the 'patriotic duty' of all Central Asians." In the process, officials ignored the ecological realities of their designs. Cotton production did increase to a point that allowed the U.S.S.R. to become a net exporter of cotton, yet the policy did not take into account the well-being of those who lived at the mouth of the Amu Darya. Similarly, the mouth of the Syr Darya, choked by diversions, became a twisting wasteland of dust composed primarily of chemical

Figure 16 Agricultural pesticides pose a threat to animals, plants, and humans if ingested. This Charles O'Rear photograph illustrates the efforts taken by Imperial County to cordon off the barrels that bring the agents of death to the border oasis. (National Archives and Records Administration photograph)

residue from agricultural pesticides. Public health declined, and the local fishing economy practically vanished. To solve the problem, Soviet engineers suggested that a canal be built to carry water from the Ob and Irtysh Rivers in Siberia to the Aral Sea. Mikhail Gorbachev shelved the grandiose plan.[10]

Law professor David H. Getches has linked the tragedy at the Aral Sea with that of the Wellton-Mohawk project, noting, "Both Wellton-Mohawk and the Aral Sea are public policy disasters created by government officials determined to accomplish a single-minded goal. They pursued only the mission of making the desert bloom." Calling for more public participation and greater ecological sensitivity in the process of water policy formulation, Getches argues that the largely closed decision-making process in both nations during the height of the cold war led to disasters. He notes, however, that the prospects for change were better in the delta than in Central Asia. "We know Central Asians are capable of violence against their neighbors," he observed, "[and there] is no prior history of cooperation, mutual problem-solving, and regional statesmanship that is needed to solve the Aral Sea problem."[11] Yet the Aral Sea outlines a situation that very well could occur in the delta unless efforts are made to assure that development throughout the basin does not encourage further ecological decline there.

Ideology also plays a significant role in water conflict. In the Colorado River Delta, nationalistic rhetoric periodically politicized binational water negotiations. The threat of Communist infiltration of local political groups in the Mexicali Valley during the salinity crisis kept the attention of U.S. officials. Yet U.S. control of the Mexicali Valley's water supply and agribusiness complex also alarmed Mexican officials and influenced their policies in the region. Despite these differences, binational cooperation often prevented nationalistic tensions in the delta from descending into violence.

In contrast, ideological differences have characterized Arab and Israeli water conflict in the Jordan River watershed. In the modern era, the need for water, religious attitudes toward water, and political nationalism have been subsumed into one conflict. In the wake of the establishment of Israel in 1948, the new nation nationalized water resources in the region. Additionally, during the Arab-Israeli War in 1967, Israel targeted the source of the Jordan River and controlled its flow into the Sea of Galilee by taking the Golan Heights and the West Bank. These actions not only aggravated tensions between Palestinians and Jews but also reinforced the ideological differences that divided the two peoples. Recently, however, Jordan and Israel have made progress by signing a 1994 water-sharing accord for the Jordan and Yarmuk Rivers as well as for attendant groundwater aquifers.[12]

The ability to overcome ideological differences suggests that almost any group of willing parties involved in water conflict can find at least minimal grounds for sharing a resource needed by all humankind. On the other hand, the growing shortage of fresh water throughout the world also suggests that water could serve as an extremely divisive force during the twenty-first century.[13] The challenges and triumphs of other arid watersheds should inspire residents of the Colorado River Delta to take steps to protect the region's ecosystem and promote sustainable development on both sides of the border, in spite of institutional and cultural obstacles.

water and the U.S.-Mexican Relationship: A Happy Marriage?

If the comparative approach yields any insights into improving U.S.–Mexican water relations, those solutions must be adapted to the particular historical and institutional circumstances that have shaped U.S.–Mexican water policy in the delta. In retrospect, while Mexican and U.S. federalism differed markedly in the distribution of power between national, state, and local governments as well as in legal jurisdiction over surface water and groundwater rights, strong similarities in the actual administration of natural resources and immigration in the delta region allowed tremendous growth on both sides of the border. Federal control, both Mexican and U.S., over water resources increased on both sides of the border, while immigration policies generally left enough doors open to accommodate industrial and agricultural expansion in the region. Economic development of the delta, exponential levels of emigration to the region, the ambivalent political posturing of both "neighbors," and the dynamics of the world economy threatened the very lifeline, the Colorado

River, that had given birth to the region's dual legacy of agricultural abundance and ecological impoverishment.

The development of water resources in the region offered a candid portrait of both nations' pursuit of those resources during the twentieth century, particularly during the post–World War II era. In Mexico, efforts to modernize encouraged Mexicali Valley farmers to produce crops destined for export or for the palates of Mexico's emerging middle class.[14] The capitalist orientation of crop production in the Mexicali Valley was demonstrated by the large number of ejidatarios who produced cotton primarily for market sales. Ultimately, the push to develop the border region strained available water resources. Rehabilitation of the Mexicali Valley served as official recognition that scarce resources limited opportunities on the border.

The presence of the two national water commissions, the IBWC and the CILA, has provided a degree of stability in water relations, despite complaints that they possess little power, focus narrowly on technical issues, and do not allow sufficient public input into policy decisions. Nevertheless, the IBWC at least offered a forum for interaction on water issues and resolution of water conflict. Particularly during the years prior to 1975, it often served as a buffer between individuals in both governments whose actions were not in the best interests of both nations. The executive organization in the U.S. government of BECC and NADBank in the wake of NAFTA offers some hope for greater levels of public involvement in border water issues and perhaps an expansion into broader environmental issues that impact the region.[15]

While strong laws and institutions are critical to effective water management, they are of little worth if they are ignored in times of crisis. What is needed is a commitment by regional and national officials to promote sustainable development in the delta. The practical reality of such a commitment would be the recognition on the part of both nations that environmental degradation in the border region cannot take a back seat to development. Furthermore, it is imperative that the flow of information and communication regarding water issues remain open, regardless of which paradigm for institutional monitoring is adopted. Open communication must be accompanied by a commitment to avoid unilateral actions that impact the neighboring nation, states, and communities.[16]

From a historical perspective, sewage, pesticides, and increased salinity are merely by-products of more fundamental issues related to regional development in the delta during the twentieth century. As the environmental group the Defenders of Wildlife has noted, "Rampant human population, concomitant growing water use, and massive riparian habitat degradation have greatly harmed the lower Colorado River Basin, the wetlands that feed into the Gulf of California and the broader Sonoran Desert Ecosystem." Other scholars concerned about water resources in the delta have offered similar critiques of the region's development. Paul Ganster has observed, "*Unmanaged growth* in the region has produced serious transborder environmental problems, including air and water pollution, contamination from improper disposal of hazardous and solid wastes, and urban and development impacts on plant and animal species and critical ecosystems." Similarly, Marco Antonio Alcazar Ávila, an official at the Dirección General de Fronteras, has noted that all along the border "a planning effort that permits the anticipation of measures to decrease the negative impact of demographic expansion" is needed to counteract the unmanaged depletion of water resources. He also suggests that if regional population continues to grow exponentially and the two economies become even more polarized, "it is possible to foresee . . . national and bi-national crises of greater proportion, with unforeseen effects, as a product of the different inequalities that could produce the abusive use and deterioration of existing natural resources."[17]

Ultimately, the ecological problems in the region are not the exclusive domain of either the United States or Mexico. Instead, they are shared problems that demand complex solutions from both countries. As the historical perspective illustrates, compartmentalizing responsibility for these problems only breeds fear and mistrust between Mexicans, Americans, and Native groups in the delta. If we continue with a reductionist outlook, the border relationship truly will remain "[an unhappy] marriage without possibility of divorce."[18] Viewing the region's development from a more holistic point of view suggests that change can be brought about despite international boundaries, differing models of federalism, and cultural differences. In the end, the Colorado River Delta must be seen as an integrated, binational region. To approach the region in any other way denies the realities of a shared history, ecosystem, and regional identity.

Coda

The Contemporary Delta

For nearly three decades, Anita Alvarez Williams has served as a cultural voice for Cocopah natives living in the delta. As she astutely observes, "The most deeply rooted knowledge of the Colorado River rests with the Native Americans whose ancestors have lived by, with, on, and in the river for several thousand years or more."[1] The following vignette examines some of her trips on the river over the years.

As she made her way up the Colorado River one Sunday, en route to the Imperial National Wildlife Refuge, Alvarez Williams noted the influence of miners and steamboats on the river. She lamented the fact that "Native American farms and gardens mentioned by early travelers on the river seem to have been lost to us." Birds attended her party as they plied northward. Killdeer, herons, egrets, and ducks chimed in with the sound of the boat's engine. Beaver caves revealed signs of life, and coyotes hid behind the tules, straining to steal a peak at the human intruders.[2]

On another occasion, Alvarez Williams paid a visit to a friend in the Cocopah settlements south of Mexicali in the wake of river flooding. The floods had carried away most of the Cocopah homes at El Mayor on the Hardy River and had filled the dry canal from the Laguna Salada to the Colorado River with fish. She accompanied her friend on a fishing trip into the heart of the Laguna Salada. This was an unusual experience for Alvarez Williams, "since most of my life," she noted, "I had known the Laguna Salada as a barren, dry salt flat. . . . There I was boating along on cloud-reflecting water between the Sierra Cucupa and the Sierra de Juárez. And in the company of friends whose ancestors had probably been fishing river and lake here for a couple of thousand years." The floods of 1983 brought back memories of an earlier time, when fishing sustained the Cocopah. Visions of the present mixed with images of the Cocopah centuries earlier, fishing on the lake from reed rafts. The recent floods had filled the lagoons and canals with fish again. "My friends were pleased," she wrote. "They would have plenty to eat and sell to the Mexicali fish merchant who regularly transported fish to Mexicali in his refrigerated truck."[3]

Several years later, on January 1, 1989, Alvarez Williams and her husband headed back to the Laguna Salada and found a very different scene. After their car sunk into a muddy salt flat, Alvarez Williams and her children searched for material to rescue their vehicle from the mud. "About halfway to the bushes we came upon a seemingly endless curving windrow of desiccated fish, hundreds of them," she recalled. "This had to have been where the Laguna Salada finally dried up, and these fish were the last to go. They were so perfectly desiccated that they didn't stink. Lightly dusted with glistening sand, their forms and even their scales intact, these fish were preparing to become fossils. They were beautiful." She and the children gathered the brittle fish in order to dig their vehicle out of the mud flat. The gift of the desert proved invaluable in rescuing their car from the mud, but Alvarez Williams remembered that other fish still remained, "their iridescent scales finely coated with sand, glistening faintly in the moonlight."[4]

Three years later, Alvarez Williams went fishing with some Cocopah friends and a CNN news crew investigating the plight of Cocopah living at the mouth of the Colorado River. Although it was sweltering in the middle of June, Cocopah fishermen and women took their boats to a spot near the mouth of the river and waited with their nets for the tide to come in. The Cocopah fished there because the Hardy River was too highly contaminated with pesticides from farms in the Mexicali Valley. When the tide reached eight feet, the Cocopah put in their boats and cast their nets while a pelican watched. Over a period of two hours, fishers in Alvarez Williams's boat caught only three corvina, each a foot long. Another Cocopah had better luck, filling two ice chests with corvina. They ended the day with a dinner of fresh fish, tortillas, and salsa prepared on the shores of the river.

In her writing, Alvarez Williams expresses her hope that the Cocopah's fishing prospects will improve and that they will once again be able to cultivate crops in the delta as they had in the days of José Joaquín Arrillaga (see "Deltascape: The Spanish Delta"). Alvarez Williams recalled a wild grain, *Distichlis palmeri,* that the Cocopah used to plant during the late nineteenth century. In 1885, an American researcher recorded that it "covered forty to fifty thousand acres." It was irrigated by tidewaters from the Gulf of California. By the end of the twentieth century, it was nearly gone, "a mere fringe along the river."[5]

On a reconnaissance trip to locate regional flora and fauna for a local museum exhibit in 1996, Alvarez Williams and her associates went to the eastern bank of the Colorado River near its mouth. She found some seeds of the vanishing grain in the remains of the high tide. They then looked for some of the blue crabs that often lived among the grain stalks. "I walked through the Distichlis patches," she recalled, "looking for the little blue crabs that like to keep it company, and found many of their mud hills, but no crabs, except for a few expired shells or claws. No live crabs." She remembered the crabs from earlier trips on the river, "clicking and snapping around us, very busy at the base of the Distichlis stems."[6] An ecologist living in the region alerted them to a muddy mound where one of the crabs was living.

Alvarez Williams completed her 1996 trip by going with the ecologist down to La Laguna del Indio, where many of the natural wonders of the delta continued to thrive, despite drastic changes in conditions. "We drove along the river and then along canal banks of some lovely lagoons edged with grasses, cattail, arrow weed, mesquite, and willow. Ducks, egrets, moorhen, heron, and others cruised water and sky, resting and nesting in the greenery—a birdwatcher's heaven." With a voice of hope amid the formidable challenges that confront the delta, Alvarez Williams reminded us, "The river needs friends . . . not only do the [Cocopah] need the river, so do we. And the riparian habitat needs the river. A healing thought: the Colorado River flowing through her delta once again, restoring life to the land and to the Sea of Cortez."[7]

Notes

Abbreviations Used in the Notes

ADLAPR	Arizona Division of Libraries, Archives, and Public Records, Phoenix
	AD Archives Division
	GO Record Group Governor's Office
	RL Research Library
AGN	Archivo General de la Nación
	AC Record Group Manuel Ávila Camacho
	LC Record Group Lázaro Cárdenas
	LM Record Group Adolfo López Mateos
	RC Record Group Adolfo Ruíz Cortines
AHA	Archivo Histórico del Agua
AHE	Archivo Histórico del Estado de Baja California
DOI	U.S. Department of the Interior
	RL Research Library
HLDAM	Hayden Library, Arizona State University, Department of Archives and Manuscripts, Tempe
	CHP Carl Hayden Papers
	JRP John J. Rhodes Papers
IID	Imperial Irrigation District Research Library
NACP	National Archives II
	DF Decimal File
	POL Political-Thematic File
	MEX-US U.S.–Mexican Relations File
UABCUM	Universidad Autónoma de Baja California, University Museum, Archives, Mexicali
YCWUA	Yuma County Water Users Association Historical Papers

Book Epigraph

1. Mulford Winsor Jr., "The Menace of the Colorado," Mulford Winsor Jr. Papers, RG 36, Historical Notes and Working Papers on Various Subjects, 1901–53, box 4, folder 33, ADLAPR-AD.

Introduction

1. Smythe, "An International Wedding," 293–94.
2. Ibid., 286.
3. Ibid.
4. Ibid., 288.
5. Ibid., 289.
6. Ibid.
7. Ibid., 292.
8. Ibid., 291.
9. Ibid.
10. See Kresen, "A Geologic Tour"; Simon, *The Date Palm,* 128–36; Tuttle, "Bats"; Heisey, "Sky-High over the Sonoran"; Lopez and Aurness, "A Worldly Wilderness"; Dunbier, *The Sonoran Desert.*
11. Smythe, "An International Wedding," 299–300.
12. Ibid., 300.
13. Ibid.
14. Clifford, "Plotting a Revival"; Yozwiak, "Two Waterways 'Endangered'"; Stan Grossfield, "A River Runs Dry."
15. The New River is not the only river that feeds the Salton Sea. In fact, the Alamo River contributes 600,000 acre-feet of water per year to the Salton Sea, while the New River only contributes 475,000 acre-feet. The Whitewater River and various other minor streams also contribute in excess of 250,000 acre-feet of water per year. See UC-MEXUS Border Water Project, *Alternative Futures,* 8–9.
16. Dillin, "Pollution Seeps"; "New River Named"; "In Health There Are No Borders"; LaRue, "Taking the Initiative."
17. Nevertheless, numerous studies from scholars on both sides of the border help us understand the development of specific parts of the binational region, including Anguiano Téllez, *Agricultura y migración;* Walther Meade, *El valle de Mexicali;* Martínez, *Historia de Baja California;* Instituto de Investigaciones Históricas, *Mexicali: Una historia;* deBuys and Meyers, *Salt Dreams;* Worster, *Rivers of Empire,* 194–212; Hundley, *The Great Thirst;* Fradkin, *A River No More,* 291–318; Metz, *Border,* 272–90.
18. Influential theoretical studies for this work included Martínez, *Troublesome Border;* Hall, *Social Change;* Piñera Ramírez, *Historiografía;* Langley, *Mexico and the United States;* Schoultz, *Beneath the United States;* Greenberg, "The Tragedy of Commoditization"; Sheridan, "Arizona."
19. Joaquín Arrillaga, *Diary of His Surveys,* 76.
20. Ibid.
21. Ibid., 78.

22. Ibid., 86. "Yurimuri" were probably tepary beans.

23. Ibid., 87.

24. Ibid., 89.

Chapter 1. The Twentieth-Century Ghost of William Walker

1. Comisión Encargada del Desarrollo de los Territorios Federales, "Cincuenta Pensamientos," November 11, 1936, AGN-LC, 437.1/413.

2. Moyano, "William Walker," 1:217–18; see also May, "Manifest Destiny's Filibusters."

3. Salas-Porras Soule, "Baja California," 45.

4. See Ceballos-Ramírez and Martínez, "Conflict and Accommodation."

5. See Chamberlin, "Mexican Colonization." Pablo Martínez explores Abelardo L. Rodríguez's efforts to stimulate Mexican development of the northern peninsula in *Historia de Baja California,* 540–44.

6. On American investment in Mexico during the Porfiriato, see Hart, *Revolutionary Mexico,* 129–62.

7. Herrera Carrillo, *Colonización del valle de Mexicali.*

8. Piñera Ramírez, "Guillermo Andrade."

9. Grijalva Larranaga, "Colonización del valle de Mexicali."

10. Ibid., 235.

11. See Henderson, "Agriculture and Livestock," 254.

12. Theodore Roosevelt, "Message from the President of the United States," January 12, 1907, in U.S. Department of State, *Papers Relating to the Foreign Relations of the United States, 1911,* 528–34.

13. Edwin A. Meserve, "Synopsis Statement of the History of the California Development Company and of the Diversion of the Colorado River into What Is Now Known as the Imperial Valley," in U.S. Senate, S. Doc. 212, 4:30–37.

14. Richard A. Ballinger to Philander C. Knox, October 17, 1910, in U.S. Department of State, *Papers Relating to the Foreign Relations of the United States, 1911,* 543–44.

15. Ibid., 543.

16. See Buffington, "Prohibition in the Borderlands."

17. Metz, *Border,* 265.

18. Blanquel, "Pensamiento filosófico," 356.

19. U.S. Department of State to the Mexican Embassy, February 12, 1911, in U.S. Department of State, *Papers Relating to the Foreign Relations of the United States, 1911,* 556.

20. Ibid., 557–60; Cosio Villegas, *Historia moderna de México,* 6:383–86, 429–31.

21. Acting Chief of the Division of Mexican Affairs, Hanna, to the First Secretary of the Mexican Embassy, Tellez, November 9, 1921, in U.S. Department of State, *Papers Relating to the Foreign Relations of the United States, 1921,* 2:521.

22. Message from Chargé in Mexico, Summerlin, to the Secretary of State, December 5, 1921, in ibid.

23. Hundley discusses the division of the Colorado River among seven states in the United States in *Water and the West.*

24. "Mexico Registers 'No Sale.'"

25. Ibid.

26. "Ashurst's Folly."

27. Cárdenas del Río, *Obras,* 1:293.

28. Ibid.

29. Ernesto Aguirre Colorado to Cárdenas, November 3, 1935, AGN-LC, 437.1/413.

30. Ibid.

31. To that end, the Mexican government curtailed Chinese, southern European, Indian, and Japanese immigration, and many foreigners were forced to leave the country. See Duncan, "The Chinese."

32. Lázaro Cárdenas, "A la Nación," AGN-LC, 437.1/413.

33. Comisión Encargada del Desarrollo de los Territorios Federales, "Cincuenta Pensamientos."

34. Anguiano Tellez, *Agricultura y migración,* 90–94.

35. Ibid., 113.

36. Lázaro Cárdenas to the Secretaría de Agricultura y Fomento, AGN-LC, 437.1/413.

37. Lázaro Cárdenas to the Secretaría de Relaciones Exteriores, AGN-LC, 437.1/413.

38. Lázaro Cárdenas to Navarro Cortina, January 20, 1937, AGN-LC, 437.1/413.

39. Antonio Basich and Bernardo Batiz to the Comisión Mixta Intersecretaría del Territorio Norte de Baja California, "Aguas Internacionales," December 24, 1935, AGN-LC, 437.1/413.

40. For early developments in the U.S. delta, see Pisani, *From Family Farm to Agribusiness,* 89–92, 309–19.

41. Cárdenas del Río, *Obras,* 1:441–42.

42. Ibid.

43. See Limerick, *The Legacy of Conquest.*

44. Ibid., 15, emphasis added.

45. See Whiteford, "Troubled Waters."

46. Anguiano Téllez, *Agricultura y migración*, 105–7.

47. Knight assesses the Cárdenas legacy in "Cardenismo"; Hernández Chávez also examines the Cárdenas era in *La mecánica cardenista*.

48. See "The End of U.S. Intervention."

49. Ceballos-Ramírez and Martínez, "Conflict and Accommodation," 157.

50. Henry Frauenfelder to Carl Hayden, March 5, 1937, YCWUA.

Chapter 2. "Our 'Good Neighbors'"

1. The title of this chapter is taken from a letter from E. Aguirre Camacho to President Manuel Ávila Camacho, n.d., AGN-AC, 561.3/11-2.

2. Hugo Farmer, Testimony, Arizona Commission of the Colorado River Basin States, June 22–23, 1938, Phoenix, ADLAPR-RL, 42–43.

3. E. Aguirre Camacho to Ávila Camacho.

4. Governor Crel R. Sánchez Taboada to J. Jesus González Gallo, October 29, 1941, AGN-AC.

5. Ezequiel Padilla, "Condiciones en que se encuentran las plantas de bombeo para regar las tierras ribereñas del río Colorado, B.C.," Departamento Jurídico y Consultativo, Oficina de Límites y Aguas, August 24, 1942, AGN-AC, 561.3/11-1.

6. Ibid.

7. Armando Lizarraga to Ávila Camacho, April 8, 1943; Sanchez Taboada to Ávila Camacho, April 12, 1943; Sanchez Taboada to Ávila Camacho, April 15, 1943; Distribuidora del Pacífico, S.A., to Ávila Camacho, April 30, 1943; Sánchez Taboada to Ávila Camacho, April 30, 1943, AGN-AC, 561.3/11-2.

8. U.S. Department of State, *Foreign Relations of the United States: Diplomatic Papers, 1943*, 6:611–13.

9. Ibid., 6:614–15; Sánchez Taboada to Ávila Camacho, June 16, 1943; Sánchez Taboada to Ávila Camacho, November 17, 1943, AGN-AC, 561.3/11-2.

10. On July 4, 1944, Sánchez Taboada informed Ávila Camacho that the releases from Boulder and Parker Dams had been decreased considerably. Mexicans were again prohibited from building a temporary dam below Alamo Canal. See AGN-AC, 561.3/11-2.

11. See Langley, *Mexico and the United States*, 21–36.

12. Spruille Braden, Acting Secretary of State, to Ambassador Thurston in Mexico, August 16, 1946, in U.S. Department of State, *Foreign Relations of the United States: Diplomatic Papers, 1946*, 11:1030–33.

13. Ugo Carusi, Commissioner of the Immigration and Naturalization Service, to the Secretary of State, Philadelphia, January 11, 1954, in U.S. Department of State, *Foreign Relations of the United States: Diplomatic Papers, 1945*, 9:1140.

14. Ibid., 9:1139.

15. Ibid., 9:1140.

16. Memorandum of Conversation by the First Secretary of the Mexican Embassy, S. E. O'Donoghue, Mexico City, January 31, 1946, in U.S. Department of State, *Foreign Relations of the United States: Diplomatic Papers, 1946,* 11:1018.

17. Memorandum of Telephone Conversation by Mr. William G. MacLean of the Division of Mexican Affairs, Washington, D.C., December 11, 1944, in U.S. Department of State, *Foreign Relations of the United States: Diplomatic Papers, 1944,* 7:1333.

18. See Carusi to the Secretary of State, in U.S. Department of State, *Foreign Relations of the United States: Diplomatic Papers, 1945,* 9:1140; Ambassador White to the Secretary of State, Mexico City, August 14, 1953, in U.S. Department of State, *Foreign Relations of the United States: Diplomatic Papers, 1952–1954,* 4:1341–46.

19. See E. F. Sanguenetti to Carl Hayden, October 7, 1942; A. O. Broussard (employee of Sanguenetti) to Hayden, November 28, 1942; Don Gustin, Secretary, L. M. McLaren Produce Company, to Senator Hayden, HLDAM-CHP, MS 1, box 548, folder 15.

20. See Henry Frauenfelder to Carl Hayden re: Farm Labor on Yuma Project, October 9, 1942, HLDAM-CHP, MS 1, box 548, folder 15.

21. Ambassador White to Secretary of State, Mexico City, December 31, 1946, in U.S. Department of State, *Foreign Relations of the United States: Diplomatic Papers, 1946,* vol. 11.

22. Carusi to the Secretary of State, in U.S. Department of State, *Foreign Relations of the United States: Diplomatic Papers, 1945,* 9:1140.

23. Philip G. Bruton to Carl Hayden, October 21, 1944; Albert Del Guercio, September 23, 1944, Los Angeles, HLDAM-CHP, MS 1.

24. Metz, *Border,* 269.

25. Ibid.; Board of Governors, March 6, 1944, YCWUA.

26. Henry Frauenfelder to Ernest W. McFarland, March 27, 1944, YCWUA.

27. Ibid.

28. U.S. Senate Committee on Foreign Relations, *Water Treaty with Mexico,* 234–35.

29. Ibid., 226.

30. See *Congressional Record,* 79th Cong., 1st sess., April 18, 1945, 91, pt. 3:3492.

31. Enríquez Coyro, *El tratado entre México y los Estados Unidos,* 1:612–16.

32. Adolfo Orive Alba, "Address of Engineer Adolfo Orive Alba, Secretary of Hydraulic Resources upon the Inauguration of the 'Morelos Dam,' September 23, 1950," ADLAPR-AD-GO, box 45.

33. Piñera Ramírez, "El oro blanco en Mexicali," 109.

34. Martínez Zepeda, "Entrevista," app. 18.

35. Ibid.

36. Espinoza, "Estudio agrológico preliminar," 89; Federico Ibarra Muñóz, "Rehabilitación del distrito de riego no. 14 río Colorado, B.C.," n.d., n.p., AHA, 9.

37. Minutes from April 20, 1955, Meeting between General Government Secretary and Mexicali Interest Groups, AGN-RC, 404.2/296.

38. Mexicali and San Luis Valley Representatives to President Adolfo Ruiz Cortines, April 22, 1955, AGN-LM, 404.1/502.

39. Notes on the Irrigation District and Mexican Subsidiary Company, June 13, 1935, Compañía de Terrenos y Aguas de la B.C., S.A., Various Subjects—1911–57, IID.

40. Presidential Decree Regarding Coordination of Works for Entire Use of Colorado River Water, under Supervision of National Irrigation Commission, July 21, 1941, Compañía de Terrenos y Aguas de la B.C., S.A., Various Subjects—1911–57, IID.

41. IID officials feared that if the dam caused a flood it would take the path of least resistance, down into El Centro and the Imperial Valley.

42. Eng. Méndez to Cia. de T. y A. Regarding Use and Ownership of Alamo Canal, July 14, 1953, Compañía de Terrenos y Aguas de la B.C., S.A., Various Subjects—1911–57, IID.

43. Atty. Barcenas to Atty. Orcí, July 5, 1951, Compañía de Terrenos y Aguas de la B.C., S.A., Negotiations with Mexico re: Water Service to All American Canal and Sale of Assets, IID.

44. Memorandum Relative to Interview with Secretary of Hydraulic Resources in Order to Define Situation of Compañía in Relation to Inauguration of the Morelos Dam, September 21, 1951, Compañía de Terrenos y Aguas de la B.C., S.A., Negotiations with Mexico re: Water Service to All American Canal and Sale of Assets, IID.

45. Memorandum re: Arturo Orcí's Petition to the Secretary of Foreign Relations for 5-Year Extension of Duration of Compañía, June 23, 1960; Department of Foreign Relations to Atty. Orcí Denying Petition for 5-Year Extension of Duration of Cia., August 16, 1960, Compañía de Terrenos y Aguas de la B.C. Negotiations with Mexico re: Water Service Subsequent to AAC Sale of Assets of Compañía, vol. 2, 1960–62, IID.

46. Official Registration of Minutes of August 22, 1960, August 25, 1960, Compañía de Terrenos y Aguas de la B.C. Negotiations with Mexico re: Water Service Subsequent to AAC Sale of Assets of Compañía, vol. 2, 1960–62, IID.

47. Orcí to Bowker, November 19, 1960, Compañía de Terrenos y Aguas de la

B.C. Negotiations with Mexico re: Water Service Subsequent to AAC Sale of Assets of Compañía, vol. 2, 1960–62, IID.

48. Memorandum re: Interviews that Messrs. Bowker and Orcí Had with Secretary of Hydraulic Resources, February 8, 1961, Compañía de Terrenos y Aguas de la B.C. Negotiations with Mexico re: Water Service Subsequent to AAC Sale of Assets of Compañía, vol. 2, 1960–62, IID.

49. Compañía to Orcí, February 17, 1961, Compañía de Terrenos y Aguas de la B.C. Negotiations with Mexico re: Water Service Subsequent to AAC Sale of Assets of Compañía, vol. 2, 1960–62, IID.

50. Revised Offer Made by Secretary of Hydraulic Resources to Representatives of Compañía, June 21, 1961; Liquidators to IID Board of Directors Transmitting Two Notes Issued by Treasury Department of Mexican Government, August 22, 1961, Compañía de Terrenos y Aguas de la B.C. Negotiations with Mexico re: Water Service Subsequent to AAC Sale of Assets of Compañía, vol. 2, 1960–62, IID.

51. Leopold, *A Sand County Almanac,* 150–56.

52. Ibid., 157–58.

Chapter 3. Saline Solutions

1. At the time, Warne was assistant commissioner of the Bureau of Reclamation. See U.S. House Committee on Irrigation and Reclamation, *Reauthorizing Gila Project,* 14.

2. Engineer Luís Cabrera explained the geographic relationship between the various valleys in the delta: "[The] Mexicali Valley, [the San Luis Valley], the Imperial Valley, and the Yuma Valley are really all one valley and . . . all of the irrigation districts in this one big valley are, taken together, the last user on the river" ("Use of the Waters," 30–33).

3. Lenora Werley, "U.S. Takes Sudden Interest in Mexicali Water," *Arizona Daily Star,* December 17, 1961, HLDAM-CHP, MS 1, box 253, folder 8.

4. Ibid.

5. Hundley discusses the salinity crisis as an extension of the Mexican Water Treaty of 1944 in *Dividing the Waters,* 173–81. Fradkin focuses on the environmental and international ramifications of the crisis in *A River No More,* 291–318. Metz underscores Carl Hayden's reluctance to help Mexico in *Border,* 272–90. Furnish and Landham provide the best study of the Mexicali area prior to and during the crisis in "El convenio de 1973."

6. See Baker, "History of Irrigation in Yuma County," in *Colorado River Water.*

7. Refnes, Ely, Beck and Co., "Mohawk Municipal Water Conservation District and Gila Valley Power District," HLDAM-CHP, MS 1, box 652, folder 1.

8. See the Gila Project Association, *A Small Appropriation for the Gila Project This Year Will Start Canal Work to Take Colorado River Water to the Thirsty Lands of the Mohawk Valley,* 1940, ADLAPR-RL.

9. Hugo Farmer to Hayden, January 25, 1941, HLDAM-CHP, MS 1, box 120, folder 25.

10. William Warne to Hayden, September 9, 1944, HLDAM-CHP, MS 1, box 652, folder 21.

11. Farmer to H. W. Bashore, September 23, 1944, HLDAM-CHP, MS 1, box 652, folder 21.

12. Leon Jacobs to Farmer, August 18, 1944, HLDAM-CHP, MS 1, box 652, folder 21.

13. U.S. House Committee on Irrigation and Reclamation, *Reauthorizing Gila Project,* 10, 12–13.

14. Farmer to Hayden, January 14, 1941, HLDAM-CHP, MS 1, box 120, folder 25.

15. Farmer, "The Gila Project," Statement of Hugo B. Farmer, April 17, 1945, HLDAM-CHP, MS 1, box 120, folder 25.

16. The Colorado River Compact was proposed in 1921 by Colorado politicians who feared that the lower basin states, particularly Arizona and California, would appropriate all the river's water. The compact apportioned each state in the basin a predetermined quantity of water. It was signed without Arizona's approval in 1921. See Hundley, *Water and the West.*

17. Houghton, "Problems of the Colorado River."

18. Ibid., 639.

19. Farmer to Hayden, January 15, 1941, HLDAM-CHP, MS 1, box 120, folder 25.

20. Farmer to Hayden, January 25, 1941, HLDAM-CHP, MS 1, box 120, folder 25.

21. Ibid.

22. U.S. House Committee on Irrigation and Reclamation, *Reauthorizing Gila Project,* 534–35.

23. Farmer to Hayden, HLDAM-CHP, MS 1, box 610, folder 7.

24. Rice, *Carl Hayden,* 71.

25. John Page to Hayden, February 13, 1941, HLDAM-CHP, MS 1, box 120, folder 1.

26. Ibid.

27. Ibid.

28. Ibid.

29. U.S. House Committee on Irrigation and Reclamation, *Reauthorizing Gila Project,* 387.

30. U.S. Senate Committee on Foreign Relations, *Water Treaty with Mexico,* 271.

31. Farmer to Hayden, April 3, 1944, HLDAM-CHP, MS 1, box 652, folder 23.

32. U.S. Senate Committee on Irrigation and Reclamation, *Hearings: Arizona Water Resources,* 200. Hundley has noted that 450 ppm was the desired level of salt for water delivered to Mexico (*Dividing the Waters,* 173).

33. U.S. Senate Committee on Irrigation and Reclamation, *Hearings: Arizona Water Resources,* 204, 205, 208, 213.

34. Ibid., 209.

35. Ibid.

36. Ibid.

37. Ibid., 210.

38. Ibid., 211.

39. Ibid., 201.

40. Ibid., 212.

41. U.S. House Committee on Irrigation and Reclamation, *Reauthorizing Gila Project,* 46.

42. Ibid.

43. Carson, "Arizona's Interest."

44. U.S. House Committee on Irrigation and Reclamation, *Reauthorizing Gila Project,* 770–71.

45. Reisner, *Cadillac Desert,* 479–83.

46. Baker, *Colorado River Water.*

47. Hundley, *Dividing the Waters,* 173.

48. W. A. Dexheimer to Hayden, February 4, 1957, HLDAM-CHP, MS 1, box 479, folder 7, emphasis added.

49. Exhibit E, "1958, 1959, and 1960 Crop Histories of 13 Farms Selected at Random Through the District," HLDAM-CHP, MS 1, box 300, folder 27.

50. Ibid.

51. Ibid., 5.

52. USBR—Gila Project, "Wellton-Mohawk Drainage Facilities," HLDAM-CHP, MS 1, box 330, folder 27.

53. Ibid.

54. Wilburn J. Brown to Frank Batley, February 24, 1961, HLDAM-CHP, MS 1, box 330, folder 27.

55. J. D. Mansfield to Paul Eaton, June 23, 1959, HLDAM-CHP, MS 1, box 330, folder 27.

56. Rollie Hoyt Keller to Hayden, January 23, 1959, HLDAM-CHP, MS 1, box 330, folder 27.

57. I have adapted my discussion of western perceptions of victimization from Limerick, *The Legacy of Conquest,* 35–54.

58. Fred G. Aandahl to Hayden, HLDAM-CHP, MS 1, box 330, folder 27.

59. John Haugh to Paul Fannin, May 8, 1964, HLDAM-CHP, MS 1, box 330, folder 31.

60. Sam Dick to Hayden, March 13, 1962, HLDAM-CHP, MS 1.

61. Gustavo Vildosola Almada to Hayden, February 9, 1962, HLDAM-CHP, MS 1, box 253, folder 8.

62. Hayden, "Remarks by Senator Carl Hayden, April 26, 1962, Concerning Complaints by Mexico on Quality of Colorado River Water," HLDAM-CHP, MS 1, box 293, folder 1.

63. Hayden to Dean Rusk, December 20, 1961, HLDAM-CHP, MS 1.

64. Hayden, "Remarks by Senator Carl Hayden, April 26, 1962," HLDAM-CHP, MS 1, box 293, folder 4.

65. William A. Couple to Hayden, July 28, 1964, HLDAM-CHP, MS 1, box 352.

66. Metz, *Border,* 280.

67. Hundley, *Dividing the Waters,* 179.

68. Westover, Keddie, and Choules to Hayden, September 21, 1967, HLDAM-CHP, MS 1, box 352.

69. Ibid.

70. Betty Lucas to Stewart Udall, September 5, 1965, HLDAM-CHP, MS 1, box 333, folder 15.

71. USBR Commissioner to Hayden, September 24, 1965, HLDAM-CHP, MS 1, box 333, folder 15.

72. Fradkin notes, "It was Echeverria's task, as one writer commented, to 'restore the revolutionary mask,' which had slipped badly in recent years" (*A River No More,* 305).

73. Ibid., 308.

74. Fradkin observes: "While subject to 'real domestic pressures,' the Mexican President 'had consciously agitated the problem and lent official support to exaggerated claims apparently in an effort to arouse the country and make it a national issue' according to a confidential Department of State memorandum sent to Kissinger from the White House" (ibid., 307–8).

75. Sheridan discusses the interaction between political systems and the environment in *Arizona.* Also see Worster, *An Unsettled Country.*

76. Bernal Aguire, *Compendio histórico-biográfico.*

77. Ibid.

78. For an overview of the topic of salinity in river basins throughout world history, see Pillsbury, "The Salinity of Rivers."

79. McCully, *Silenced Rivers*, 40–41.

80. Postel offers an excellent historical overview of salinity in arid regions as well as possible solutions to combat salinity in *Pillar of Sand*, 18–29, 102–9.

Chapter 4. Water and the Landscapes of Power in the Mexicali Valley

1. Cavise, "Because of NAFTA"; for a detailed documentary history of the Chiapas uprisings, see Womack, *Zapata and the Mexican Revolution;* Golden, "Hate, Neglect."

2. Woodward to Chayes, Memorandum, "Delivery of Colorado River Water to Mexico," November 14, 1961, NACP, RG 59, DF, 1960–63, 611.12322/11-1461.

3. Woodward to Udall, November 17, 1961, NACP, RG 59, DF, 1960–63, 611.12322/11-1761.

4. Ibid.

5. Ibid.

6. Ibid.

7. Carrillo to Rusk, November 9, 1961, NACP, RG 59, DF, 1960–63, 611.12322/11-961.

8. Carr to Rusk, December 11, 1961, NACP, RG 59, DF, 1960–63, 611.12322/12-1161.

9. Rusk to Carrillo, December 20, 1961, NACP, RG 59, DF, 1960–63, 611.12322/11-961.

10. U.S. Department of State, Memorandum of Conversation, "Salinity of Colorado River Water," December 20, 1961, NACP, RG 59, DF, 1960–63, 611.12322/12-2061.

11. Rusk to Carrillo, January 16, 1962, NACP, RG 59, DF, 1960–63, 611.12322/11-961.

12. Memorandum of Conversation, "Salinity of Water in the Colorado," December 22, 1961, NACP, RG 59, DF, 1960–63, 611.12322/12-2261.

13. U.S. Department of State, "Joint Action Being Considered to Alleviate Salinity on Lower Colorado River," February 9, 1962, NACP, RG 59, DF, 1960–63, 611.12322/2-962.

14. Dispatch from Boyd to U.S. Department of State, February 13, 1962, NACP, RG 59, DF, 1960–63, 611.12322/2-1362.

15. Gulick to Rusk, March 6, 1962, NACP, RG 59, DF, 1960–63, 611.12322/3-662.

16. Memorandum of Conversation, "Colorado River Salinity Problem," March 9, 1962, NACP, RG 59, DF, 1960–63, 611.12322/3-962.

17. Leon Bernstein and Joseph Friedkin, "Salinity of Colorado River Waters," November 21, 1961, NACP, RG 59, DF, 1960–63, 611.12322.

18. Mexican Ministry of Agriculture and Livestock, "The Salt Water Problem of the Mexicali and San Luis Valleys," in Julian Rodríguez Adame to Mann, February 12, 1962, NACP, RG 59, DF, 1960–63, 611.12322.

19. Bill Blackledge, Report, February 1962, contained in J. F. Friedkin to Robert M. Sayre, March 6, 1962, NACP, RG 59, DF, 1960–63, 611.12322/3-662.

20. Martin to McGhee, "Study of Colorado River Salinity Problem," NACP, RG 59, DF, 1960–63, 611.12322/4-2562.

21. A draft of the study is included in "Joint Report of United States and Mexican Expert Panels on Colorado River Salinity Problems," May 8, 1962, NACP, RG 59, DF, 1960–63, 611.12322/5-2862; see also Martin to Rusk, "Letter to Foreign Minister Tello of Mexico on Salinity Problem," June 8, 1962, NACP, RG 59, DF, 1960–63, 611.12322/6-862.

22. "Comments of Department of Health, Education, and Welfare on Report of United States Advisory Panel International Boundary and Water Commission," in Secretary of Health, Education, and Welfare to Rusk, October 30, 1962, NACP, RG 59, DF, 1960–63, 611.12322/10-2462.

23. McGhee to Martin, "Mexican Program for Rehabilitation of Mexicali Valley," June 5, 1962, NACP, RG 59, DF, 1960–63, 611.12322/6-562.

24. John Hugh Crimmins to Martin, "Colorado River Salinity Problem," July 19, 1962, NACP, RG 59, DF, 1960–63, 611.12322/7-1962.

25. U.S. Department of the Interior/Bureau of Reclamation, "Special Studies: Delivery of Water to Mexico," February 1963, vii, DOI-RL.

26. Ibid., 77.

27. Carrillo to Rusk, May 17, 1963, NACP, RG 59, POL 33-1 MEX-US, 1963.

28. Mann to Rusk, August 21, 1963, NACP, RG 59, POL 33-1 MEX-US, 1963.

29. Blackledge to Robert Allen, February 7, 1964, enclosed with Allen to U.S. Department of State, "Evidence of Effects Suffered Due to Increase in Salinity [of] Colorado River Waters Delivered to Mexico," February 13, 1964, NACP, RG 59, POL 33-1 MEX-US, 1963, folder 1/1/64.

30. Carrillo and Sayre, Memorandum of Conversation, "Colorado River Salinity Problem," January 6, 1964, NACP, RG 59, POL 33-1 MEX-US, 1963, folder 1/1/64.

31. Memorandum of Conversation, "Joint Communiqué on Meeting of Presidents of United States and Mexico," February 21, 1964, NACP, RG 59, POL 33-1 MEX-US, 1963, folder 1/1/64.

32. Sayre to Mann, Memorandum, "Salinity Problem on Lower Colorado," March 13, 1964, NACP, RG 59, POL 33-1 MEX-US, 1963, folder 3/1/64.

33. Friedkin to Sayre, April 18, 1964, NACP, RG 59, POL 33-1 MEX-US, 1963, folder 4/1/64.

34. "Report by Committee of 14 on Mexican Salinity Problem," May 9, 1963, NACP, RG 59, POL 33-1 MEX-US, 1963.

35. James Boyd, Dispatch, "Salinity of Colorado River Waters—Mexicali Reaction," NACP, RG 59, DF, 1960–63, 611.12322/12-761.

36. Journalist Lenora Werley estimated that there were as many as 35,000 protesters on December 14, 1961. See chapter 4.

37. Mann to Secretary of State, December 15, 1961, NACP, RG 59, DF, 1960–63, 611.12322/12-1561.

38. Boyd to U.S. Department of State, Dispatch, December 15, 1961, NACP, RG 59, DF, 1960–63, 611.12322/12-1561.

39. Bernal Aguire, *Compendio histórico-biográfico,* 382–85.

40. Boyd to Rusk, January 29, 1962, NACP, RG 59, DF, 1960–63, 611.12322/1-2962.

41. Ibid.

42. Mann to Rusk, December 18, 1961; Boyd to Rusk, NACP, RG 59, DF, 1960–63, 611.12322/12-1861.

43. Mann and Sayre, Memorandum of Conversation, "Salinity of Colorado River Water," December 20, 1961, NACP, RG 59, DF, 1960–63, 611.12322/12-2061.

44. Boyd to U.S. Department of State, Dispatch, February 6, 1962, NACP, RG 59, DF, 1960–63, 611.12322/2-662.

45. Mann to U.S. Department of State, "Salinity of Colorado River Waters," February 16, 1962, NACP, RG 59, DF, 1960–63, 611.12322/2-1662.

46. American Embassy, Mexico City, to U.S. Department of State, "President López Comments on Colorado River Salinity Problem," February 16, 1962, NACP, RG 59, DF, 1960–63.

47. Mann to U.S. Department of State, "Salinity of Colorado River Waters," February 21, 1962, NACP, RG 59, DF, 1960–63, 611.12322/2-2162.

48. Robert W. Adams to U.S. Department of State, Foreign Post Dispatch, "Ejido Leader Garzón of Mexicali Approaches Embassy on Claim Against the U.S.," June 6, 1962, NACP, RG 59, DF, 1960–63, 611.12322/6-662.

49. Memorandum, Liga Agraria Estatal de Baja California, March 6, 1962; Moises Maislin Leal, "Informa situación prevalenciente en el distrito de riego," March 8, 1962; Memorandum, n.d.; Dirreción de Agricultura y Ganadería del Estado, "Informes de labores correspondiente a los meses de marzo y abril de 1962," AHE, Fondo Territorio Norte, Sección Agricultura y Fomento, Serie Agricultura y Ganadería, box 368.

50. Alfonso Garzón to Oscar González Lugo, December 13, 1962, AHE, Fondo Territorio Norte, Sección Agricultura y Fomento, Serie Agricultura y Ganadería, box 368.

51. Garzón to Eligio Esquivel Méndez, February 13, 1963; Comisionado Ejidal del Ejido Xochimilco, Municipio de Mexicali, Estado de Baja California, to Alfredo del Mazo, February 18, 1963; Garzón to Adolfo López Mateos, n.d., AHE, Fondo Territorio Norte, Sección Agricultura y Fomento, Serie Agricultura y Ganadería, box 366.

52. Minutes, March 9, 1963, AHE, Fondo Territorio Norte, Sección Agricultura y Fomento, Serie Agricultura y Ganadería, box 366.

53. Garzón to Juan Muñoz Martinez, March 23, 1963, AHE, Fondo Territorio Norte, Sección Agricultura y Fomento, Serie Agricultura y Ganadería, box 366, 671.12/571.

54. Freeman to Rusk, May 21, 1964, NACP, RG 59, POL 33-1, MEX-US, folder 5/1/64.

55. Federación Estatal Campesina de Sonora to President Johnson, November 7, 1964, AHE.

56. Boyd to U.S. Department of State, "Salinity of the Colorado River Waters: Committee for Defense of Mexicali Valley Reactivated," March 17, 1964, NACP, RG 59, POL 33-1, MEX-US, folder 3/1/64.

57. The Mexican chief of immigration in Mexicali, for example, reported to the American consulate that "the protest demonstrations . . . were interfering with the current political contest [in reference to the presidential election]." See Boyd to U.S. Department of State, "Salinity of Colorado River Waters—Demonstrations Against," May 15, 1964, NACP, RG 59, POL 33-1, MEX-US, folder 5/1/64. An example of Mexican officials using radical protest (something they generally detested) to their advantage can be seen in an exchange between Mexican senator Vildosola and Ambassador Freeman. Vildosola warned Freeman of an upcoming "mammoth" demonstration on July 12, 1964, and suggested that the United States find a resolution to the problem before then. As Freeman explained the complications of finding a resolution because of domestic concerns with the Colorado River Basin states in the United States, Vildosola warned that he might not be able to guarantee that these demonstrations would be peaceful like those in the past. "He expressed his full understanding of the dangers of communists and other extremists in seeking to turn the demonstrations to their own ends," Freeman noted, "but he in no way accepted the inference of the desirability of postponing the scheduled nation-wide demonstrations on July 12." See Freeman to Rusk, June 19, 1964, NACP, RG 59, POL 33-1, MEX-US, folder 6/6/64.

58. Boyd to U.S. Department of State, "Salinity of Colorado River Waters—Demonstrations Against."

59. Freeman to Rusk, August 6, 1964, NACP, RG 59, POL 33-1, MEX-US, folder 8/1/64; see also Comité de Defensa del Valle de Mexicali to Centrales Obreras y

Campesinas, Organizaciones de la Initiativa Privada, y la Opinión Pública Nacional, August 5, 1964, AHE, Fondo Territorio Norte, Sección Agricultura y Fomento, Serie Agricultura y Ganadería, box 368.

60. Garzón to Aurelio Flores Valenzuela, August 9, 1964, AHE, Fondo Territorio Norte, Sección Agricultura y Fomento, Serie Agricultura y Ganadería, box 368.

61. Feldman to U.S. Department of State, "Salinity Demonstration Postponed," November 19, 1964, NACP, RG 59, POL 33-1, MEX-US, folder 10/1/64.

62. Feldman to U.S. Department of State, "Round-up of Mexicali Reaction to the Solution of the Salinity Problem," April 5, 1965, NACP, RG 59, POL 33-1, MEX-US, folder 4/1/65.

63. Humberto Hernández to J. William Fulbright, May 23, 1964, UABCUM, Fondo Rafael Martínez Retes, folder 10 (1964).

64. See chapter 6.

65. Kleinman and Brown, *Colorado River Salinity*, 8.

66. Gardner and Stewart, "Agriculture and Salinity Control," 65.

67. Bernal, *A Report on Salinity Operations;* for other helpful references on water quality, see Richards, ed., *Diagnosis and Improvement.*

68. Smith, "Rebels Take to Heartland"; McGirk, "Mexico's Rebellious Road Show."

69. Fradkin, *A River No More,* 319.

70. Ibid., 324.

71. Ibid., 327.

72. Ibid., 338–39.

73. Ibid., 339.

Chapter 5. Salt of the River, Salt of the Earth

1. Rafael Martínez Retes to Manuel J. Tello, November 19, 1963, UABCUM, Fondo Rafael Martínez Retes, folder 8, "Plan Udall, Estados Unidos."

2. El Comité de Defensa del Valle de Mexicali to Gustavo Diaz Ordaz, October 28, 1965, AHE, Fondo Territorio Norte, Sección Agricultura y Fomento, Serie Agricultura y Ganadería, box 368.

3. Feldman to U.S. Department of State, "Local Reaction to Drilling of Yuma Mesa Wells," November 12, 1965, NACP, RG 59, POL 33-1, MEX-US, folder 11/1/65.

4. Hayden to Rusk, December 13, 1965, NACP, RG 59, POL 33-1, MEX-US, folder 12/13/65.

5. Sayre to Rusk, "Lower Colorado River Groundwater and Salinity Problem with Mexico," March 22, 1966, NACP, RG 59, POL 33-1, MEX-US, folder 3/18/66.

6. Friedkin to Terry Leonhardy, June 16, 1966, NACP, RG 59, POL 33-1, MEX-US, folder 5/4/66.

7. Sayre and Friedkin to U.S. Embassy, Mexico City, May 27, 1967, NACP, RG 59, POL 33-1, MEX-US, folder 1/1/67.

8. Feldman to U.S. Department of State, "An International Treaty on the Use of Subterranean Water Is Still an Issue," December 12, 1967, NACP, RG 59, POL 33-1, MEX-US, folder 1/1/67.

9. Antonio Coria to Antonio Rodríguez L., "Aguas del subsuelo en la región de Sonoita a S. Luís Río Colorado, Son.," AHA, Fondo Consultativo Técnico, box 871, expediente 8231. The ban on additional wells was in place as early as 1960. See letter from Roberto Barrios to C. Secretario de Recursos Hidráulicos, "Se solicita se considera proposición para poder aprovechar los terrenos comprendidos en la región de Sonoita a San Luís Río Colorado," November 1, 1960, AHA, Fondo Consultativo Técnico, box 871, expediente 8231.

10. Heinz Lessert Jones, Eduardo Paredes Arellano, and Luis Hernandez Torrens to Aurelio Benassini V., Chief of Technical Consultation, July 9, 1968, AHA, Fondo Consultativo Técnico, box 871, expediente 8231.

11. "Conclusiones y recomendaciones de la junta celebrada el día 2 de marzo en relación con la explotación de aguas subterráneas en la Mesa de San Luís, Sonora," author unknown, n.d., AHA, Fondo Consultativo Técnico, box 871, expediente 8231.

12. J. F. Friedkin to Chris G. Petrow, February 6, 1970, NACP, RG 59, POL 33-1, MEX-US, folder 1/1/70.

13. McBride to Rogers, February 1972, NACP, RG 59, POL 33-1, MEX-US, folder 1/25/72.

14. Feldman to State, "Steps to Protect Mexicali Valley Water Table," May 26, 1972, NACP, RG 59, box 2482, folder 1/25/72; see Benjamin Granados Dominguez, "Distrito de riego no. 14, río Colorado, B.C. y Son.—Generalidades," in Secretaría de Recursos Hidráulicos, *Memoria de la primera reunión,* 47–55; Walther Meade, *El valle de Mexicali,* 155–65.

15. McBride to Rogers, NACP, RG 59, box 2482, folder 6/1/72.

16. Commissioner Friedkin to Country Director Robert A. Stevenson, "Groundwaters—Lower Colorado River Basin, Technical Joint Meeting—United States and Mexican Engineers, Phoenix—December 12, 1972," NACP, RG 59, box 2482, folder 10/3/72.

17. Feldman to U.S. Department of State, "Salinity Still in the News," June 7, 1966, NACP, RG 59, POL 33-1, MEX-US, folder 5/4/66.

18. Memorandum of Conversation, "Colorado River Salinity, Meeting between

President Johnson and President Diaz Ordaz," December 3, 1966, NACP, RG 59, POL 33-1, MEX-US, folder 11/22/66.

19. Freeman to U.S. Embassy, Mexico City, April 3, 1965, NACP, RG 59, POL 33-1, MEX-US, folder 4/1/65.

20. U.S. Embassy, Mexico City, to Rogers, August 8, 1969, NACP, RG 59, POL 33-1, MEX-US, folder 11/1/69.

21. Feldman to U.S. Department of State, "Wheat Producers Claim Damage Caused by Salinity," April 7, 1965, NACP, RG 59, POL 33-1, MEX-US, folder 4/1/65.

22. Ibid.; Freeman to U.S. Department of State, April 3, 1965, NACP, RG 59, POL 33-1, MEX-US, folder 4/1/65.

23. Sayre to Terrance Leonardy, June 3, 1965, NACP, RG 59, POL 33-1, MEX-US, folder 6/1/65.

24. Freeman to Rusk, June 8, 1965, NACP, RG 59, POL 33-1, MEX-US, folder 6/1/65.

25. Rusk to U.S. Embassy, Mexico City, June 17, 1965, NACP, RG 59, POL 33-1, MEX-US, folder 6/17/65.

26. Feldman to U.S. Department of State, "Comments of the Secretary of Hydraulic Resources on Salinity and a Columnist's Reaction," March 11, 1969, NACP, RG 59, POL 33-1, MEX-US, folder 1/1/69.

27. Feldman to U.S. Department of State, "Salinity Still an Issue," April 3, 1969, NACP, RG 59, POL 33-1, MEX-US, folder 1/1/69.

28. Feldman to U.S. Department of State, "Salinity Still an Issue," July 11, 1969, NACP, RG 59, POL 33-1, MEX-US, folder 1/1/69.

29. Feldman to U.S. Department of State, "Conflicting Mexican Opinions on Salinity," July 11, 1969; McBride to Rogers, August 8, 1969, NACP, RG 59, POL 33-1, MEX-US, folder 11/1/69.

30. "Problema de la salinidad creado por la calidad de las aguas, que Estados Unidos entrega a México conforme al Tratado de 1944," AHA, Fondo Consultativo Técnico, box 13, expediente 61, 2–3.

31. Ibid., 5.

32. Ibid., 18.

33. Ibid., 19.

34. Ibid., 20.

35. Ibid., 20–21.

36. Charles H. McBride to Rogers, March 16, 1970, NACP, RG 59, POL 33-1, MEX-US, folder 1/1/70.

37. Memorandum of Conversation, "Means of Improving U.S. Performance under 1965 Salinity Agreement with Mexico," February 13, 1970; Memorandum of

Conversation, "Lower Colorado River Salinity Problem with Mexico," April 16, 1970, NACP, RG 59, POL 33-1, MEX-US, folder 1/1/70.

38. Carrillo Flores and Hernandez Teran, "Conclusiones de la reunión celebrada en la SRE," July 24, 1969[?], AHA, Fondo Consultativo Técnico, box 13, expediente 61.

39. McBride to Rogers, June 2, 1970, NACP, RG 59, POL 33-1, MEX-US, folder 1/1/70; Kubish to Rogers, October 23, 1970, NACP, RG 59, POL 33-1, MEX-US, folder 7/1/70.

40. McBride to Rogers, May 5, 1970, NACP, RG 59, POL 33-1, MEX-US, folder 1/1/70.

41. McBride to Rogers, June 2, 1970, NACP, RG 59, POL 33-1, MEX-US, folder 1/1/70.

42. Kubish to Rogers, September 25, 1970, NACP, RG 59, POL 33-1, MEX-US, folder 7/1/70.

43. Feldman to U.S. Department of State, November 25, 1969, NACP, RG 59, POL 33-1, MEX-US, folder 11/1/69.

44. CEPES Estado de Baja California, Asamblea Popular de Desarrollo Estatal, "Estado de Baja California, Salinidad," Luis Castellanos, December 28, 1969, AHA, Fondo Consultativo Técnico, box 13, expediente 61.

45. Feldman to U.S. Department of State, "New Positions Being Advocated on Salinity Problem," April 21, 1972, NACP, RG 59, POL 33-1, MEX-US, folder 1/25/72.

46. Memorandum of Conversation, "Colorado River Salinity Problem with Mexico: Reply to Mexican Counter-Proposal of February 2, 1971," NACP, RG 59, POL 33-1, MEX-US, folder 2/1/71. IBWC commissioner Friedkin believed that the greatest problem in the future would not be Wellton-Mohawk drainage but increased water use upstream from Imperial Dam. See J. F. Friedkin to William P. Rogers, January 9, 1971, NACP, RG 59, POL 33-1, MEX-US, folder 1/1/71.

47. McBride to Rogers, May 1971, NACP, RG 59, POL 33-1, MEX-US, folder 5/1/71.

48. Roger Morton to Rogers, July 16, 1971, NACP, RG 59, POL 33-1, MEX-US, folder 6/29/71.

49. Friedkin to Robert A. Stevenson, August 5, 1971, NACP, RG 59, POL 33-1, MEX-US, folder 6/29/71.

50. McBride to Rogers, September 1971, NACP, RG 59, POL 33-1, MEX-US, folder 6/29/71.

51. Rogers to U.S. Embassy, Mexico City, August 14, 1971, NACP, RG 59, POL 33-1, MEX-US, folder 6/29/71.

52. Feldman to U.S. Department of State, "The Interest of U.S. Ecological Activist Groups in the Salinity Problem," September 21, 1971, NACP, RG 59, POL 33-1, MEX-US, folder 9/25/71.

53. U.S. Embassy, Mexico City, to U.S. Department of State, "Meetings on Salinity, November 8–11, 1971," NACP, RG 59, POL 33-1, MEX-US, folder 9/25/71.

54. Memorandum of Conversation, "US-Mexican Relations: Colorado River Salinity, Wednesday, November 24, 1971; Mexico City," December 10, 1971, NACP, RG 59, POL 33-1, MEX-US, folder 9/25/71.

55. Feldman to U.S. Department of State, "New Positions Being Advocated on Salinity Problem," April 21, 1972, NACP, RG 59, POL 33-1, MEX-US, folder 1/25/72.

56. McBride to Rogers, March 1972, NACP, RG 59, POL 33-1, MEX-US, folder 1/25/72.

57. David A. Gantz, "Meeting with Committee of Fourteen on October 29, 1971," November 1, 1971, NACP, RG 59, POL 33-1, MEX-US, folder 9/25/71. The Committee of Fourteen even expressed a willingness to part with additional water if necessary to meet salt balance under the new treaty but wanted a guarantee from Mexico that no lawsuits (which might ultimately impair U.S. water rights or the continued existence of the Wellton-Mohawk district) would be brought against the United States; Rabasa explained the Mexican government's rationale for accepting a twelve-month extension in McBride to Rogers, November 1971, NACP, RG 59, POL 33-1, MEX-US, folder 9/25/71.

58. Meyer to Hurwitch, "Salinity," November 19, 1971, NACP, RG 59, POL 33-1, MEX-US, folder 9/25/71.

59. Feldman to U.S. Department of State, "Reaction to Prolongation of Minute 218 (Salinity Problem of Colorado River)," November 22, 1971, NACP, RG 59, POL 33-1, MEX-US, folder 9/25/71.

60. McBride to Rogers, September 1972, NACP, RG 59, POL 33-1, MEX-US, folder 6/1/72.

61. U.S. Embassy, Mexico City, to Rogers, "Brownell Visit to Mexicali"; U.S. Embassy, Mexico City, to U.S. Department of State, "Brownell Meeting with Mexican Media Leaders," December 4, 1972, NACP, RG 59, POL 33-1, MEX-US, folder 10/3/72.

62. This section has been adapted from Ward, "Geo-Environmental Disconnection."

63. Hess, *Viva Las Vegas,* 103–6.

64. Liskey, "The Mirage."

65. Kopytoff, "Computers Are Balanchine"; Hughes, "Wynn Win."

66. Brooks-Dillard, "Cirque du Soleil"; Lampert-Greaux, "The Wizardry of O."

67. Hughes, "Wynn Win."

Chapter 6. "The Politics of Place"

1. Greenberg, "The Tragedy of Commoditization."

2. These various geopolitical perspectives were represented by two sets of bills discussed in the House and Senate. The solution promoted by the Nixon administration and the Department of State was set forth in H.R. 12,384 and S.R. 3094, also referred to as Title I. These bills made provisions only for those measures that would solve the immediate problems in Mexicali. Supporters of these bills wanted to construct the desalinization plant near Yuma, extend the wastewater drainage channel to the Gulf of California, provide financial and technical assistance for Mexicali farmers, and provide clean water while the plant was under construction. H.R. 12,384 and S.R. 3094 also included appropriations for the lining of the Coachella Canal (above the Imperial Valley in California) with concrete in order to conserve the water that would be needed to fulfill U.S. responsibilities under the Mexican Water Treaty.

In contrast, H.R. 12,165 and S.R. 2940 (drawn up by Congressman Johnson [CA] and Senator Fannin [AZ]) included everything mentioned in the administration-sponsored bills plus an ambitious plan known as Title II, which provided for the construction of a 34-million-dollar groundwater pumping well field near Yuma in order to combat Mexican pumping of a binational aquifer. Additionally, Title II included millions of dollars for the removal of natural salt sources throughout the basin. Herbert Brownell played a critical role in helping national leaders realize that western leaders would roadblock international interests unless their local interests were satisfied. When the administration initially objected to Brownell's suggestion that the federal government pay for the desalinization plant, he reminded them that "without their [the basin states'] support one does not have a solution to the problem with Mexico" (Fradkin, *A River No More,* 313).

3. Kemmis, *Community and the Politics of Place,* 7.

4. Brownell with Burke, *Advising Ike,* 155.

5. Ibid.

6. U.S. House Subcommittee on Water and Power Resources, *Hearings before the Subcommittee on Water and Power Resources,* 128. Hereafter cited as House hearings.

7. Brownell with Burke, *Advising Ike,* 3.

8. Van Der Werf, "Desalting Plant."

9. House hearings, 95.

10. Ibid., 213–14.

11. Ibid.

12. Ibid., 88–89; U.S. Senate Subcommittee on Water and Power Resources, *Hearings before the Subcommittee on Water and Power Resources,* 46–50. Hereafter cited as Senate hearings.

13. Sale discusses political changes in the contemporary environmental movement in *The Green Revolution.*

14. House hearings, 306.

15. Ibid.

16. Ibid., 311.

17. Ibid.

18. Ibid.

19. Reisner, *Cadillac Desert,* 297.

20. Hayes, *Beauty, Health and Permanence,* 2–5.

21. House hearings, 311.

22. Ibid., 81–82.

23. U.S. Office of Saline Water, *Saline Water Conversion Summary Report,* 51.

24. Ken Lucas, *Arizona Farmer-Ranchman* (May 1975): 1–4.

25. Atomic Energy Commission, *Nuclear Power and Water Desalting Plants.*

26. Lucas, *Arizona Farmer-Ranchman.*

27. House hearings, 116.

28. Ibid., 268–87.

29. Senate hearings, 291.

30. Ibid., 227.

31. Ibid., 111.

32. House hearings, 289.

33. Ibid., 167.

34. Senate hearings, 313–15.

35. House hearings, 289–90.

36. Ibid., 167.

37. Senate hearings, 313–15.

38. House hearings, 215.

39. Senate hearings, 181–82.

40. Ibid., 185.

41. House hearings, 116.

42. Ibid., 75.

43. Ibid., 133.

44. Ibid., 96, 192.

45. Ibid., 189.

46. Pisani, "The Irrigation District."

47. Senate hearings, 231.

48. House hearings, 292.

49. Ibid., 180.

50. Senate hearings, 313–14.

51. House hearings, 262.

52. Ibid., 261.

53. Senate hearings, 284–85.

54. House hearings, 262.

55. Ibid., 267.

56. C. C. Tabor to Ken Lucas, May 1975, HLDAM-JRP, MS 2, box 130, folder 19.

57. Lenora Werley, "U.S. Takes Sudden Interest in Mexicali Water," *Arizona Daily Star,* December 17, 1961, copy found in HLDAM-CHP, MS 1, box 253, folder 8.

58. House hearings, 252.

59. Ibid.

60. Ibid.

61. Ibid.

62. Ibid., 253.

63. Henry Frauenfelder to Senator Ernest McFarland, April 4, 1945, YCWUA.

64. U.S. Senate Committee on Interior and Insular Affairs, *Yuma, Arizona Groundwater Problems,* 25. Hereafter cited as Senate committee.

65. Ibid., 5.

66. Ibid., 42–43.

67. Ibid., 46–49.

68. Sam Dick to A. B. West, October 12, 1962, HLDAM-JRP, MS 2, box 88:35, folder 3.

69. U.S. Department of the Interior, Minutes of Meeting, re: Yuma Valley Drainage Problem, February 6, 1963, HLDAM-JRP, MS 2, box 88:35, folder 2.

70. H. M. Corey to John J. Rhodes, May 24, 1963, HLDAM-JRP, MS 2, box 88:35, folder 3.

71. Senate committee, 50–51.

72. W. S. Gookin, Memorandum, December 1963, HLDAM-CHP, MS 1, box 708, folder 6.

73. Author unknown, Confidential Memorandum, HLDAM-CHP, MS 2, box 333, folder 18.

74. Senate hearings, 341–42.

75. Kelly, *Cocopah Ethnography,* 2.

76. Hawley Atkinson to Stan Womer, December 3, 1973, ADLAPR-AD-GO, box 726.

77. Robert S. Barley to Governor Jack Williams, ADLAPR-AD-GO, box 726.

78. Senate hearings, 263.

79. Ibid., 265.

80. Ibid., 267.

81. W. A. Dexheimer to Carl Hayden, February 4, 1957, HLDAM-CHP, MS 1, box 479, folder 7.

82. Fradkin, *A River No More,* 315.

83. Martin, "Economic Magnitudes."

84. Glenn, Felger, Burquez, and Turner, "Ciénaga de Santa Clara."

85. Van Der Werf, "Desalting Plant"; LaRue, "Technology on Tap."

86. Greenberg, "The Tragedy of Commoditization," 133–49.

87. This section has been adapted from information in U.S. Bureau of Reclamation, "Yuma Desalting Plant General Information."

Epilogue

1. House, *Frontier on the Rio Grande,* 123–27. The 1990s drought increased the strain on goodwill in both nations in relation to water from the Rio Grande and its tributaries. See Brye, "Environment"; Pinkerton, "Mexico Holding Back Water." Pinkerton's article illustrates that American farmers were just as frustrated with unilateral actions related to water on the other side of the border.

2. House, *Frontier on the Rio Grande,* 119–20; see also O'Driscoll, "Colorado Fights Texas."

3. Sanchez, "To the World Commission on Dams."

4. T. R. Martin, "Meeting of Presidents Johnson and Lopez Mateos in California, February 20–22, Background Paper, Salinity on the Lower Rio Grande," February 14, 1964, Declassified Documents Reference System, CDROM ID 1977010100401, Fiche 1977-66G.

5. Hector Fuentes quoted in "Transboundary Pollution: Joint U.S., Mexican Manufacturing Program May Be Causing Pollution in Texas, Arizona," *International Environment Report* (BNA), June 14, 1989, quoted in Paule, "Underground Water," 1129.

6. Berger, "Precious Resource."

7. Clark, "International Aquifer Management."

8. Getches, "Essays from Askhabad"; Hinrichsen, "Sea Change"; Nasar, "How the Soviets Murdered a Sea"; Burke, "Sea Change Threatens Aral Sea"; Keller, "Developers Turn Aral Sea into a Catastrophe."

9. Nasar, "How the Soviets Murdered a Sea."

10. Getches, "Essays from Askhabad," 526–29.

11. Ibid., 534, 530; see also Thoenes, "Central Asians Reach Common Ground." Plans for rehabilitation of the Aral Sea are discussed in Williams, "The Sinking Sea."

12. See Hassoun, "Water between Arabs and Israelis."

13. See Kaplan, *The Coming Anarchy*, 20–25, 35–37, 51.

14. See Spalding, *The Mexican Food Crisis*.

15. See Varady, Colnic, Meredith, and Sprouse, "The U.S.–Mexican Border Environment Commission"; Sprouse and Mumme, "Beyond BECC"; Mumme, "In Focus"; Milich and Varady, "Openness, Sustainability."

16. Control of water from the delta's aquifers currently represents the most controversial aspect of natural resource exploitation in regional relations. The American plan to line the All-American Canal serves as the latest manifestation of that controversy. Jesús Román Calleros explores this issue in "El Acta 242: Revestimiento del canal All-American. Una nueva diferencia international, México–Estados Unidos," in Trava Manzanilla, Román Calleros, and Bernal Rodríguez, comps., *Manejo ambientalmente adecuado del agua*, 97–128.

17. Defenders of Wildlife, "The Ecological Realities"; Ganster, "Environmental Issues," emphasis added; Alcazar Ávila, "El papel del agua."

18. John Gavin as quoted in Limerick, *The Legacy of Conquest*, 346.

Coda

1. Alvarez Williams, "People and the River," 331.

2. Ibid., 333, 335.

3. Ibid., 336–37, 338.

4. Ibid., 339.

5. Ibid., 345.

6. Ibid., 347.

7. Ibid., 349.

Bibliography

Archives and Research Libraries

Mexico

Archive and Library, Secretaría de Relaciones Exteriores, Mexico City
Archives, Museo Universitario, Universidad Autónoma de Baja California, Mexicali, Baja California
Archivo General de la Nación, Mexico City
Archivo Histórico del Agua, Mexico City
Archivo Histórico del Estado de Baja California, Mexicali

United States

Arizona Division of Libraries, Archives, and Public Records, Phoenix
Hayden Arizona Archives, Hayden Library, Arizona State University, Tempe
Imperial Irrigation District Research Library, Imperial, CA
Library of Congress, Washington, D.C.
National Archives II, College Park, MD
U.S. Bureau of Reclamation, Yuma, AZ
U.S. Department of the Interior Research Library, Washington, D.C.
Yuma County Water Users Association Historical Papers, Yuma, AZ

General Bibliography

Aboites Aguilar, Luís. *La irrigación revolucionaria: Historia del sistema nacional de riego del río Conchos, Chihuahua, 1927–1938.* Mexico City: Secretaría de Educación Pública/Centro de Investigaciones y Estudios Superiores en Antropología Social, 1987.

Alcazar Ávila, Marco Antonio. "El papel del agua como frontera entre México y los Estados Unidos de Norteamérica." *Ingeniería Hidráulica en México* (January–April 1989): 19–29. Archivo Histórico del Agua, Mexico City.

Alvarez Williams, Anita. "People and the River." *Journal of the Southwest* 39 (1997): 331–51.

Anderson, Kurt. "Somber Prelude to the Fourth: A Faulty Bridge and an Untamable River Claim Eight Lives." *Time,* July 11, 1983, 14.

Anguiano Tellez, María Eugenia. *Agricultura y migración en el valle de Mexicali.* Tijuana: COLEF, 1995.

"Ashurst's Folly." *Outlook and Independent,* January 21, 1931, 87.

Atomic Energy Commission. *Nuclear Power and Water Desalting Plants for South-west United States and Northwest Mexico, Preliminary Assessment Conducted by the Joint United States–Mexico International Atomic Energy Agency Study Team. Executive Summary.* Washington, D.C.: GPO, 1968.

Babbitt, Bruce. "Western Water Policy—From Reclamation to Restoration." www .doigov/secretary/univ.htm. December 7, 1999. No longer available on-line.

Baker, Denise L., et al. *Pre-Reconnaissance Investigation of Water Quality, Bottom Sediment, and Biota Associated with Irrigation Drainage in Yuma, Valley, Arizona.* Phoenix: U.S. Fish and Wildlife Service, Fish and Wildlife Enhancement Department, 1992.

Baker, Thadd. *Colorado River Water: Yuma County Lifeline.* Yuma, AZ: Yuma County Chamber of Commerce, 1977.

Balz, Dan. "Water Wars: Booming Town of El Paso Casts an Eye on New Mexico's Trove." *Washington Post,* February 13, 1981, A2.

Beard, Betty. "Be Cool, Mister, Dew Your Job." *Arizona Republic,* April 29, 1995, D1.

Bee, Robert L. *Crosscurrents along the Colorado: The Impact of Government Policy on the Quechan Indians.* Tucson: University of Arizona Press, 1981.

Berger, David. "Precious Resource: Water Issues in the Lower Rio Grande Basin." October 1995. www2.planeta.com/mader/ecotravel/border/sabal.html. September 11, 2000.

Bernal, John M. *A Report on Salinity Operations on the Colorado River under Minute No. 242, January 1–December 31, 1997.* El Paso: International Boundary and Water Commission, 1998.

Bernal Aguire, Celso. *Compendio histórico-biográfico de Mexicali, 1531–1966.* Mexicali: Published by the author, 1966.

Bigler, David L., and Will Bagley, eds. *Army of Israel: Mormon Battalion Narratives.* Spokane, WA: Arthur H. Clark Company, 2000.

Billington, Ray Allen. *The Far Western Frontier: 1830–1860.* New York: Colophon Books, 1956.

Blair, R. E. *The Work of the Yuma Reclamation Project Experiment Farm in 1918.* U.S. Department of Agriculture Circular 75. Washington, D.C.: GPO, 1920.

Blaisdell, Lowell L. *The Desert Revolution, 1911.* Westport, CT: Greenwood Press, 1986.

——. "Was It Revolution or Filibustering? The Mystery of the Flores Magón Revolt in Baja California." *Pacific Historical Review* 23 (1954): 147–64.

Blanquel, Eduardo. "Pensamiento filosófico de Flores Magón." In Miguel Mathes, ed., *Baja California: Textos de su historia*. Mexico City: Instituto de Investigaciones, 1988. 2:351–61.

Boyle, Robert H. "Life—or Death—for the Salton Sea?" *Smithsonian* 27, no. 3 (June 1996): 86.

Brass, Kevin. "High-End Mix on Manmade Lake near Las Vegas." *New York Times,* December 28, 1997, sec. 11, p. 5.

Brooks-Dillard, Sandra. "Cirque du Soleil Artistry Conjures up Water Circus." *Denver Post,* November 1, 1998, A1.

Brownell, Herbert, with John P. Burke. *Advising Ike: The Memoirs of Attorney General Herbert Brownell.* Lawrence: University Press of Kansas, 1993.

Brye, Robert. "Environment: Troubled Waters." *Guardian,* June 14, 1995, T6.

Buffington, Robert. "Prohibition in the Borderlands: National Government–Border Community Relations." *Pacific Historical Review* 63 (winter 1993): 19–38.

Burke, Justin. "Sea Change Threatens Aral Sea." *Christian Science Monitor,* October 9, 1990, Habitat sec., p. 12.

Cabrera, Luís. "Use of the Waters of the Colorado River in Mexico: Pertinent Technical Commentaries." *Natural Resources Journal* 15, no. 1 (January 1975): 27–34.

Cannon, Lou. "Desert City Looks to Sea for Water; Las Vegas Focusing on Desalination Plant." *Washington Post,* July 5, 1992, A3.

——. "When It Comes to Development, Las Vegas Plays without Limits." *Washington Post,* February 2, 1997, A3.

Capra, Fritjof. *The Web of Life: A New Understanding of Living Systems.* New York: Anchor Books, 1995.

Cárdenas del Río, Lázaro. *Obras: I—Apuntes, 1913–1940.* Vol. 1. Mexico City: Universidad Nacional Autónoma de México, Dirección General de Publicaciones, 1972.

Carrier, Jim. "The Colorado: A River Drained Dry." *National Geographic* (June 1991): 4–32.

Carson, Charles A. "Arizona's Interest in the Colorado River." *Rocky Mountain Law Review* 19 (1947): 352–57.

Cavise, Leonard L. "Because of NAFTA, Annihilation Is in Store for the Indians of Chiapas." *Houston Chronicle,* March 20, 1994, Outlook sec., p. 4.

Ceballos-Ramírez, Manuel, and Oscar J. Martínez. "Conflict and Accommodation on the Border, 1848–1911." In Jaime E. Rodríguez and Kathryn Vincent, eds., *Myths, Misdeeds and Misunderstandings: The Roots of Conflict in U.S.–Mexican Relations.* Wilmington, DE: Scholarly Resources, 1997. 135–57.

Cervantes Ramírez, Maximiliano, and Francisco A. Bernal Rodríguez. "Comportamiento de la salinidad en el agua del río Colorado." In José Luís Trava Manzanilla, Jesús Román Calleros, and Francisco A. Bernal Rodríguez, comps., *Manejo ambientalmente adecuado del agua: La frontera México–Estados Unidos*. Tijuana: COLEF, 1991. 129–34.

Chabra, Ranbir. *Soil Salinity and Water Quality*. Rotterdam: A. A. Balkema, 1996.

Chamberlin, Eugene Keith. "Mexican Colonization versus American Interests in Lower California." *Pacific Historical Review* 20 (1951): 43–55.

Cházaro, Sergio L., coordinator. *Uso sustenible del agua en México*. Mexico City: Seguros Comercial América, 1999.

Clark, J. C. "International Aquifer Management: The Hueco Bolsón on the Rio Grande River." *Natural Resources Journal* 18 (January 1978): 163–77.

Clifford, Frank. "Plotting a Revival in a Delta Gone to Dust." *Los Angeles Times,* March 24, 1997, A1.

Cohen, Michael J., et al. *Haven or Hazard: The Ecology and Future of the Salton Sea. Executive Summary.* www.sci.sdsu.edu/salton/EcoSaltonSeaPacInst ExeSum.html. September 7, 2000.

"Colorado River Flooding Peaks." *Engineering News-Record,* July 7, 1983, 7.

Cook, O. F. *Cotton Farming in the Southwest*. U.S. Department of Agriculture Circular 132-B. Washington, D.C.: GPO, 1913.

Corbett, Peter. "Vegas vs. Valley for Tourism Title." *Arizona Republic,* July 19, 1999, A1.

Cosio Villegas, Daniel. *Historia moderna de México*. Vol. 6. Mexico City: Editorial Hermes, 1963.

Cronon, William. *Changes in the Land: Indians, Colonists, and the Ecology of New England*. New York: Hill and Wang, 1983.

——. *Nature's Metropolis: Chicago and the Great West*. New York: W. W. Norton, 1991.

DeBuys, William, and Joan Meyers. *Salt Dreams: Land and Water in Low-Down California*. Albuquerque: University of New Mexico Press, 1999.

Defenders of Wildlife. "The Ecological Realities of the Salton Sea, August 1998." www.sci.sdsu.edu/salton/DOWPositionSaltonSea.html. September 7, 2000.

De la Fuente, Marco Antonio. "Examen jurídico de aguas y límites entre México y los E.U." In Victor Carlos García Moreno, comp., *Análisis de algunos problemas fronterizos y bilaterales entre México y los Estados Unidos*. Mexico City: Universidad Nacional Autónoma de México, 1982. 59–102.

De la Torre, Jorge Ceballos, et al. *Agua y desarrollo regional*. Mexicali: Colegio de Economistas de Baja California, 1989.

Del Rio, Ignacio. "Inquietud de marqués de León, 1878." In Miguel Mathes, ed.,

Baja California: Textos de su historia. Mexico City: Instituto de Investigaciones, 1988. 2:18–23.

"Deterioration of the Salton Sea: Ten-Year Chronology of Events and Actions Taken." In *Saving the Salton Sea: A Research Needs Assessment*. Appendix B. www.sci.sdsu.edu/salton/deterioration_salton_sea.htm. September 7, 2000.

DeVoss, David. "How the Bugs Finally Won." *Los Angeles Times*, September 20, 1987, Magazine sec., p. 18.

DeVoto, Bernard. *The Year of Decision, 1846*. Boston: Houghton Mifflin Company, 1960.

De Williams, Anita. *Travelers among the Cucupa*. Los Angeles: Dawson's Book Shop, 1975.

Dillin, John. "Pollution Seeps from Mexico to U.S." *Christian Science Monitor*, December 28, 1989, 6.

Drake, Joan. "Man-Made Lakes: A Splash with Home Buyers." *Los Angeles Times*, August 20, 1989, sec. 8, p. 1.

Dunbier, Roger. *The Sonoran Desert: Its Geography, Economy, and People*. Tucson: University of Arizona Press, 1968.

Duncan, Robert H. "The Chinese and the Economic Development of Northern Baja California." *Hispanic American Historical Review* 74 (November 1994): 616–47.

Dunning, Harrison C. "Confronting the Environmental Legacy of Irrigated Agriculture in the West: The Case of the Central Valley Project." *Environmental Law* 23 (1993): 943–69.

Dwyer, John J. "The End of U.S. Intervention in Mexico: Franklin Roosevelt and the Expropriation of American-Owned Agricultural Property." *Presidential Studies Quarterly* 28, no. 3 (summer 1998): 495–509.

Egan, Timothy. "Las Vegas Stakes Claim in 90's Water War." *New York Times*, April 10, 1994, sec. 1, p. 1.

——. "Urban Sprawl Strains Western States." *New York Times*, December 29, 1996, sec. 1, p. 1.

Eisenberg, Evan. *The Ecology of Eden: An Inquiry into the Dream of Paradise and a New Vision of Our Role in Nature*. New York: Vintage, 1998.

Enríquez Coyro, Ernesto. *El tratado entre México y los Estados Unidos de América sobre ríos internacionales*. Vol. 1. Mexico City: Universidad Nacional Autónoma de México, 1975.

Environmental Protection Agency. *U.S.–Mexico Border XXI, Frontera XXI*. www.epa.gov/usmexicoborder/index.htm. September 11, 2000.

Espinoza, M. Perez. "Estudio agrológico preliminar del distrito de riego del río

Colorado." *Ingeniería Hidráulica en México* (October–December 1958). Archivo Histórico del Agua, Mexico City.

Farmer, Hugo. "Testimony." Arizona Commission of the Colorado River Basin States, June 22–23, 1938. Arizona Division of Libraries, Archives, and Public Records, Phoenix.

Fernández, Raúl A. *La frontera México–Estados Unidos: Un estudio socioeconómico.* Mexico City: Terra Nova, 1980.

Fite, Gilbert. *Cotton Fields No More: Southern Agriculture, 1865–1980.* Lexington: University of Kentucky Press, 1984.

Fletcher, Colin. *River: One Man's Journey down the Colorado, Source to Sea.* New York: Vintage, 1997.

Foley, Neil. "Mexicans, Mechanization, and the Growth of Corporate Cotton Culture in South Texas: The Taft Ranch, 1900–1930." *Journal of Southern History* 62, no. 2 (May 1996): 275–302.

Fradkin, Philip. *A River No More: The Colorado River and the West.* New York: Knopf, 1981.

——. "The River Revisited." *Los Angeles Times,* October 29, 1995, Magazine sec., p. 16.

Furnish, Dale, and Jerry Landham. "El convenio de 1973 sobre la salinidad del río Colorado y el valle de Mexicali." *Revista de la Facultad* (Universidad Nacional Autónoma de México) 20 (January 1975): 103–29.

Ganster, Paul. "Environmental Issues of the California–Baja California Border Region." *Border Environmental Research Reports,* no. 1, June 1996. Southwest Center for Environmental Research and Policy. www.scerp.org. September 11, 2000.

Gardner, B. Delworth, and Clyde E. Stewart. "Agriculture and Salinity Control in the Colorado River Basin." *Natural Resources Journal* 15, no. 1 (January 1975): 63–82.

Gerhard, Peter. "The Socialist Invasion of Baja California, 1911." *Pacific Historical Review* 15 (1946): 295–304.

Getches, David H. "Essays from Askhabad, to Wellton-Mohawk, to Los Angeles: The Drought in Water Policy." *Colorado Law Review* 4. Lexus-Nexis website.

Gill, Mario. "Flores Magón y los filibusteros." In Miguel Mathes, ed., *Baja California: Textos de su historia.* Mexico City: Instituto de Investigaciones, 1988. 2:286–310.

Gleik, Peter. "Water, War, and Peace in the Middle East." *Environment* 36, no. 3 (1994): 6–42.

——. *The World's Water: The Biennial Report on Fresh Water.* Washington, D.C.: Island Press, 1998.

Glenn, Edward P., Richard S. Felger, Alberto Burquez, and Dale S. Turner. "Ciénaga de Santa Clara: Endangered Wetland in the Colorado River Delta, Sonora, Mexico." *Natural Resources Journal* 32 (1992): 817–24.

Golden, Arthur. "Hate, Neglect Provided Fuel for Rebellion." *San Diego Union-Tribune,* January 5, 1994: News sec., pp. 1–6.

Golfen, Bob. "Golf Stuck in Trap between Tourism, Nature Activists." *Arizona Republic,* October 17, 1993, B1.

González de León, Antonio. "Factores de tensión internacional en la frontera." In Roque González Salazar, ed., *La frontera del norte: Integración y desarrollo.* Mexico City: Colegio de México, 1981.

Gottlieb, Robert, and Margaret Fitzsimmons. *Thirst for Growth: Water Agencies as Hidden Government in California.* Tucson: University of Arizona Press, 1991.

Graham, Frank, Jr. "Gambling on Water." *Audubon* 94, no. 4 (July 1992): 64–69.

——. "Midnight at the Oasis." *Audubon* 100, no. 3 (May 1998): 82–89.

Greenberg, James B. "The Tragedy of Commoditization: Political Ecology of the Colorado River's Destruction." *Research in Economic Anthropology* 19 (1998): 133–49.

Grijalva Larranaga, Edna Aide. "Colonización del valle de Mexicali, 1902." In Miguel Mathes, ed., *Baja California: Textos de su historia.* Mexico City: Instituto de Investigaciones, 1988. 2:234–48.

Grossfield, Stan. "A River Runs Dry; A People Wither; Their Water Taken, Mexico's Cocopah Cling to Arid Homeland." *Boston Globe,* September 21, 1997, A1.

Hall, Thomas D. *Social Change and the Southwest, 1350–1880.* Lawrence: University Press of Kansas, 1989.

Hansberger, Edwin L., Delia Fuquay Hansberger, and James LeRoy Hansberger. *Dates, Pecans, and Ostriches: Some Memories of Life in the Yuma Valley.* Yuma, AZ: Yuma County Historical Society, 1970.

Hansen, Niles. *The Border Economy: Regional Development in the Southwest.* Austin: University of Texas Press, 1981.

Harris, Tom. *Death in the Marsh.* Washington, D.C.: Island Press, 1991.

Hart, John. *Anarchism and the Mexican Working Class, 1860–1931.* Austin: University of Texas Press, 1978.

——. *Revolutionary Mexico.* Berkeley: University of California Press, 1987.

——. *Storm over Mono Lake: The Mono Lake Battle and the California Water Future.* Berkeley: University of California Press, 1996.

Hassoun, Rosina. "Water between Arabs and Israelis: Researching Twice Promised Resources." In John M. Donahue and Barbara Rose Johnston, eds., *Water, Culture, and Power: Local Struggles in a Global Context.* Washington, D.C.: Island Press. 313–38.

Hayes, Samuel P. *Beauty, Health and Permanence: Environmental Politics in the United States, 1955–1985.* Cambridge: Cambridge University Press, 1987.

Heisey, Adriel. "Sky-High over the Sonoran." *National Geographic* (October 2000): 31–49.

Henderson, David Allen. "Agriculture and Livestock Raising in the Evolution of the Economy and Culture of the State of Baja California, Mexico." Ph.D. dissertation, UCLA, 1964.

Hernández Chávez, Alicia. *La mecánica cardenista.* Vol. 16, *Historia de la revolución mexicana.* Mexico City: Colegio de México, 1980.

Herrera Carrillo, Pablo. *Colonización del valle de Mexicali.* Mexicali: Universidad Autónoma de Baja California, 1976.

Herrick, Thaddeus. "Water Woes." *Houston Chronicle,* February 14, 1999, State sec., p. 1.

Hess, Alan. *Viva Las Vegas: After Hours Architecture.* San Francisco: Chronicle Books, 1993.

Hinrichsen, Don. "Sea Change." *Amicus Journal* (spring 1995). www.igc.apc.org/ nrdc/nrdc/eamicus/clip01/dhsea.html. No longer available on-line.

Houghton, N. D. "Problems of the Colorado River as Reflected in Arizona Politics." *Western Political Quarterly* 4, no. 4 (1951): 634–43.

House, John. *Frontier on the Rio Grande: A Political Geography of Development and Social Deprivation.* Oxford: Clarendon Press, 1982.

Huffman, Bill. "State Riding Crest as Public Demands More Courses." *Arizona Republic,* February 2, 1999, Arizona Golf sec., p. 8.

Hughes, Robert. "Wynn Win." *Time,* October 26, 1998, 76.

Hundley, Norris, Jr. *Dividing the Waters: A Century of Controversy between the United States and Mexico.* Berkeley: University of California Press, 1966.

——. *The Great Thirst: Californians and Water, 1770s–1990s.* Berkeley: University of California Press, 1992.

——. *Water and the West: The Colorado River Compact and the Politics of Water in the American West.* Berkeley: University of California Press, 1975.

Indian Lakes. www.indianlakes.net. January 7, 2000.

"In Health There Are No Borders." *Newsweek,* August 1, 1988, 47.

Instituto de Investigaciones Históricas. *Mexicali: Una historia.* 2 vols. Mexicali: Universidad Autónoma de Baja California, 1991.

International Boundary and Water Commission. "Transboundary Aquifer and Binational Ground-water Data Base." www.ibwc.state.gov/RIOGRAND/bina tional_waters.htm. September 7, 2000.

Jackson, Kenneth T. *Crabgrass Frontier: The Suburbanization of the United States.* New York: Oxford University Press, 1985.

Jenkins, Virginia Scott. *The Lawn: A History of an American Obsession.* Washington, D.C.: Smithsonian Institution Press, 1994.

Jervis, Robert. *Complexity in Political and Social Life.* Princeton, NJ: Princeton University Press, 1997.

Joaquín Arrillaga, José. *Diary of His Surveys of the Frontier.* Trans. Froy Tiscareno, ed. John W. Robinson. Los Angeles: Dawson's Book Shop, 1966.

Johnson, Rich. *The Central Arizona Project, 1918–1968.* Tucson: University of Arizona Press, 1977.

Jordan, Fernando. *El otro México: Biografía de Baja California.* Mexico City: Secretaría de Educación Pública, Frontera, 1976.

Kaplan, Robert. *The Coming Anarchy: Shattering the Dreams of the Post Cold War.* New York: Random House, 2000.

Kearney, Thomas H., and William A. Peterson. *Egyptian Cotton in the Southwestern United States.* Bureau of Plant Industry Bulletin 128. Washington, D.C.: GPO, 1908.

——. *Experiments with Egyptian Cotton in 1908.* Bureau of Plant Industry Circular 29. Washington, D.C.: GPO, 1909.

Keller, Bill. "Developers Turn Aral Sea into a Catastrophe." *New York Times,* December 20, 1988, C1.

Kelly, William. *Cocopah Ethnography.* Tucson: University of Arizona Press, 1977.

Kemmis, Daniel. *Community and the Politics of Place.* Norman: University of Oklahoma Press, 1991.

Kieran, Evelyn. "Getaway." *San Diego Union-Tribune,* February 19, 1987, C2.

King, Kirke A., and Brenda J. Andrews. *Contaminants in Fish and Wildlife Collected from the Lower Colorado River and Irrigation Drains in the Yuma Valley, Arizona.* Phoenix: U.S. Fish and Wildlife Service, Arizona Ecological Services Field Office, 1996.

Kirshenbaum, James. "Rising Waters and Mismanagement on the Colorado." *Sports Illustrated,* June 11, 1984, 11.

Kleinman, Alan P., and F. Bruce Brown. *Colorado River Salinity: Economic Impacts on Agricultural, Municipal, and Industrial Users.* U.S. Department of the Interior, Colorado River Water Quality Office, Engineering and Research Division. Washington, D.C.: GPO, 1980.

Knight, Alan. "Cardenismo: Juggernaut or Jalopy?" *Journal of Latin American Studies* 26 (February 1994): 73–107.

Kopytoff, Verne G. "Computers Are Balanchine behind Those Dancing Fountains." *New York Times,* October 21, 1999, G7.

Krakauer, Jon. *Into the Wild.* New York: Villard, 1996.

Kresen, Peter L. "A Geologic Tour of the Lower Colorado River Region of Arizona and Sonora." *Journal of the Southwest* 39 (1997): 566–82.

LaFranchi, Howard. "U.S., Mexico Hear Drip, Drip, Drip of Water Draining from Border." *Christian Science Monitor,* March 5, 1996, World sec., p. 1.

Lake Las Vegas. www.lakelasvegas.com. September 7, 2000.

Lampert-Greaux, Ellen. "The Wizardry of O." *Entertainment Design* 33, no. 2 (February 1999): 36–41.

Langley, Lester D. *Mexico and the United States: The Fragile Relationship.* Boston: Twayne Publishers, 1991.

LaRue, Steve. "In but Not Out." *San Diego Union-Tribune,* July 1, 1998, E1.

———. "Taking the Initiative: The New River Cleanup." *San Diego Union-Tribune,* December 26, 1992, A1.

———. "Technology on Tap: New Treatments May Offer a Clearer Solution." *San Diego Union-Tribune,* April 22, 1998, E1.

Leopold, Aldo. *A Sand County Almanac: With Essays on Conservation from Round River.* New York: Ballantine Books, 1970.

Limerick, Patricia. *The Legacy of Conquest: The Unbroken Past of the American West.* New York: W. W. Norton, 1987.

Liskey, Eric. "The Mirage." *Grounds Maintenance* 32, no. 8 (August 1997): C34.

Lopez, Barry, and Craig Aurness. "A Worldly Wilderness: California Desert." *National Geographic* (January 1987): 42–77.

López Zamora, Emilio. *El agua, la tierra: Los hombres de México.* Mexico City: Fondo de Cultura Económica, 1977.

———. "La contaminación de las aguas del río Colorado: Un conflicto internacional." *Política,* March 1, 1963, 3–13.

Luckingham, Bradford. "Phoenix: The Desert Metropolis." In Richard M. Bernard and Bradley R. Rice, eds., *Sunbelt Cities.* Austin: University of Texas Press, 1983. 309–27.

Lytle, Mark. "An Environmental Approach to American Diplomatic History." *Diplomatic History* (spring 1996): 279–300.

MacLaclan, Colin M. *Anarchism and the Mexican Revolution: The Political Trials of Ricardo Flores Magón in the United States.* Berkeley: University of California Press, 1991.

Maerowitz, Marlene Pontrelli. "Town Lake Shows Dreams Do Come True." *Arizona Republic,* May 29, 1999.

Mann, Dean E. *The Politics of Water in Arizona.* Tucson: University of Arizona Press, 1963.

Marcum, Diana. "California and the West: Turning Desert into an Aquatic Paradise." *Los Angeles Times,* September 19, 1999, A28.

Martin, J. G., and G. C. White. *Handling and Marketing Durango Cotton in the Imperial Valley.* U.S. Department of Agriculture Bulletin 458. Washington, D.C.: GPO, 1917.

Martin, W. E. "Economic Magnitudes and Economic Alternatives in Lower Basin Use of Colorado River Water." *Natural Resources Journal* 15, no. 1 (1975): 229–39.

Martínez, Oscar J. *Troublesome Border.* Tucson: University of Arizona Press, 1988.

Martínez, Pablo L. *Historia de Baja California.* Mexico City: Consejo Editorial del Gobierno del Estado de B.C.S., 1991.

———. "Polémica contra los sentimientos nacionales." In Miguel Mathes, ed., *Baja California: Textos de su historia.* Mexico City: Instituto de Investigaciones, 1988. 2:391–403.

Martínez Zepeda, Jorge. "Entrevista al Sr. Juan Buenrostro Guerrero." In Instituto de Investigaciones Históricas, ed., *Mexicali: Una historia.* Mexicali: Universidad Autónoma de Baja California, 1991.

May, Robert. "Manifest Destiny's Filibusters." In Sam W. Haynes and Christopher Morris, eds., *Manifest Destiny and Empire: American Antebellum Expansionism.* Arlington: University of Texas at Arlington Press. 146–79.

McCully, Patrick. *Silenced Rivers: The Ecology and Politics of Large Dams.* London: Zed Books, 1996.

McCurdy, Mary Kyle. "Symposium on the Public Trust and the Waters of the American West: Yesterday, Today, and Tomorrow." *Environmental Law* 19 (spring 1989): 683–721.

McGirk, Jan. "Mexico's Rebellious Road Show Reaches Its Destination." *Independent* (London), March 12, 2001, News sec., p. 12.

McLachlan, Argyle. *Community Production of Durango Cotton in the Imperial Valley.* U.S. Department of Agriculture Bulletin 324. Washington, D.C.: GPO, 1915.

McPhee, John. *Encounters with the Archdruid.* New York: Farrar, Straus and Giroux, 1971.

Merchant, Carolyn. *The Death of Nature: Women, Ecology, and the Scientific Revolution.* New York: Harper and Row, 1983.

Metz, Leon. *Border: The U.S.–Mexican Line.* El Paso: Magnan Books, 1989.

"Mexico Registers 'No Sale' of Lower California." *Literary Digest,* January 21, 1931, 13.

Meyer, Michael. *Water and the Hispanic Southwest: A Social and Legal History, 1550–1850.* Tucson: University of Arizona Press, 1984.

Milich, Lenard, and Robert G. Varady. "Openness, Sustainability, and Public Participation in Transboundary River-Basin Institutions: Part III, Adapting the U.S.–Mexico Paradigm." *Arid Lands Newsletter,* no. 44 (fall–winter 1998). www.ag.arizona.edu/OALS/ALN/aln44/varady-milich3.html. May 26, 1999.

Milstein, M. "Water Woes." *National Parks* 66, nos. 5–6 (May–June 1992): 39–45.

Morgantau, Tom, et al. "The Colorado: Man-Made Flood." *Newsweek,* July 11, 1983, 28.

Moyano, Angela. "William Walker en la Península." In Miguel Mathes, ed., *Baja California: Textos de su historia.* Mexico City: Instituto de Investigaciones, 1988. 1:202–24.

Mumme, Stephen. "In Focus: NAFTA and the Environment." *Foreign Policy in Focus* 4, no. 26 (October 1999). www.foreignpolicy_infocus.org/briefs/vol4/v4n26nafta.html. June 4, 2002.

Murphy, Michael. "The High Cost of Green: Conservation Takes a Back Seat to Lush Lawns." *Phoenix Gazette,* October 28, 1993, A1.

Nasar, Rusi. "How the Soviets Murdered a Sea." *Washington Post,* June 4, 1989, B3.

Nash, Roderick. *Wilderness and the American Mind.* Rev. ed. New Haven, CT: Yale University Press, 1973.

Nemecek, Sasha. "Frankly, My Dear, I Don't Want a Dam: How Dams Affect Biodiversity." *Scientific American* (October 1997). www.sciam.com/0897issue/0897scicit3.html. September 11, 2000.

Newberg, Julie. "Even in the Desert, Water's Everywhere." *Arizona Republic,* September 21, 1997, special sec., p. 22.

"New River Named One of Nation's Most Threatened Rivers." *U.S. Newswire,* April 16, 1997.

"NLA Fights Turf Restrictions in Las Vegas." *Landscape Management* 37, no. 11 (November 1998): 14.

Noble, E. G. *The Work of the Yuma Reclamation Project Experiment Farm in 1919 and 1920.* U.S. Department of Agriculture Circular 221. Washington, D.C.: GPO, 1922.

Nomani, Asra. "Backyard Works of Art: Pools Feature Waterfalls, Fountains." *Arizona Republic,* June 12, 1999, E1.

Nye, David. *American Technological Sublime.* Cambridge, MA: MIT Press, 1994.

O'Driscoll, Patrick. "Colorado Fights Texas for Rio Grande Flow; Wasted Water Would Have Wiped out Debt, Officials Say." *Denver Post,* April 14, 1996, C1.

Orcutt, C. R. "A Visit to Lake Maquata." *West American Scientist* 7, no. 59 (1891): 158–64.

Pacific Institute for Studies in Development, Environment, and Security. "Salton Sea Assessment: Scoping Comments." September 30, 1998. www.sci.sdsu.edu/salton/PISaltonSeaRestorationPlan.html. September 7, 2000.

Pare, Madeline Ferrin. *Arizona Pageant: A Short History of the 48th State.* Phoenix: Arizona Historical Foundation, 1965.

Paule, Adrienne. "Underground Water: A Fugitive at the Border." *Pace Environmental Law Review* 13 (spring 1996): 1129–70.

Pauw, Ted. "New River Pollution in Mexico (NEW)." American University Case Study no. 142. www.sci.sdsu.edu/salton/NEW_RIVER.htm. June 4, 2002.

Perry, Tony. "After Fifty Years, New Hope for Detoxifying New River." *Los Angeles Times,* November 4, 1995, A1.

Peterson, W. A. *The Work of the Yuma Experiment Farm in 1912.* Bureau of Plant Industry Circular 126B. Washington, D.C.: GPO, 1913.

Petrie, Bob. "Town Lake Water 'Scape; Half-Billion Gallons a Year Expected to Evaporate." *Arizona Republic,* March 30, 1999, EV1.

Pierson, Jay Dexter. "The Growth of a Western Town: A Case Study of Yuma, Arizona, 1915–1950." M.A. thesis, Arizona State University, August 1987.

Pillsbury, A. F. "The Salinity of Rivers." *Scientific American* (January 1981): 54–65.

Piñera Ramírez, David. "Guillermo Andrade, pionero del valle de Mexicali." In Miguel Mathes, ed., *Baja California: Textos de su historia.* Mexico City: Instituto de Investigaciones, 1988. 2:228–29.

——. *Historiografía de la frontera norte de México: Balance y metas de investigación.* Mexicali: Universidad Autónoma de Baja California, 1990.

——. "El oro blanco en Mexicali." In David Piñera Ramírez, ed., *La frontera en nuestros días.* Vol. 6 of David Piñera Ramírez, coordinator, *Visión histórica de la frontera norte de México.* Mexicali: Universidad Autónoma de Baja California, Instituto de Investigaciones Históricas, 1991.

——, coordinator. *Visión histórica de la frontera norte de México.* 6 vols. Mexicali: Universidad Autónoma de Baja California, Instituto de Investigaciones Históricas, 1987–91.

Pinkerton, James. "Mexico Holding Back Water, Farmers Claim; Angry South Texans Call for Trade Sanctions." *Houston Chronicle,* February 18, 2000, Business sec., p. 2.

Pisani, Donald J. *From Family Farm to Agribusiness.* Berkeley: University of California Press, 1984.

——. "The Irrigation District and the Federal Relationship: Neglected Aspects of Water History." In Gerald D. Nash and Richard Etulian, eds., *The Twentieth-Century West: Historical Interpretations.* Albuquerque: University of New Mexico Press, 1989. 257–92.

Pitt, Jennifer, and Dan Luecke. *A Delta Once More: Restoring Riparian and Wetland Habitat in the Colorado River Delta.* New York: Environmental Defense Fund, 1999.

Poljakoff-Mayber, Alexandra. *Plants in Saline Environments.* Ecological Studies 15. New York: Springer-Verlag, 1975.

Post, Tom. "Splash." *Forbes,* April 19, 1999: 126.

Postel, Sandra. *Pillar of Sand: Can the Irrigation Miracle Last?* New York: Norton, 1999.

Raat, Dirk W. *Revoltosos: Mexico's Rebels in the United States, 1903–1923.* College Station: Texas A&M University Press, 1981.

Rambo, A. Terry. *Conceptual Approaches to Human Ecology.* Research Report no. 14, East-West Environment and Policy Institute. Honolulu: East-West Center, 1983.

Reinman, T. R. "Desert Bloom; Arizona Leaves S.D. in Dust of Golf-Course Building Boom." *San Diego Union-Tribune,* February 2, 1999, D1.

Reisner, Marc. *Cadillac Desert: The American West and Its Disappearing Water.* New York: Viking Penguin, 1986.

Rice, Ross. *Carl Hayden: Builder of the American West.* Lanham, MD: University Press of America, 1994.

Richards, L. A., ed. *Diagnosis and Improvement of Saline and Alkali Soils, USDA.* Washington, D.C.: GPO, 1954.

Riding, Alan. *Distant Neighbors.* New York: Vintage Books, 1989.

Riley, Michael. "Dead Cats, Toxins, and Typhoid: Clean-up Time for the New River, an International Irritant." *Time,* April 20, 1987, 68.

Rio Salado. www.tempe.gov/rio/. September 7, 2000.

Roderick, Kevin. "Las Vegas' Thirst for Water Upsets Many in Arid West." *Los Angeles Times,* May 6, 1991, A1.

Roosevelt, Theodore. "Theodore Roosevelt on Conservation, December 3, 1907." In Richard Hofstadter, ed., *The Progressive Movement, 1900–1915.* Englewood Cliffs, NJ: Prentice-Hall, 1963. 69–72.

Ropp, Thomas. "Add 'Green' to Landscaping." *Arizona Republic,* September 10, 1999, B5.

Ruíz, Ramon. *On the Rim of Mexico: Encounters of the Rich and Poor.* Boulder, CO: Westview Press, 1998.

Salas-Porras Soule, Alejandra. "Baja California: Vanguardia del movimiento popular en la frontera." In Alejandra Salas-Porras Soule, Alejandro Covarrubias V., Jorge Carrera Robles, and Sandra Arenal, coordinators, *Nuestra frontera norte (. . . tan cerca de los EUA).* Mexico City: Editorial Nuestro Tiempo, S.A., 1989. 43–80.

Sale, Kirkpatrick. *The Green Revolution: The American Environmental Movement 1962–1992.* New York: Hill and Wang, 1993.

Sanchez, Raul M. "To the World Commission on Dams: Don't Forget the Law, and Don't Forget Human Rights—Lessons from the U.S.-Mexico Border." *University of Miami Inter-American Law Review* 30 (winter-spring 1999): 629-57.

Sanchez, Rene. "Water Creations Spring from the Edge of the Desert." *Los Angeles Times,* July 6, 1999, C1.

——. "West Wages a New Sort of Turf War; Water Conservation Pushed as Desert Communities Struggle with Growth." *Washington Post,* May 16, 1999, A3.

Sandez, Daniel. "Los primeros pobladores del valle de Mexicali." In Miguel Mathes, ed., *Baja California: Textos de su historia.* Mexico City: Instituto de Investigaciones, 1988. 2:230-33.

Schoultz, Lars. *Beneath the United States: A History of U.S. Policy toward Latin America.* Cambridge, MA: Harvard University Press, 1998.

Scofield, Carl. *Egyptian Cotton Culture in the Southwest.* Bureau of Plant Industry Circular 123C. Washington, D.C.: GPO, 1913.

Scofield, C. S., et al. *Community Production of Egyptian Cotton.* U.S. Department of Agriculture Bulletin 332. Washington, D.C.: GPO, 1916.

Secretaría de Recursos Hidráulicos. *Memoria de la primera reunión nacional de residentes de zonas de riego.* Mexico City: Secretaría de Recursos Hidráulicos, 1971.

Sellew, Francis L. "The Colorado River Siphon at Yuma, Arizona." *Engineering News* 68, no. 9 (1912): 377-85.

Shadowlake Estates. www.shadowlakeestates.com. December 10, 1999.

Shainberg, I., and J. D. Oster. *Quality of Irrigation Water.* Bet Dagan, Israel: International Irrigation Information Center, 1978.

Sheridan, Thomas E. *Arizona: A History.* Tucson: University of Arizona Press, 1995.

——. "Arizona: The Political Ecology of a Desert State." *Journal of Political Ecology* 2 (1995): 41-57.

Simon, Hilda. *The Date Palm: Bread of the Desert.* New York: Dodd, Mead and Company, 1978.

Sklair, Leslie. *Assembling for Development: The Maquila Industry in Mexico and the United States.* Winchester, MA: Unwin Hyman, 1989.

Smith, Felix E. "The Kesterson Effect: Reasonable Use of Water and the Public Trust." *San Joaquin Agricultural Law Review* 6 (1996): 45-67.

Smith, James F. "Rebels Take to Heartland of Mexican Revolution." *Los Angeles Times,* March 9, 2001, A1, 4.

Smythe, William. "An International Wedding: The Tale of a Trip on the Borders of Two Republics." *Sunset* (October 1900): 286-300.

Snape, W. J., III. "Adding an Environmental Minute to the 1944 Water Treaty: Impossible or Inevitable?" www.sci.sdsu.edu/salton/Snape1998Environ Minute.html. September 11, 2000.

Spalding, Rose. *The Mexican Food Crisis: An Analysis of SAM*. Research Report Series 33. San Diego: Center for U.S.-Mexican Studies, University of California-San Diego, 1984.

Spencer, Leslie. "Water: The West's Most Misallocated Resource." *Forbes,* April 27, 1992, 68.

Sprouse, Terry, and Stephen Mumme. "Beyond BECC: Envisioning Needed Institutional Reforms for Environmental Protection on the Mexico-U.S. Border." Udall Center for Public Policy. www.udallcenter.arizona.edu/publications/ beyondbecc/html. September 7, 2000.

Stammer, Larry B. "Pipe Break Sends Raw Sewage into Salton Sea." *Los Angeles Times,* April 19, 1985, A3.

Stapells, Cathy. "Praising Arizona Snowbirds Know What They Like—and It's Scottsdale, for Its Golf, Arts, Shopping, and Southwest Flavor." *Toronto Sun,* January 4, 1998, T10.

Steele, Bob. "Siphon: Our Water's Been Coming under the River for 75 Years." *Yuma Daily Sun,* October 25, 1987, 12–14.

Sykes, Godfrey. *The Colorado Delta*. American Geographical Society, Special Publication no. 19. Port Washington, NY: Kennikat Press, 1970.

Taylor, Paul S. *Mexican Labor in the United States*. New York: Arno Press, 1970.

Thoenes, Sander. "Central Asians Reach Common Ground over Water." *Financial Times,* April 9, 1996, 3.

Tiano, Susan. *Patriarchy on the Line: Labor, Gender, and Ideology in the Mexican Maquila Industry*. Philadelphia: Temple University Press, 1994.

Trafzer, Clifford. *Yuma: Frontier Crossing of the Far Southwest*. Wichita, KS: Western Heritage Books, 1980.

Trava Manzanilla, José Luís, Jesús Román Calleros, and Francisco A. Bernal Rodríguez, comps., *Manejo ambientalmente adecuado del agua: La frontera México–Estados Unidos*. Tijuana: COLEF, 1991.

Trevino Arrendondo, Rene. "La industrialización y el desarrollo económico del estado de Baja California." Thesis, Escuela Nacional de Economía, Universidad Nacional Autónoma de México, Mexico City, 1962.

Tuttle, Merlin D. "Bats: The Cactus Connection." *National Geographic* (June 1991): 130–40.

Tyler, Daniel. *A Concise History of the Mormon Battalion*. Waynesboro, VA: M&R Books, 1964.

UC-MEXUS Border Water Project. *Alternative Futures for the Salton Sea*. Issue

Paper 1. Riverside: University of California Institute for Mexico and the United States, 1999.

Ulloa, Berta. "The U.S. Government versus the Mexican Revolution, 1910–1917." In Jaime E. Rodríguez and Kathryn Vincent, eds., *Myths, Misdeeds and Misunderstandings: The Roots of Conflict in U.S.–Mexican Relations*. Wilmington, DE: Scholarly Resources, 1997. 159–68.

U.S. Bureau of Reclamation. "Reconnaissance Investigation of Water Quality, Bottom Sediment, and Biota Associated with Irrigation Drainage in the Lower Colorado River Valley, Arizona, California, and Nevada." Abstract. www.usbr.gov/niwqp/biblio/niwqp.abs/radtke.txt. September 11, 2000.

———. "Salton Sea: Challenges and Opportunities." www.sdsu.edu/salton/Salton_Sea.html. September 11, 2000.

———. "The Source, Transport, and Fate of Selenium and Other Contaminants in Hydrological and Biological Cycles of the Salton Sea Area." In *USBR Salton Sea Study*. February 1998. No longer available on-line.

———. "Special Studies: Delivery of Water to Mexico." February 1963.

———. "Yuma Desalting Plant General Information." www.yao.lc.usbr.gov/Desalt.htm. June 2, 2001.

U.S. Bureau of the Census. *14th Census of the United States, 1920, Agriculture*. Vol. 6, pt. 3. Washington, D.C.: GPO, 1922.

———. *15th Census of the United States, 1930, Agriculture*. Vol. 2, pt. 3. Washington, D.C.: GPO, 1932.

———. *United States Census of Agricultural, 1925*. Pt. 3. Washington, D.C.: GPO, 1927.

U.S. Department of State. *Foreign Relations of the United States: Diplomatic Papers, 1943*. Vol. 6. Washington, D.C.: GPO, 1965.

———. *Foreign Relations of the United States: Diplomatic Papers, 1944*. Vol. 7. Washington, D.C.: GPO, 1967.

———. *Foreign Relations of the United States: Diplomatic Papers, 1945*. Vol. 9. Washington, D.C.: GPO, 1969.

———. *Foreign Relations of the United States: Diplomatic Papers, 1946*. Vol. 11. Washington, D.C.: GPO, 1969.

———. *Foreign Relations of the United States: Diplomatic Papers, 1952–1954*. Vol. 4. Washington, D.C.: GPO, 1983.

———. *Papers Relating to the Foreign Relations of the United States, 1911*. Washington, D.C.: GPO, 1918.

———. *Papers Relating to the Foreign Relations of the United States, 1921*. Vol. 2. Washington, D.C.: GPO, 1936.

U.S. Geological Survey. "Methods to Identify Areas Susceptible to Irrigation-

Induced Selenium Contamination in the Western United States." www.water
.usgs.gov/pubs/FS/FS-038-97/. September 11, 2000.

U.S. House Committee on Interior and Insular Affairs. *Hearings on Colorado River
Management.* 98th Cong., 1st sess. Serial no. 98-20. Washington, D.C.: GPO,
1983.

U.S. House Committee on Irrigation and Reclamation. *Reauthorizing Gila Project:
Hearings before the Committee on Irrigation and Reclamation.* 79th Cong.,
2nd sess. H.R. 5434. Washington, D.C.: GPO, 1947.

U.S. House Subcommittee on Water and Power Resources. *Hearings before the
Subcommittee on Water and Power Resources of the Committee on Interior and
Insular Affairs, House of Representatives.* 93rd Cong., 2nd sess. H.R. 12,165
and Related Bills. Washington, D.C.: GPO, 1974.

U.S. Office of Saline Water. *Saline Water Conversion Summary Report, 1971–1972.*
Washington, D.C.: GPO, 1972.

U.S. Senate. S. Doc. 212. 59th Cong., 2nd sess. Vol. 4. Washington, D.C.: GPO,
1907.

———. *Survey of Conditions of Indians in the United States.* Washington, D.C.: GPO,
1931.

U.S. Senate Committee on Foreign Relations. *Water Treaty with Mexico: Hearings
before the Committee on Foreign Relations.* 79th Cong., 1st sess. Washington,
D.C.: GPO, 1945.

U.S. Senate Committee on Interior and Insular Affairs. *Yuma, Arizona Groundwater Problems: Hearings before the Committee on Interior and Insular Affairs.* Washington, D.C.: GPO, 1956.

U.S. Senate Committee on Irrigation and Reclamation. *Hearings: Arizona Water
Resources.* 78th Cong., 2nd sess. S.R. 304. Washington, D.C.: GPO, 1944.

U.S. Senate Subcommittee on Water and Power Resources. *Hearings before the
Subcommittee on Water and Power Resources of the Committee of Interior and
Insular Affairs. S. 1807, S. 2940, S. 3094, Salinity Control Measures on the
Colorado River.* 93rd Cong., 2nd sess. Washington, D.C.: GPO, 1974.

Van Der Werf, Martin. "Desalting Plant: White Elephant in the Desert." *Arizona
Republic,* November 14, 1993, A8.

Van Leeuwen, Thomas A. P. *The Springboard in the Pond: An Intimate History of the
Swimming Pool.* Cambridge, MA: MIT Press, 1998.

Varady, Robert G., David Colnic, Robert Meredith, and Terry Sprouse. "The U.S.–
Mexican Border Environment Commission: Collected Perspectives on the
First Two Years." *Journal of Borderlands Studies* 11, no. 2 (fall 1996). Udall
Center for Studies in Public Policy. www.udallcenter.arizona.edu/publica
tions/jbs__becc.html. September 7, 2000.

Villa, Clifford J. "Comment: California Dreaming: Water Transfers from the Pacific Northwest." *Environmental Law* 23 (1993): 997–1026.

Walker, Sam. "Nevada Body of Water Set to Become Bone of Contention." *Christian Science Monitor,* June 6, 1997, United States sec., p. 1.

Walsh, Patricia. "Everybody's Been Passing the Buck since the Whole Thing Started." Regional News, Arizona-Nevada. UPI. September 3, 1983.

———. "It's Unhealthy Having Good People Throwing Rocks at One Another." Regional News, Arizona-Nevada. UPI. September 6, 1983.

Walther Meade, Adalberto. *El valle de Mexicali.* Mexicali: Universidad Autónoma de Baja California, 1996.

Ward, Evan R. "Crossroads on the Periphery: Yuma County Water Relations, 1922–1928." M.A. thesis, University of Georgia, Athens, 1997.

———. "Geo-Environmental Disconnection and the Colorado River Delta: Technology, Culture, and the Political Ecology of Paradise." *Environment and History* 7, no. 2 (May 2001): 219–46.

———. "The Mexican Water Treaty." In Char Miller, ed., *Water and the Environment since 1945: Global Perspectives.* Vol. 7 of *History in Dispute.* Farmington Hills, MI: St. James Press, 2001.

———. " 'The Politics of Place': Diplomatic and Domestic Priorities of the Colorado River Salinity Control Act (1974)." *Journal of Political Ecology* 6 (1999): 31–56.

———. "Saline Solutions: Arizona Water Politics, Mexican-American Relations, and the Wellton-Mohawk Valley." *Journal of Arizona History* (fall 1999): 267–92.

———. "Salt of the River, Salt of the Earth: Politics, Science, and Ecological Diplomacy in the Mexicali Valley, 1961–1965." *Frontera Norte* 26.

———. "The Twentieth-Century Ghosts of William Walker: Conquest of Land and Water as Central Themes in the History of the Colorado River Delta." *Pacific Historical Review* 70 (August 2001): 359–85.

———. "Two Rivers, Two Nations, One History: The Transformation of the Colorado River Delta since 1940." *Frontera Norte* 22 (July–December 1999): 113–40.

Warren, Jennifer. "Well-Made Plans Keep Palm Springs an Oasis in the Drought." *Los Angeles Times,* April 28, 1991, A3.

Waters, Frank. *The Colorado.* New York: Rinehart and Company, 1961.

Weatherford, Gary D., and F. Lee Brown, eds. *New Courses for the Colorado River.* Albuquerque: University of New Mexico Press, 1986.

Webb, Walter Prescott. *The Great Plains.* Lincoln: University of Nebraska Press, 1981.

Weber, Devra. *Dark Sweat, White Gold: California Farm Workers, Cotton, and the New Deal.* Berkeley: University of California Press, 1994.

Western, Ken. "Legends of the Falls a New Lure at Pointe." *Arizona Republic,* June 5, 1996, E1.

Westover, William H. *Yuma Footprints.* Tucson: Arizona Pioneers Historical Society, 1966.

Whiteford, Scott. "Troubled Waters: The Regional Impact of Foreign Investment and State Capital in the Mexicali Valley." In Ina Rosenthal-Uray, ed., *Regional Impacts of U.S.–Mexican Relations.* San Diego: Center for U.S.–Mexican Studies, University of California–San Diego, 1986. 17–36.

Williams, Daniel. "The Sinking Sea: Dike Splitting Kazakhstan's Aral Dims Hopes for Its Salvation." *Washington Post,* November 12, 1998, A23.

Wittfogel, Karl. *Oriental Despotism.* New York: Penguin, 1981.

Womack, John, Jr. *Zapata and the Mexican Revolution.* New York: Vintage Books, 1968.

Wood, Daniel B. "Pirate Ships, Fountains: Extravagant Water Use Hits Upper Limits." *Christian Science Monitor,* February 1, 1995, Points of Compass sec., p. 10.

Worster, Donald. *Rivers of Empire: Water, Aridity, and the Growth of the American West.* New York: Pantheon, 1985.

——. *An Unsettled Country: Changing Landscapes of the American West.* Albuquerque: University of New Mexico Press, 1994.

Wright, Harold Bell. *The Winning of Barbara Worth.* New York: A. L. Burt Company, 1911.

Yost, Barbara. "Imponderables; Water Features Are Backyard Oases for the Soul." *Arizona Republic,* March 3, 1996, Arizona Style sec., p. 22.

Yozwiak, Steve. "Two Waterways 'Endangered'; Pinto on Roster Third Year, Colorado's Delta Is Added." *Arizona Republic,* April 6, 1998, B1.

Yuma Chamber of Commerce. *Yuma Project: The Land of Perpetual Sunshine.* Yuma, AZ: Yuma Chamber of Commerce, 1923.

Index

Roosevelt, Theodore, 6–7
Ruíz Cortines, Adolfo, 38–39
Rusk, Dean, 58, 67, 69–70, 99

Sagebrush Rebellion, 86
Saline Water Act (1952), 122
salinity, 45–49, 63–64, 66–84, 91–111, 119–128, 145–146
Salinity Control Act. *See* Colorado River Salinity Control Act
Salton Sea, xxv
Salt River Valley, 47–50, 54
Sánchez Taboada, Rodolfo, 25, 27, 28
San Luís Mesa. *See* San Luís Río Colorado
San Luís Río Colorado, 93–98, 135–136
Sayre, Robert, 78, 95
Sea of Cortés, xxviii, 42, 140, 155. *See also* Gulf of California
Sierra Club, 120–121
Smythe, William Ellsworth, xvii–xxv, xxvii
Sonoran Desert, 152. *See also* Colorado Desert
Southern Pacific Railroad, 8
Steiner, Wesley, 126–127

Tello, Manuel, 81
Treaty of Guadalupe Hidalgo, xxx
Tunney, John, 124

Udall, Morris, 119
Udall, Stewart, 70, 95
Union Agrícola Regional, 96
U.S. Bureau of Reclamation (USBR): and Gila Project, 54; groundwater flows study, 97; and Mexicali Valley

salinity crisis, 71–72, 73, 76–78; and Minute 218, 100–103; unilateral study of Mexicali Valley salinity crisis, 76–77; and western politicians, 86
U.S. Border Patrol, 29–31
U.S. Department of Health, Education and Welfare, 75–76
U.S. Department of State: and groundwater pumping wars, 94–95; and impact of salinity on bi-national relations, 108; and Mexicali Valley, 68–72; policy during salinity crisis, 86; position on water releases, 25, 27; and salinity control policy, 119
U.S. Department of the Interior: authorization to protect CRLC lands in Mexico, 9; and Cocopah, 138; conflict with USDS policy, 86; and desalinization plant site, 122; and groundwater pumping near San Luís Río Colorado, 92; and groundwater pumping wars, 94–95; and impact of salinity on bi-national relations, 108; and Mexicali Valley, 68–70
USDS. *See* U.S. Department of State
U.S. Immigration and Naturalization Service, 21–22, 29–31
U.S.–Mexican War, 4

Vietnam conflict, 60–61, 119

Walker, William, 3–4, 12–13, 18–21
Warne, William E., 44, 47, 123
Weatherford, Gary, 88–90
Wellton-Mohawk Irrigation and Drainage District, 66–78. *See also* Wellton-Mohawk Valley

About the Author

Evan Ward is an assistant professor of history at the University of North Alabama, where he teaches courses on Latin America and the American West. His articles on the Colorado River Delta have appeared in several journals, including the *Pacific Historical Review, Frontera Norte,* and *Environment and History.*